HE RESTORETH MY SOUL

UNDERSTANDING AND BREAKING THE
CHEMICAL AND SPIRITUAL CHAINS OF
PORNOGRAPHY ADDICTION THROUGH
THE ATONEMENT OF JESUS CHRIST

Donald L. Hilton Jr., MD

Published by:
Forward Press Publishing, LLC
P.O. Box 592681
San Antonio, TX 78259
www.ForwardPress.org

Proceeds from this book are dedicated to the anti-pornography effort.

Library of Congress Cataloging-in-Publication Data Applied For

ISBN # 978-0-9819576-0-9

Second Printing, Revised Edition, November, 2009

3 5 7 9 10 8 6 4 2

Printed in the United States of America
Print and Bind Direct!
www.PrintAndBind.com

In loving memory of my father
Donald Long Hilton, MD
who healed and loved many

He was afraid; and beginning to sink,
he cried, saying, Lord, save me.
And immediately Jesus stretched
forth his hand, and caught him.

Matthew 14:30-31

And the spirit and the body are the soul of man.

Doctrine and Covenants 88:15

He restoreth my soul: he leadeth me in
the paths of righteousness for his name's sake.

The 23rd Psalm

CONTENTS

APPENDICES

ACKNOWLEDGMENTS

It is not possible to adequately thank all who have helped this work come together. I must give special thanks to my editor, Mary Lou Terry, whose skill and insight were indispensable in manuscript preparation. David and Toni Handy, who serve as missionaries ministering to those in addiction, have shared the knowledge and experience they have gained. The Handys, and many of those recovering from addiction with whom they serve, have assisted in reading and critiquing the manuscript, and their insights and perspective have been invaluable.

I am grateful to many others who have read and otherwise assisted in manuscript preparation. Richard Miller, my bishop and close friend, spent many hours reading and editing, and shared his experience as a bishop. I thank my friend, Robert Steuer, for his valuable perspective as a medical doctor and experienced spiritual leader. Randal Wright assisted in so many essential ways, from his knowledge of the publishing process to his encouragement and support in bringing this sensitive subject to light. My mother, Irene Hilton, read and edited several versions of the manuscript, and has the ability to see both the big picture and the smallest detail. I am grateful to her for reading to me as a child, and for teaching me to love God. She has always been a pillar of strength in my life.

Finally, I am grateful to my wife, Jana, who helped with every phase of this work, tirelessly editing and reviewing the manuscript, critiquing wording and content. She is my truest critic, best friend, and constant companion. Many of the ideas and words are hers, and this book is as much her work as it is mine.

Permissions for use of the figures were obtained through appropriate journal-specific web sites. I thank Walter Rane, a remarkable and gifted artist, for allowing his painting, "Lord Save Me," to be used on the cover.

INTRODUCTION

While preparing this manuscript, I read an article in *USA Today* published December 13, 2007 entitled "Study: Young adults now find porn more acceptable." It referenced an article, which was later published in January 2008 in the *Journal of Adolescent Research*[1] describing the cultural mainstreaming of pornography in college-age young adults. Perhaps the most sobering statistic was that 87 percent of young men from six universities have sought out and viewed pornography in the last year, with 20 percent viewing it daily or nearly every day. More alarming was this statistic in view of a recent *Church News* article: *"Latter-day Saints with the problem are no different when it comes to prevalence or magnitude of sexual addictions."*[2]

This book was written in response to what I regard as the primary threat to our peace as individuals, families, Church members, and as a society, culture, nation, and world. These thoughts are mine alone and should not be taken to represent the official position or doctrine of the Church of Jesus Christ of Latter-day Saints.

I began writing some thoughts after searching the current medical literature on the chemical aspects of sexual addictions and then focused on pornography addiction. In medical school I was assigned to a substance abuse addiction recovery clinic for my psychiatry rotation. I now find that this early introduction helped me understand the high recidivism of the addicted. During my senior year of medical school I worked with rat models of Parkinson's disease, which is a defect in one component of the dopaminergic system of the brain, just as addiction is an imbalance in another dopaminergic system. I

---

[1] Jason S. Carroll, Laura M. Padilla-Walker, Larry J. Nelson, Chad D. Olson, Carolyn McNamara Barry, Stephanie D. Madsen, "Generation XXX: Pornography Acceptance and Use Among Emerging Adults," *Journal of Adolescent Research*, Vol. 23(1) 2008, 6-30.

[2] "Defending the Home Against Pornography," *Church News*, April 21, 2007, archives, http://www.desnews.com/cn/view/1,1721,470006290,00.html.

placed dopamine pumps in the rats' brains to try to cure Parkinson's disease, and although the dopamine deficiency obviously has different effects in addiction versus Parkinson's disease, my interest in this drug and neurotransmitter was kindled.

Most, if not all, families will be affected by pornography. If you are a man, you must first safeguard yourself. If you are secretly involved, hopefully this work will convince you there will never be peace for you until you are healed. If you are free from addiction now, you must still guard yourself against future addiction, as all are vulnerable who are not "sober and vigilant,"[3] as Peter warned. If you are a father, it is essential to understand what your sons will be exposed to and that he will be at serious risk for addiction at some point in his life. If you are a woman please understand that this problem is real and must be confronted head on. You also need to be aware of the profound risk your sons face.

It is important for those who have daughters to understand that although the numbers are smaller for girls, there is still a risk, both from visual pornography and primarily from chat rooms, text messaging, and verbal pornography. Also, studies are showing that the young men whom they will date and consider for marriage have virtually all been exposed and many have been or are addicted, to a lesser or greater degree. It is imperative that every young woman understands the scope and seriousness of this problem. Her awareness will help her to be discerning in dating and eventually choosing a marriage partner. Our extended family members are also at risk: sons and daughters-in-law, grandchildren and their spouses, and other loved ones.

Hopefully, bishops and ecclesiastical leaders will find this work to be helpful in understanding the difficulty of treating pornography and sexual addiction adequately from a spiritual perspective alone.

This problem is at least as serious as I have represented it to be and it will continue to escalate. *Knowledge is power:* we will become more *empowered* with each bit of *knowledge* we accrue in regard to pornography addiction. While we have been appropriately concerned about devastating physical diseases such as AIDS, with more under-

---

[3] 2 Peter 5:8

standing and emphasis we will also be able to protect ourselves and our loved ones from this other "overflowing scourge"[4] of pornography. I sincerely hope this work will be helpful to all, both men and women, boys and girls, who struggle with addictions of any kind, including related sexual addictions and compulsions such as same sex attraction, compulsive promiscuity, and also drug addictions.

The first part of this book defines components of the problem, while the second explores healing. Please do not become discouraged by the early chapters as the problems caused by pornography are discussed. It is necessary to describe the problem frankly because there are those who doubt they even need to change. Stories written by those in strong recovery are woven throughout the book and are also found in the appendices. I am grateful to them for their willingness to share. The final chapters focus on the healing and peace that comes through Jesus Christ, and how repentance *and* recovery allow His Atonement to become effective in the lives of those who seek Him.

WHAT CAN WE DO?

It may seem unusual to do this at the start rather than at the end of this book, but I will summarize what I feel are critical and immediate steps we can and should take to address this issue. When a patient comes in to see a physician with a cough, he must decide whether the person only has a cold, or whether he has pneumonia. If he admits each patient with a cold to the intensive care unit on intravenous antibiotics, he will be over-reacting, and will be unable to care for all of the other patients who need his care. Likewise, if he doesn't recognize those with pneumonia as being critically ill, he will send them out with cough syrup instead of admitting them to the hospital.

This is what is currently happening to those afflicted and addicted to pornography, and also to others affected by their choices. Although we are not doing this knowingly, we have not recognized fully the scope and nature of this problem, and we are paying a terrible price, a price which will be realized more and more as time

---

[4]   *Doctrine and Covenants* 45:31

passes and it becomes more obvious that there has been a paradigm shift. One who is an experienced warrior in this battle from many perspectives recently told me, "We are currently losing this war." What can we do differently as a people to begin to change the direction of this problem?

- **Treat pornography and sexual addiction as a full addiction, and not from a behavioral/spiritual perspective alone.** We have not accorded pornography and sexual addiction the respect and weight needed to take into account the tremendous effort required *to save even one.* To assist in the recovery process, 12 Step support groups specific to pornography addiction must be available to all. The current scenario of sending the young man on a mission after three to six months of 'white-knuckle' sobriety is only setting him up for intermittent struggling throughout his mission, and/or quick relapse upon return and re-introduction into the overwhelming media barrage he will surely face.

- **Individuals struggling with pornography and sexual addiction must understand that because this is a true addiction, they will not be able to stop unless they seek help from appropriate sources.** The rationalization that "this is my private sin, and I can resolve it privately with God" will only produce escalation of the addiction, and entrench them in a double life. They must have the personal desire to seek and obtain repentance and recovery.

- **Disclosure of each incident of viewing or sexually acting out is essential to obtain both repentance and recovery.** For the married person, repentance requires that the spiritual leader (bishop for the LDS person) and the spouse know the extent and scope of the problem. Disclosure to the spouse may for some be best undertaken after conferring with their bishop, a counselor, and/or an experienced support person who has years of sobriety and is strong in recovery.

- While we have emphasized prevention in the past, and should continue to do so, we must also recognize that virtually all of our young men and many of our young women are already seriously exposed, and are therefore already in need of treatment. By continuing to emphasize avoidance only, we shame the majority who are already caught in the addiction into secrecy and guilt. We must extend a hand of healing and support to those trapped in secrecy, so there is a safe place for them to seek help.

- Understand that the majority of young men returning from missions are slipping quickly into addiction, and we must be ready to support them with 12 Step support groups specific to pornography addiction immediately upon return from their mission. We should be as determined to support them as the adversary is to capture them as they emerge from a spiritual high and enter the world again. If we can change the current pattern of quick relapse after mission, we can begin to see dating and marriage patterns return to normalcy.

- Recognize that many married men are secretly addicted, and have support groups ready to help them emerge from addiction. Otherwise, we risk a natural acceptance of the secret pornography addiction that is already endemic in every demographic and religious body in the world, including our own. As men lose hope, they will accept that pornography is, for them, a reality that they will never overcome in this life. Support groups can lead them to recovery and hope.

- We must provide support groups for the spouse who has been harmed by the pornography/sexual addiction of her husband. In this way, she will have access to women who have healed from anger and betrayal, and will feel the love and empathy that only a woman with like experience can provide.

- Realize the importance of educating young women as to the prevalence and tenacity of pornography addiction, so they will understand and be fully informed as they enter the world of dating. In this sobering environment, we should counsel our young women to prepare to support themselves financially, as marriage is likely to occur later than in previous years, and divorce may be more likely. They must also be carefully nurtured themselves, as addiction to pornography and masturbation is increasing among young women.

- Educate and train leaders to understand addiction and the importance of addressing both repentance *and* recovery. Many spiritual leaders address the repentance aspect of pornography and sexual addiction alone without understanding that the person will continue to relapse long after he or she has left the care of the leader, unless a separate process of recovery is also initiated. In support groups, virtually every person there has been "through" multiple bishops. No discerning spiritual leader would tell an alcoholic to pray, repent, and move forward, without also sending them to Alcoholics Anonymous (AA) and/or therapy. Leaders must understand that the recidivism rates for pornography and sexual addiction are as high or higher than substance abuse addiction, and therefore require the same support for long-term sobriety and strong recovery.

- While therapy and counseling are integral for many, 12 Step support groups should be the backbone of recovery, as not all will have access to therapists experienced in treating sexual addiction. We must establish support groups specific to pornography and sexual addiction in every area of the Church. Ideally, these would be multi-stake, similar to the more mature and successful programs in Utah, thus 'pooling' sobriety and allowing more to have access to facilitators who are strong in recovery and have years of sobriety. This is the key: the person who has gained strong recovery shares *what works for them* with those new in recovery, and serves as a support person. This type of disclosure is *not* confession. The person in recovery has already gone through the repentance process, and is now sharing the gift of recovery with others. We may more appropriately term this type of disclosure *recovery sharing*. Although the facilitator is not a counselor, he has the credibility of experience, and provides hope to one seeking recovery. Alcoholics Anonymous has no therapists or counselors, yet is considered by many now strong in recovery to be the most effective factor in their recovery. Thus, a "buddy system" is developed where daily phone calls and support allow the person to gain longer periods of sobriety until recovery and healing become strong. While therapy can be extremely helpful for many, there simply aren't enough therapists with LDS values trained in addiction, particularly outside of Utah. By harvesting facilitators we can provide healing for future individuals emerging from addiction.

Technology has accelerated our fascination with pleasure. Indeed, the power of pleasure has been underestimated, and Internet pornography is changing the world in a fundamental way. Over 200 years ago the poet Robert Burns said, "But pleasures are like poppies spread, You seize the flow'r, its bloom is shed; Or like the snow falls in the river, A moment white – then melts forever." Yet to the person in addiction, the momentary pleasure is irresistible and all-important. The price of acting out in addiction seems paltry compared to the temporary payoff, yet the despair in between episodes of acting out increases as losses accumulate. In this work we explore the power of addiction, not just from a moral and spiritual perspective, but with the scrutiny of modern science, which now tells us that there is little difference in the physical or chemical changes in the pleasure and control centers of the brain regardless of whether the addiction is "from a chemical or an experience," as stated in the journal *Science*.[5] It is imperative that we treat pornography and sexual addiction with the respect accorded any drug addiction, for, as we shall see, that is precisely what it is.

---

[5] Constance Holden, "Behavioral Addictions: Do They Exist? *Science*, 294 (5544) 2 November 2001, 980.

PART ONE

ADDICTION

*The Zambezi River in Africa with the Zambian Escarpment
in the background, June 2004*

CHAPTER 1

OUT OF THE MOUTH
OF THE LION

Be sober, be vigilant; because your adversary the devil,
as a roaring lion, walketh about, seeking whom he may devour.

1 Peter 5:8

A few years ago my family and I were on safari in Africa. I have loved the continent ever since I served as a missionary in South Africa many years ago and wanted my wife and children to experience the majesty and primal beauty uniquely felt in the bush. One afternoon we were driving in open air Land Rovers along the banks of the Zambezi River.

Our guide referred to the high grass growing along the flats near the river as "adrenaline grass." I asked about the label "adrenaline." As we drove slowly through the grass he asked if we could see the lion. I didn't see it until the last minute, but there it was. A lion was

Adrenaline Grass along the banks of the Zambezi

This photo is a close up of the previous picture
with illumination and magnification.

hiding in the shade under the grass (turn back to the photo on the previous page . . . do you see it now?). With a little change in the angle of the light we could see it. As we watched the lion looking back at us from the shade and realized there were no doors or glass between her and us, I felt my heart rate quicken as the adrenaline kicked in. We had been told if we stayed still and remained seated, the lion would just look, but the tension was still there.

Now I "understood what I did not understand,"[1] to quote the words of South African writer Alan Payton. The lions would wait until an animal came to the edge of the water to get a drink. The lion would do what lions do, which is to hold the animal by the throat, strangling it of oxygen until it succumbed. It would then devour the animal, leaving scraps for hyenas and jackals. I knew I was seeing a powerful object lesson here and took these photographs.

The apostle Peter said, "Be sober. Be vigilant, for your adversary the devil as a roaring lion walketh about seeking whom he may devour."[2] Today, perhaps the lion of the adversary is embodied in the scourge of pornography more than in any other single weapon he uses. This spiritual lion hides in the dark and waits for unsuspecting

1   Alan Payton, *Cry, the Beloved Country*, Scribner, 1987 (original 1948), 214.
2   1 Peter 5:8

victims. It grabs them by the spiritual throat and strangles the life out of happiness, joy, companionship, learning, love (both romantic and platonic), spirituality, reason, and life itself. It consumes and devours the person in addiction and leaves his life in scraps for other addictions to finish him off, completely isolating him from everything he used to love in his former life. It provides the false promise of an exciting double life where he can have the best of both worlds. Sadly, the person mired in addiction finds in the end that this double life leaves joy in neither of the worlds, with even the sexual self being ruined and consumed as the chemically altered brain is left to crave what can never be fully satisfied. Note the following excerpt from a letter a woman wrote to President Gordon B. Hinckley, which he read in General Conference:

> Please warn the brethren (and sisters). Pornography is not some titillating feast for the eyes that gives a momentary rush of excitement. [Rather] it has the effect of damaging hearts and souls to their very depths, strangling the life out of relationships that should be sacred, hurting to the very core those you should love the most.[3]

Her husband had been diagnosed with terminal cancer, and before he died confessed a long pornography addiction to her. It is significant she used the word "strangle," consistent with the lion analogy described by Peter.

What is it that allows the lion to be seen in the second picture? Light! By redirecting the focus, light allows us to penetrate the darkness and see the lion for what it is, a danger to us and to any animal that might walk by. Secrecy allows the lion to remain hidden and to continue to destroy and hurt, waiting patiently for additional victims to come get a drink.

Guilt and shame are the supporting pillars of secrecy and keep whispering rationalizations to the person trapped in addiction, such as, "You don't need to hurt anyone else," and "You can get rid of this on your own without anyone else knowing because you are stronger,

---

[3] Gordon B. Hinckley, "A Tragic Evil Among Us," *Ensign*, November 2004, 59.

smarter, somehow different from everyone else." In this latter rationalization lies the true essence of addiction—pride. "My will, not thine."[4] My. Me. I. It is in the isolation of pride that the addiction thrives and conquers and destroys the agency of the person. John Mark Haney, a counselor in Austin, Texas described the teenager trapped in pornography addiction as living in "isolated agony."[5]

RESTORING THE SOUL

This work is for all who have become entangled in this devastating neurochemical web, who have lost control of their ability to resist sin, and who feel abandoned by all that is good. I hope that both the teenager and adult struggling with addiction will find this information useful in their quest to overcome this problem and that mothers and spouses may find the knowledge to give them a clear perspective about their sons, husbands, and loved ones. Those struggling with addiction will be referred to in the male gender for convention, although I realize women and girls are becoming addicted to pornography in ever increasing numbers. For women who have become entangled in inappropriate chat rooms, consider this behavior on par with male visual pornography, for the end result in terms of human misery is the same. I hope those with same sex attraction will also gain insight, as well as those who find themselves addicted to any form of sexual promiscuity or to chemical substance abuse.

Know that there is, as Jeremiah said, "a balm in Gilead."[6] A physician is there. When asked why He was with social undesirables, the Savior said, "They that are whole have no need of the physician,"[7] implying He was The Physician. He told the Children of Israel through Moses, "I am the Lord that healeth thee."[8] In the end, there must be a connection with the Divine Presence to completely heal the brain and the soul. And when the Lord heals, it is without reservation or limit.[9]

---

[4]   Ezra Taft Benson, "Pride, The Universal Sin," *Ensign*, May 1989, 4.
[5]   John Mark Haney, Article 10, "Teenagers and Pornography Addiction: Treating the Silent Epidemic," http://counselingoutfitters.com/vistas/vistas06/vistas06.
[6]   Jeremiah 8:22
[7]   Mark 2:17
[8]   Exodus 15:26
[9]   3 Nephi 17:7-9

CHAPTER 2

WHAT IS ADDICTION?

What win I, if I gain the thing I seek?
A dream, a breath, a froth of fleeting joy.
Who buys a minute's mirth to wail a week?
Or sells eternity to get a toy?
For one sweet grape who will the vine destroy?
Or what fond beggar, but to touch the crown,
Would with the sceptre straight be strucken down?

William Shakespeare

A functional definition of pornography would be anything that induces an inappropriate sexual interest for that person. Some images are clearly pornography for anyone. Each person knows in his own heart what is a temptation for him, and that is the true test. We are our own judges.

As a physician, I like the structural definition which will be further described in Chapter 6: "Addiction represents a pathological, yet powerful, form of learning and memory."[1] We use the term "pathology" in medicine to describe a process of disease, where the body or mind has departed from the healthy, normal state. Applying this definition to pornography, addiction is simply a repetitive behavior which damages the person and others in his life and which the person is unable to stop. One young man with a pornography addiction who was new to a 12 Step program and early in the realization of the depth of his own addiction asked his group why he should even want to stop. The answer is simple: *because you can't.*

---

[1]   Julie A. Kauer & Robert C. Malenka, "Synaptic Plasticity and Addiction," *Nature Reviews Neuroscience* 8, 8440858, November 2007, 844-858.

A SPECIAL FORM OF INSANITY

Neal A. Maxwell said, "I believe that sin is a special form of insanity, that it reflects a kind of 'blackout' in which we either lack perspective about the consequence of our thoughts, words, and actions, or we lose it temporarily."[2] The *Oxford English Dictionary* definition of insanity is "not of sound mind, mentally deranged."[3] To the un-addicted, it appears inconceivable that anyone could want what the addicted seek, much less give up everything for it. For this reason, terms such as returning to "sobriety" and "sanity" are used in addiction literature. One in recovery from addiction told me, "Sometimes we act out because there seems to be nothing else to do, no other option. We've done it so many times before." An addicted person's damaged willpower alone is not enough in overcoming addictions, but we must not forget that developing willpower with the assistance of the Savior and those who help Him (bishops, facilitators, and therapists) is still the single most important factor in facilitating recovery.

I believe the basic problem in addiction is rooted in *perspective.* Pride, stemming from lack of gratitude, allows the person to entertain desires that selfishly disregard the consequences visited upon not only the addicted one, but also upon his loved ones. *Satisfaction* of the addiction becomes the ultimate priority, yet surely a greater oxymoron does not exist. There is never final satisfaction in addiction of any kind, only temporary satiation, with the next relapse made only the more inevitable by the experience. *The perspective of the person acting out in addiction is progressively constricted until nothing exists but obsession.* In this world, the only reality is relief from the craving; the only solace is knowledge that the next relapse is waiting. Addiction is the very definition of selfishness, the ultimate contracture of perspective. As the pleasure centers are abused and damaged, *normal* pleasures become less recognized by the brain as desirable. Relationships are devalued in the addicted person's warped new world and become obstructional to acting out. Values change to accommodate the need to sate voracious desire, and spirituality is one of the first casualties. Honesty is disregarded; lies are rationalized as necessary to protect

---

2   Neal A. Maxwell, "Insights," *Ensign*, April 1974, 21.
3   *The Oxford English Dictionary, Volume VII, Second Edition,* Clarendon Press, 1013.

the innocent. As the one in addiction sheds relationships and values, losses accumulate. Support systems vanish. In the shrinking time he spends in the sane world, he finds it less desirable because of the pain present in true reality. His new world, "the new reality," is always waiting with the next fix, and the cycle perpetuates and deepens.

The un-addicted have a difficult time understanding the *power of the compulsion*. To help us understand this, a person in recovery from pornography addiction describes the craving:

> Probably the best analogy I can use is hunger and thirst. Imagine what it feels like to go on a ten-mile hike and not eat or drink anything before you go or during the hike. The temperature and humidity are high, and you are famished. As you near the end of the hike, you see a lodge ahead on the hill. They are preparing a meal for you, and the smell of the cooking food wafts through the air as you approach. You begin to picture in your mind's eye what the food will look and taste like, and upon entering, are invited to sit at the table. Now the aroma of the food is over-powering, and at that moment someone sets a delicious meal in front of you. You also see a glass of cold ice water next to your plate, and you are so thirsty and your mouth is so dry you can hardly talk.
>
> Imagine at that moment deciding not to eat or drink, or worse yet, only taking a small bite of food or a small sip of water, then getting up and walking out. More than likely, when you start to drink, you will likely drain the glass. Think of the feeling you experience when you drink and eat when you are *that* thirsty and hungry. That is similar to the craving to view pornography in one who is addicted. *When craving begins, reasoning ends!*

Of course, one should not suppose that addiction is an appetite like food that *must* be satisfied. While we die if we don't eat when in starvation, those who are addicted heal when they seek comfort in Christ instead of the addiction. Indeed, there are many who are now in strong recovery who don't feel this powerful compulsion anymore, and who are careful to avoid the triggers that create these compulsions.

THE ADDICTIVE CYCLE

Patrick Carnes, Ph.D., is widely considered to be one of the world's foremost experts on sexual addictions. He first wrote *Out of the Shadows*[4] in 1983 and has followed up with other relevant works, including *Don't Call it Love,*[5] *Facing the Shadow,*[6] and *In the Shadows of the Net.*[7] In *Out of the Shadows* he first defined the Addiction Cycle, consisting of four phases.[8] While this cycle is intended to apply to all sexual addictions, we will consider it in the context of pornography addiction.

- *Preoccupation* consists of obsessive thoughts entering the addicted person's consciousness, with memories of past images returning to create a private viewing in their mind. During this phase the person begins to withdraw and isolate from those he loves.

- *Ritualization* follows, during which the person places himself in a position in which he is ready to act out, even while consciously telling himself he is not going to view pornography again. For instance, he may tell himself he is strong, yet he begins to surf the Internet alone late at night, or flip channels on a TV where he knows unfiltered satellite or cable will likely contain pornography. He may rationalize and tell himself if he does see pornographic images he will quickly click off the channel.

- *Acting Out* inevitably follows, with a viewing binge, usually associated with masturbation.

---

[4] Patrick Carnes, *Out of the Shadows,* Hazelden, 2001.

[5] Patrick Carnes, *Don't Call It Love,* Bantam, 1991.

[6] Patrick Carnes, *Facing the Shadow: Starting Sexual and Relationship Recovery,* Gentle Path Press, 2005.

[7] Patrick Carnes, *In the Shadows of the Net: Breaking Free of Compulsive Online Sexual Behavior,* Hazelden, 2001.

[8] This cycle is described in several of the books listed.

- *Despair* ensues as the binge ends, and the addicted one feels shame and guilt. These emotions drive him deeper into secrecy and deception, while paradoxically pride tells him he is different, that he can get over this alone, that no one else needs to know. Depending on religious and social forces unique to his life and how much resistance these forces provide, the despair phase may last for days or even months until despair fades and preoccupation returns, continuing the cycle.

Carnes also defines a belief cycle based on an "addictive system" in which impaired thinking allows the one in addiction to think that he can survive in the addiction cycle.[9] As unmanageability increases secondary to the effects of the addiction, the impaired thinking alters the belief system, and the acting out becomes the drug that reinforces the impaired beliefs.[10]

As resistance evaporates, the time between one viewing of pornography and the next lessens. Their world becomes completely sexualized. Brain chemicals and the adversary synergistically act in an unholy alliance of soul-searing destruction. Dr. Victor Cline describes a four-stage escalation in addiction based on his vast experience counseling those struggling with pornography:

1. *Addiction.* The person finds he compulsively views pornography.
2. *Escalation.* The addicted person seeks progressively harder core pornography to get the same effect.
3. *Desensitization.* Tolerance increases to progressively explicit material.
4. *Acting Out Sexually.* The person seeks to act out fantasies viewed in the pornography (prostitution, adultery, etc.).[11]

---

[9] Patrick Carnes, *Out of the Shadows*, Hazelden, 1983, 29-31.
[10] Ibid.
[11] Victor Cline, *Pornography Effects on Adults and Children.* Morality in Media, http://mentalhealthlibrary.info/library/porn/pornlds/pornldsauthor/links/victorcline/porneffect.htm.

The addicted one will only suffer more loss as the behavior continues. Like a cat chasing its tail, there is no final solution, satiation, or satisfaction in addiction. It is a "futile cycle" which prevents the addicted one from moving forward.

When the pain of the losses accumulated exceeds the payoff of viewing pornography, the person will do what it takes to stop. Successful recovery will likely be the hardest task they have ever accomplished, but in the end will be worth any price paid, since it is the only way back to sanity and peace.

CHAPTER 3

THE MONEY TRAIL

*Money can't buy happiness, but it can
buy you the kind of misery you prefer.*

Author Unknown

Money often costs too much.

Ralph Waldo Emerson

Forbes magazine placed global profits from pornography at 56 billion dollars a year, with *Fortune* magazine estimating at least 10 billion a year in the U.S. alone.[1] A more recent estimate is 100 billion and 13 billion dollars, respectively.[2] Janet LaRue, Chief Counsel for Concerned Women for America describes these profits and names specific companies in "The Porn Ring Around Corporate White Collars: Getting Filthy Rich."[3] According to LaRue, companies such as AT&T, MCI, Time-Warner, Comcast, Echo Star Communications, GM's DirecTV, Hilton, Marriott, Sheraton, Radisson, VISA, MasterCard, and American Express profit financially from selling this damaging material while individuals and families suffer. A quote from an underwriter at Centrex Securities sums it up well: "I'm not a weirdo or a pervert, it's not my deal. I've got kids and a family. But

---

[1] Janet M. LaRue, "Porn Nation," *World and I*, Aug. 1, 2001, 44.
[2] Jason S. Carroll, Laura M. Padilla-Walker, Larry J. Nelson, Chad D. Olson, Carolyn McNamara Barry, Stephanie D. Madsen, "Generation XXX: Pornography Acceptance and Use Among Emerging Adults," *Journal of Adolescent Research*, Vol. 23(1) 2008, 6-30.
[3] Janet M. LaRue, "The Porn Ring Around Corporate White Collars: Getting Filthy Rich," www.cwfa.org/images/content/wcp-report.pdf.

if I can see as an underwriter going out and making bucks on people being weird, hey, dollars are dollars. *I'm not selling drugs.* It's Wall Street."[4] (emphasis added)

Actually, pornography *is* a drug. We will go into that in more detail later. But we must realize that we are fighting some of the wealthiest people in the world, and as indicated above, not just Larry Flynn and Hugh Hefner and their associates, but mainstream companies we use every day for legitimate needs. John Harmer calls this the Sex-Industrial Complex and has spent years fighting pornography from his days as Ronald Reagan's Lieutenant Governor in California to his current leadership of the anti-pornography Lighted Candle Society, which promotes litigation against pornographers for damage inflicted on individuals and society.

With companies like On Command and LodgeNet Entertainment providing pornography to 1.5 million hotel rooms, it is no wonder "analysts cited in the *Los Angeles Times* suggest that adult features generate approximately half of total hotel pay-per-view revenue in the United States, approximately $250 million annually."[5] We think of AT&T providing us with communication, but what about the millions a year they make selling pornography? Jon Radloff, a former AT&T cable executive claimed pornography was very profitable for AT&T, but not something the company wanted to draw attention to. He said, "We wanted to provide it, but it wasn't something that we touted in our advertising campaigns."[6]

When retired FBI agent Bill Kelly wrote to AT&T advising the company that the Hot Network hard-core pornography offerings violate the federal obscenity laws, AT&T responded by saying essentially that it's OK because everyone is doing it.[7]

4   Brendon I. Koerner, "A Lust for Profits," *U.S. News & World Report*, March 27, 2000, 44.
5   Private Media Group, Inc., http://222.prvt.com/prod broadcasting.asp.
6   "Corporate America Gets Rich Off Pornography," *Capitol Hill Blue*, June 27, 2002, http://chblue.com/article.asp?ID=2895.
7   Letter to Bill Kelly from Daniel E. Somers, President and CEO, AT&T Broadband, in Janet M. LaRue, "The Porn Ring Around Corporate White Collars: Getting Filthy Rich," www.cwfa.org/images/content/wcp-report.pdf.

In ABCNews.com's "Porn Profits: Corporate America's Secret," we learn that pornography is bigger business than the NFL, NBA, and pro baseball combined.[8] The companies previously mentioned make millions off pornography each year, yet they don't show these profits in company reports.[9]

Oprah Winfrey recently had a show where she effectively mainstreamed pornography.[10] On the show, Dr. Pepper Schwartz advocated the notion of "friends with benefits," or basically the unattached sexuality. Campus psychiatrist Dr. Miriam Grossman identifies this same unbonded sexuality causing an epidemic of depression in young women at UCLA,[11] yet Schwartz flew across the world having one-night stands and then wrote a book about it. She said, "We adore each other, we respect each other, we have great sex, and that's it. It stays in that little category and it doesn't get out of it."[12] Yet it is unlikely that we would hear Schwartz, Oprah, or these other companies talking about the human exploitation and objectification that occurs making these movies: unprotected sex with young people as young as eighteen, not to mention the devastating social, mental, and spiritual consequences.

Former Surgeon General C. Everett Koop said all of these mainstream companies are eager to profit from pornography, yet consider the performers in the industry to be "throwaway people."[13] Koop says there are no government standards regulating testing in the industry; thus, America's big corporations are complicit in a public health hazard. The ABC article reveals the corporate attitude:

ABCNEWS asked the companies to discuss the revenue they derive from adult films and whether they have any re-

---

[8]   "Porn Profits: Corporate America's Secret," ABCNews.com, Jan 28, 2003, http://abcnews.go.com/Primetime/Story?id=132001&page=1.

[9]   Ibid.

[10]   "237 Reasons to Have Sex," Oprah Winfrey Show, September 25, 2007.

[11]   Grossman, Miriam, *Unprotected: A Campus Psychiatrist Reveals How Political Correctness in Her Profession Endangers Every Student.* Penguin, 2006; published under the name Anonymous, MD. She finally revealed her identity on "Dr. Laura."

[12]   "237 Reasons to Have Sex," Oprah Winfrey Show, September 25, 2007.

[13]   Porn Profits: Corporate America's Secret, ABCNews.com, Jan 29, 2003.

sponsibility for the welfare of the performers. A spokesman
for DirecTV said he was not permitted to talk about the company's profits from adult movies. Representatives of Comcast, Hilton and Marriott refused to talk on the record about
the issue. A spokesman for AOL Time Warner, Mark Harrad, said that Time Warner Cable "has traditionally offered
what they called . . . more soft-core programming." Also, he
said, "in a couple of divisions they have increased the programming to the next step up, if you will, which I think some
people would understandably call hard-core." The decision to
offer the harder material was driven by consumers, Harrad
said. Koop believes that to prompt reform, Congress should
hold hearings on regulating the industry and "subpoena some
of the people who run these shows." If nothing is done, "it'll
just get worse," he said, adding, "The appetite for pornography seems to be insatiable."[14]

Dr. Koop was spot on with his use of the word "insatiable," which
means always needing more and impossible to satisfy. Synonyms for
insatiable are voracious, greedy, ravenous, and unquenchable. It is
ironic that the insatiable appetite for money by the pornographers
and the mainstream companies who profit from them is supported
and fueled by the insatiable appetite for pornography in the addicted.

It's Just a Business

A recent development has been the proliferation of free pornographic sites, of which many, up to a fourth in one estimate, are self-
made.[15] Porn companies are feeling the pinch as consumers use the
free material and avoid the cost and risk of discovery of pay sites.
Steven Hirsch, co-founder of Vivid, a large porn company, com-
plained, "We're dealing with rampant piracy, tons of free content...

---

14   Ibid.
15   "Porn Companies Challenged by Internet Sites," *Yahoo News* (AT&T), Jan.11,
     2008, 2:21p.m.ET, http://news.yahoo.com/s/nm/20080111/bs_nm/porn_inter-
     net_dc;_ylt=AmbH2G1yR8hzIoeqfYFWKr1v24cA.

This industry is going to have to get together and look at these guys that are putting out the stuff for free ... so they are going to have to get in line and start paying for it ... If that doesn't happen and we see all of this free content out there, people are not going to be able to afford to produce movies anymore."[16] Sounds good at first: pornographers going bankrupt because they can't get people to pay, but there is a dark side to this phenomenon. The free pornography is proliferating, and it is even easier for the target audience, the teenager, to access it and become a lifelong customer. The pornographers are already looking to firm up ties with the Sex Industrial Complex, as the Yahoo article states:

> Some adult industry executives say a solution may lay in future distribution deals with big companies such as AT&T Inc (T.N), Verizon Communications Inc (VZ.N), Comcast Corp (CMCSA.O) and Apple Inc. (AAPL.O). An Apple spokeswoman said the company would not comment if it had held past talks or was interested in distributing adult product. A spokeswoman for Comcast, the largest U.S. cable provider, said the firm offered adult content in its video-on-demand service but said she knew of no talks for mobile adult distribution. Sales of sex films to mobile devices occur in Europe but have yet to take off in the United States. "We won't make money through adult content," said Verizon Wireless spokesman Ken Muche. AT&T did not comment.[17]

The pornographer Steven Hirsch, previously quoted, portrays himself as a family man who just goes to work. An interview with David Asman on *Your World with Neil Cavuto* is enlightening:

ASMAN: We all know sex sells. From dirty magazines to adult films, porn is a multibillion-dollar business. It's also a pioneer of sorts, blazing a path across the Internet. And now

16   Ibid.
17   Ibid.

it wants to teach Hollywood a lesson. On Monday, Vivid Entertainment is going to start selling downloadable movies that can be burned onto DVDs. Will Hollywood, who resisted this for a long time, be forced to follow? Steven Hirsch is CEO of Vivid Entertainment and he joins us now. Good to see you, Mr. Hirsch.

HIRSCH: Thank you.

ASMAN: I have got to ask you a question up front. I'm in the news business. When I go home, the last thing I want to do is turn on the news. Now you are in the sex business. When you go home, is sex the last thing you are interested in?

HIRSCH: I don't know if it's the last thing that I'm interested in. But it's not the first thing I'm looking forward to. *I like to hang out with my kids when I get home.*

ASMAN: All right. A lot of people wonder that, whether or not the sex industry guy—whether he burns out on sex. But you say no?

HIRSCH: *No. It's just a business.*[18] (emphasis added)

It is interesting to note the easy conversational style of Asman with Hirsch. By granting him an interview, and as evidenced by the accepting tone of the program, Fox and other news agencies help mainstream pornography. Again, no concern was voiced during the program about the "throwaway people"[19] of pornography, rather the emphasis was on the technology and economics. It is unlikely that Hirsch spends time at home worrying about the economic or emotional well being of his workers. Would Asman interview a cocaine cartel drug lord about how to better the business of addicting the world to cocaine? Hirsch mentioned how he enjoyed being at home and spending time with his kids. Is he considering the families that

[18] "Porn to Run," *Your World with Neil Cavuto*, Fox News May 12, 2006.
[19] "Porn Profits: Corporate America's Secret," ABCNews.com, Jan 29, 2003.

are broken as a result of the pornographic material he produces? Has he considered the children who have lost the love and support of a father because of addiction? The peer-reviewed literature, as we will explore later, tells us marriage and children don't thrive in the context of pornography addiction.

CONSPIRING MEN

In 1833 Joseph Smith received Section 89 of the *Doctrine and Covenants*, which we refer to as the Word of Wisdom. He said, "Behold, verily, thus saith the Lord unto you: In consequence of evils and designs which do and will exist in the hearts of conspiring men in the last days, I have warned you, and *forewarn* you, by giving unto you this word of wisdom by revelation."[20] (emphasis added) We believe it to be an inspired guide as to what we should and should not take into our bodies. No one can logically dispute the conspiracy of the tobacco and alcohol industries to profit from compulsive consumption of these products. What about application of this warning as to consumption of visual products? I believe the Lord forewarns us about conspiring men and women who trap others into consuming this electronic drug, injected, says Dr. Jeffery Satinover of Princeton, "directly into the brain through the eyes."[21] Paul also warned us that we wrestle "against the rulers of this world, against spiritual wickedness in high places."[22]

My wife, Jana, moved from Utah to Texas years ago when we married and developed allergies to pollens endemic in our area. She has been taking desensitization shots now for a couple of years. She goes regularly to get another shot, so her body slowly accommodates to the allergens in the air. In the end, she hopes she can breathe the air without it bothering her. In similar fashion, societal forces are

---

[20] D&C 89:4
[21] "Hearing on the Brain Science Behind Pornography Addiction and Effects of Addiction on Families and Communities," Senate Committee on Commerce, Science, and Transportation; Subcommittee on Science Technology, and Space; November 18, 2004, http://www.obscenitycrimes.org/Senate-Reisman-Layden-Etc.pdf.
[22] Ephesians 6:12

clearly mainstreaming pornography and desensitizing us to it.

President Thomas S. Monson described how the bark beetle caused devastation in the Dutch Elm population in England. Subtly at first, the trees show signs of illness, with wilting of the younger leaves at first. Finally, the tree dies, and entire forests are destroyed by the beetle. He relates this to pornography: "At first we scarcely realize we have been infected. We laugh and make lighthearted comment concerning the off-color story or the clever cartoon. With evangelical zeal we protect the so-called rights of those who would contaminate with smut and destroy all that is precious and sacred. The beetle of pornography is doing his deadly task—undercutting our will, destroying our immunity, and stifling that upward reach within each of us."[23] The R-rated movie of yesterday is the PG or PG-13 of today. Almost every movie will have its taste of nudity, or at least sensuality. Youth and adults now go to a movie with pornography and rationalize that since it's PG-13 and it's only nudity with implied sex, it's not that bad. *And in doing so they get their desensitization shot.* Husbands and wives sit together, watching sit-coms and movies that are suggestive and provocative, if not downright pornographic, and think they can handle it. Couples and individuals must understand that carelessness and complacency in media consumption is fertile ground for addiction.

We must confront pornography not only through public awareness, but more importantly through personal education and fortification for our families and ourselves. Few, if any, families and extended families will be untouched by this plague. As Ralph Yarro, a former Novell executive who now devotes his time to fighting pornography, said, "Wake up. Apathy will kill you here. If porn hasn't touched your life already, it is going to rip huge, gaping holes in it. You better get active real quick."[24]

---

[23] Thomas S. Monson, "Pornography, the Deadly Carrier," *Ensign*, July 2001, 2.
[24] "Fight to Stop Porn," *Church News*, April 14, 2007, http://www.desnews.com/cn/view/1,1721,470006230,00.html.

RECOVERY STORY 1

I was priviledged to spend time with this person and hear his recovery story. I thank him, and the other individuals who also share their recovery stories throughout the book.

My addiction to lust, pornography, and masturbation started when I was about twelve years old. I didn't really think much of it at the time, but being raised in the LDS church, I knew that what I was doing was wrong. I didn't think I was hurting anyone, so I continued to use the addiction as an escape from depression and loneliness (though I didn't know that was what I was doing at the time) and to cover whatever I didn't feel like dealing with. Around age sixteen, I became more rebellious and started drinking alcohol with my friends as well. I graduated and left home to go to college 600 miles away. Free at last! I got involved with the wrong crowd and partied with my newfound friends. My sexual addictions were always there in their various forms but I kept them very private. I isolated from friends at church and eventually stopped going to church completely. I was often around large groups of people but I always felt completely alone. Plain old normal TV (not cable, not satellite, not videos) was my main source of inappropriate material along with people I would see throughout the day. I was nearing rock bottom, as I would regularly use lust and alcohol to numb my pains and escape from life.

At age twenty-two, I had some experiences that led to a change of heart. I really started to care about what I was doing and how it was hurting my future wife and me and family I wanted to have some day. I found out later that this change of heart had come to me as a result of my parents' prayers, fasting, asking people in their ward to pray and fast, and continuously putting my name in the temple. When this change of heart happened, I was able to walk away from alcohol, partying, everything except the sexual addictions. At this point, I actually wanted to walk away from those too, but over the

years it had turned into a strong addiction that was much more powerful than alcohol or anything else I had experienced up to that point.
As I would soon find out, I was completely unable to overcome it on
my own.

For the next ten years, I tried to overcome my sexual addictions
and failed miserably. I would mentally beat myself up every day for
being such a failure. I went on a mission around age twenty-five. I
did get a two-year reprieve from acting out my addictions physically
during my mission, but lust was still with me throughout that period. After my mission, when the Internet had matured enough for
me to get into it more fully, is when what people would consider "real
pornography" entered my life. This newfound material locked me
into the addiction even tighter. I could find no way out of it. At this
point, I was a full tithe payer, temple recommend holder/attendee,
and active member of my ward with leadership positions.

It seemed that I was doing everything in my power to do everything else in my life perfectly to make up for the sins of my hidden
life. At times, my pride would convince me that I was such a great
person that I had to have this addiction just to keep me humble.
Thoughts like that almost got me to stop fighting against it and just
accept it as a necessary evil that, by keeping me humble, did more
good than harm. I found out later that I was completely wrong about
that! I also thought that once I got married, the problem would go
away because then this "appetite" would finally be satisfied. I found
that to be completely wrong also by talking to other people who were
married and still had the problem. I found out later that just as one
in addiction is never satisfied with one piece of pornography for their
whole life, one's wife could not satisfy lust for very long either. I
found that love was completely different than lust and that I could
only find happiness if I removed lust from my life completely. I discovered that love is personal and different for each person that I love.
I also found that lust is generic and can be transferred from person
to person. That is what is done as a person views several images of
pornography one after the other, transferring lust from one to another to another.

Around age thirty-two, one of the many bishops who had tried to help me overcome this addiction told me about a 12 Step program for sexual addiction. I didn't even know what a 12 Step program was, but my bishop told me that another member of my congregation had found success there. At this point, I was willing to try anything. I went to my first 12 Step meeting and was very nervous. It turned out that the people there were just like me and had been in predicaments similar to mine but were now changing for the better. I identified with what they were saying, and I got hope in that first meeting that this might actually work. I was no longer alone. I kept going back to the 12 Step meetings, started "working the steps," and began to see real changes in my behavior and in my level of peace and joy.

It was a rocky road in the beginning for a while, but with a lot of meetings and working the steps, I became free from these addictions and then started to work on overcoming the effects that all of those years of addiction had on me.

Those meetings increased the faith I had in my Savior. If these men in this group could identify with me and like me, even after knowing about the problems I faced, maybe Christ could like me too, and maybe I could start liking myself. The meetings also provided a safe anonymous place that allowed me to be more humble or self aware and honest. Faith in Christ and humility were the missing pieces of the puzzle for me—the pieces of the puzzle that I couldn't find at church with regard to this addiction because church wasn't a safe or appropriate place for me to share about my addiction or hear testimony of others who were, through Christ, overcoming their addictions. As my faith in Christ and my humility increased, my ability to walk away from different parts of the addiction also increased. I found underneath the numbing effects of my addiction, the broken, hurting twelve-year old from my childhood. It got worse before it got better. I would get angry, afraid, depressed, controlling, but I began to reach less and less for the drug of pornography and instead could reach more and more to Christ to heal and comfort me. I always thought I had faith in Christ, but I can see now that it was weaker than I had originally thought. I set up boundaries that helped me not fall again while I healed, much like an ankle brace protects a healing ankle. Boundaries like not accessing the Internet without someone around, etc. Most importantly, I got myself to the meetings, the only place I have found where my faith in Christ with regard to this addiction could be nurtured and strengthened sufficiently to free me from my addiction.

I didn't become free from temptation, but I no longer felt compelled to give in to temptation and I was finally free to choose to turn away from these addictions and was finally free to choose other, better things in life. So instead of fighting an addiction for 95 percent of each day, I can now peacefully walk away from temptation, which I now battle only about 1 percent of each day. I still have a lot of catching up to do since my spiritual and emotional progress stopped at age twelve, but seeing the changes in me now that the addiction is gone is extremely satisfying, liberating, and peace-inducing. And this time it feels completely different from the two years of dry-drunk temporary physical sobriety I had during my mission. I am finally happy and free. I still have to exert effort to maintain the freedom and the humility and faith in Christ necessary to keep that freedom, but it's nothing like what my life of addiction was like. I have to take care of myself spiritually and physically. I have to do my part, and Christ does what I can't.

I currently have about five years free of the addiction, and I continue to attend meetings for two reasons. First, I go to give back some of the experience, strength, and hope that I have received from others in the groups I have attended. Second, I go to be reminded of what things used to be like, and that keeps me humble. The spirit is very strong and peaceful in these meetings, and they now help me to stay on track as I work to become more Christ-like. I actually think of the meetings as a mid-week boost, like a really powerful institute class that deals with actually applying the gospel of Jesus Christ in my everyday life. I am happy and I am free, one day at a time.

CHAPTER 4

ROME RE-VISITED

Those who are unaware of history are destined to repeat it.

George Santayana

A few years ago when our oldest daughter finished high school, my wife and I visited Italy with her. We were fascinated by the twin cities of Pompeii and Herculaneum and how they were frozen in time by the eruption of Mount Vesuvius on August 24, A.D 79. We felt as if we had walked through a wormhole and emerged two thousand years earlier as we walked up and down the streets and in and out of houses. My fascination with Pompeii, however, was tempered by sadness at the moral decline already in progress, as we saw in some of the homes signs of the moral decay, which would eventually destroy Rome and had already destroyed Greece. Some of the art on the walls and statues could only be described as pornographic, intended to titillate and arouse sexually.

Will Durant, in his colossal ten-volume work *The Story of Civilization,* describes the fall of Rome in volume 3. Although external forces were important, internal implosion appeared to be the direct cause. Durant explains these factors:

> Biological factors were more fundamental. A serious decline of population appears in the West after Hadrian...Aurleius, to replenish his army, enrolled slaves, gladiators, policemen, criminals...So many farms had been abandoned...that Pertinax offered them gratis to anyone who would till them. A law of Septimius Serverus speaks of a *penuria hominum* – a shortage of men. Bishop Dionysius

said the population had halved during his time, and mourned to "see the human race diminishing and constantly wasting away." Only the barbarians and the Orientals were increasing, outside the Empire and within.

What had caused this fall in population? Above all, *family limitation*. Practiced first by the educated classes, it had now seeped down to a proletariat named for its fertility: by AD 100 it had reached the agricultural classes, as shown by the use of imperial alimnemta to encourage rural parentage...*Sexual excesses may have reduced human fertility: the avoidance or deferment of marriage had a like effect...Moral decay contributed to the dissolution...men had now, in the middle and upper classes, the means to yield to temptation...Moral and esthetic standards were lowered by the magnetism of the mass: and sex ran riot in freedom while political liberty decayed.*[1] (emphasis added)

Sadly, we are following suit today, and the cyber-acceleration of the Internet will only speed up the decline. I believe pornography is both a cause and effect of the dissolution of the family, and in particular, the institution of marriage. In this regard, pornography is an integral link in the current decline seen in western populations. Two income homes and other cultural differences obviously contribute, but as marriage fades children become irrelevant and expensive. As the West atrophies away, other cultures will replace it with new middle and upper classes until luxury softens them also and the cycle repeats itself. Just as sex ran riot in Rome, so pornography aids our society in its quest for unlimited and unrestrained sexuality.

SELECTED FOR EXTINCTION?

In selling pornography as a harmless recreational pastime, unrestrained sexuality, including homosexuality, is trumped by social liberals as freedom of expression between consenting adults. There is

---

[1] Will Durant, *The Story of Civilization, Caesar and Christ, Volume 3*, Simon and Shuster, Inc., 1944, 665-666.

no higher law, or "sin" concept to define boundaries of sexual conduct. The only restraint is what society tolerates at any given time. Secularists will look to Darwin and science, and not to a Higher Power, to define constraint on biologic processes such as sexuality. Yet from a Darwinian perspective those who selfishly practice unrestrained sexuality are selecting themselves and their DNA for extinction. Consider the following from Mona Charen, who quotes psychiatrist Norman Doidge from his book, *The Brain That Changes Itself*:

> The men (and they are overwhelmingly men) who become hooked on this bilge are often miserable about it. They know that it affects their capacity to love and be loved by real women. As Doidge explained, "Pornographers promise healthy pleasure and a release from sexual tension, but what they often deliver is an addiction, tolerance, and an eventual decrease in pleasure. Paradoxically, the male patients I worked with often craved pornography but didn't like it."[2]

She also describes men who prefer pornography to actual sexual relations with a human being in this article. This is a common scenario in men addicted to pornography. Dr Doidge describes his experience treating these men: "They reported increasing difficulty in being turned on by their actual sexual partners, spouses or girlfriends, though they still considered them objectively attractive. When I asked if this phenomenon had any relationship to viewing pornography, they answered that it initially helped them get more excited during sex but over time had the opposite effect. Now, instead of using their senses to enjoy being in bed, in the present, with their partners, lovemaking increasingly required them to fantasize that they were part of a porn script."[3] In the animal world, interventions which interfere with the ability of a species to reproduce select that species or subspecies for extinction. In humans, it seems that as we become more educated and affluent, we become obsessed with pleasure. We

2   "Tis the Season for Porn?" Mona Charen, Creators Syndicate, December 19, 2008
3   Norman Doidge, *The Brain That Changes Itself*, Penguin Books, 2007, 104.

dissociate sexuality from procreation, as did Greece and Rome, and select ourselves, biologically, for extinction. As men prefer porn and prostitution to marriage and children, their DNA lines will disappear.

As marriage becomes passé in Japan, Europe, and the West, the birthrate will only decline faster. All of these areas are now below the 2.1 birthrate needed to sustain population. A BBC News article titled "The EU's Baby Blues" says, "Europe's working-age population is shrinking as fertility rates decline. In a fit of gloom, one German minister recently warned of the country 'turning the light out' if its birth rate did not pick up."[4] An IPS article titled "Japan: Wooing Women as Birth Rates Drop" laments the birth rate. " 'The yellow signal has started flickering,' said health minister Jiro Kawasaki, referring to the birth rate and the consequent threat to the national economy."[5]

VISUAL PHEROMONES: TRAPPING AND CONFUSING

In 1869 the gypsy moth was brought to Medford, Massachusetts to produce silk for local industry. While they were good at producing silk, some escaped, and it was discovered that they were also very good at defoliating and killing trees. Since then, gypsy moths have continued to spread west and south, and have caused billions in environmental damage as they have destroyed forests.

In 1972 a paper was published in *Science* which described a novel approach to controlling the moth.[6] Rather than use toxic pesticides to kill the caterpillars and adults, it proposed using sexual attraction to stop the insects from reproducing. Although this seems paradoxical, it is now a technique used for many other insect species. It so

[4] "The EU's Baby Blues," BBC, news.bbc.co.uk/1/hi/world/europe/4768644.stm March 27, 2006.
[5] "Japan: Wooing Women as Birth Rates Drop," *IPS Tokyo*, Jan 10, 2006, http://ipsnews.net/news.asp?idnews=31709.
[6] Morton Beroza and E. F. Knipling, "Gypsy Moth Control with the Sex Attractant Pheromone." *Science*, 177 (4043): 19, July 7, 1972, 19-27.

happens that for the adult male gypsy moth to find a female, she must secrete a chemical called a pheromone which he can sense in very small amounts. The paper described using an isolate of the pheromone to either trap or confuse the male, and thus prevent mating. Since then, pheromonic control of the moth and of other insects has been a mainstay of entomologic science. For instance, consider some of the following quotes from an article in 2000:

> *Ninety per cent* of chemical insecticides have been eliminated from commercial orchards in Australia thanks to the use of chemical sex attractants. As the pheromone permeates through the walls of the *tubing it is carried on air currents* through the orchard. "The male either becomes *confused* and doesn't know which direction to turn for the female, or he becomes *desensitized* to the lower levels of pheromones naturally given out by the female and has *no incentive to mate with her*...The insects follow the pheromone trail *into the trap*," says Dr. (Richard) Vickers.[7] (emphasis added)

Consider now the direct analogy. Human males are primarily attracted to females visually. Pornography is a visual pheromone. It travels thought the air on the Internet, and confuses males who think they are following natural cues for sexual attraction. They follow this visual pheromone *into the trap*, and are *desensitized*, into an inability to reproduce. Young men now find pornography more interesting and appealing than natural sexuality in a committed relationship where shared parental responsibilities allow for the rearing of children. Also, it is interesting to note the 90% number in the article compared with the 87% male involvement in pornography described in the Carroll paper.[8]

---

[7] Anna Salleh, "Sex Pheromones Cut Pesticide Use," ABC Science Online, October 16, 2000.

[8] Jason S. Carroll, Laura M. Padilla-Walker, Larry J. Nelson, Chad D. Olson, Carolyn McNamara Barry, Stephanie D. Madsen, "Generation XXX: Pornography Acceptance and Use Among Emerging Adults," *Journal of Adolescent Research*, Vol. 23(1) 2008, 6-30.

After Will Durant wrote *The Story of Civilization*, the Durants wrote *The Lessons of History*. We would do well to listen to their warning, written long before Internet pornography became the number one business on the Net:

> Intellect is therefore a vital force in history, but it can also be a dissolvent and destructive power. Out of every hundred new ideas ninety-nine or more will probably be inferior to the traditional responses which they propose to replace. No one man, however brilliant or well-informed, can come in one lifetime to such fullness of understanding as to safely judge and dismiss the customs or institutions of his society, for these are the wisdom of generations after centuries of experiment in the laboratory of history. A youth boiling with hormones will wonder why he should not give full freedom to his sexual desires; and if he is unchecked by custom, morals, or laws, he may ruin his life before he matures sufficiently to understand that sex is a river of fire that must be banked and cooled by a hundred restraints if it is not to consume in chaos both the individual and the group.[9]

Desensitization to pornography is based on a growing emphasis on the secular, with moral relativism replacing respect for Deity. A sense of the sacred is lost as sensation becomes the new god. The new "sacred" is whatever can provide the newest, most novel shock to the senses. Thus, marriage and family become less important, and we see the social changes now becoming prevalent which disregard time tested and proven institutions and mores. The decline of marriage, same sex relationships, the acceptance of childbearing out of wedlock, and the explosion of sexualizing cosmetic surgery are among symptoms of the underlying disease of secularism. The acceptance and mainstreaming of pornography is both a symptom and a cause. Its pervasiveness, particularly in teenage boys, is most alarming because it will imprint the young male brain in a way that will be difficult to heal.

---

[9]   Will and Ariel Durant, *The Lessons of History*, Simon and Schuster, 1968, 35-36.

The Durant's warning becomes more prophetic with regard to the "youth boiling with hormones"[10] being swept away by a "river of fire."[11] Pornography allows sexual sin to take on a pervasive quality with the technology of the Age of Information distributing it widely and efficiently, burning relationships and motivation. Elder Jeffery R. Holland describes the *heat* aspect of sexual sin eloquently:

> A more important scriptural observation is offered by the writer of Proverbs: "Can a man take fire in his bosom, and his clothes not be burned? Can one go upon hot coals, and his feet not be burned?...Whoso committeth adultery...destroyeth his own soul. A wound and dishonor shall he get; and his reproach shall not be wiped away."[12]
>
> Why is this matter of sexual relationships so severe that fire is almost always the metaphor, with passion pictured vividly in flames? What is there in the potentially hurtful heat of this that leaves one's soul—or the whole world, for that matter—destroyed if that flame is left unchecked and those passions unrestrained?[13]

If the Internet is a river of information, it is now swelling beyond its banks and drowning many before they even see the storm. It is sweeping away homes and marriages, trust, love, and industry. We can't expect change in the weather anytime soon. The storms of greed and lust continue to rain more pornography into the torrent. To avoid being swept away, we must move to higher ground and build on a firm foundation. As the Psalmist said, we must "ascend into the hill of the Lord"[14] and "stand in His holy place."[15] To do so, we must have "clean hands and a pure heart,"[16] not lifted up in vanity, or pride, and be free from deceit.

---

[10] Ibid, 36.
[11] Ibid.
[12] Proverbs 6:27, 28, 32, 33
[13] Jeffery R. Holland, "Personal Purity," *Ensign*, November 1998, 75-76.
[14] Psalms 24:3-4
[15] Ibid, verse 3.
[16] Ibid, verse 4.

CHAPTER 5

EVEN AMONG US

We have found the enemy, and he is us.

Walt Kelly

In the November 2004 Priesthood Session of General Conference, President Gordon B. Hinckley spoke about pornography and said, "I am convinced this is a very serious problem even among us."[1] In 2007 the LDS *Church News* ran a seven-part series on pornography. Some of the statements illustrate the extent of the problem:

> *Hundreds of bishops and stake presidents list pornography as their No. 1 concern for Church members.*
> Research indicates that by their senior year in high school, *100 percent of males have viewed pornography,* said Fred M. Riley, commissioner of LDS Family Services. In addition, *the average first exposure of males to pornography is age 11.*[2] (emphasis added)

> Experts say that as many as 40 percent of Americans suffer from a compulsive sexual behavior or addiction. The average age of beginning addiction is 11 years old. *Latter-day Saints with the problem are no different when it comes to prevalence or magnitude of sexual addictions.*[3] (emphasis added)

---

[1]   Gordon B. Hinckley, "A Tragic Evil Among Us," *Ensign*, November 2004, 61.
[2]   "Protecting homes from pornography," *Church News*, March 10, 2007, http://www.desnews.com/cn/view/1,1721,470005888,00.html.
[3]   "Defending the home against pornography," *Church News*, April 21, 2007, http://www.desnews.com/cn/view/1,1721,470006290,00.html.

It has been my privilege to work with men and boys who have struggled with pornography addiction. Most were exposed as young men between ten and fifteen years of age, and some even younger. All of these young men had already involved their bishop, most had seen a counselor, and some had been exposed to a 12 Step meeting format. Despite these efforts they have continued to struggle. They are good people who were blinded when very young, who had their agency suspended, almost before they knew what was happening to them.

Nevertheless, unless they are freed from this poison, they will be destroyed by it regardless of the reason they initially became involved and without regard to the reasons they can't stop. *It is becoming clear we are dealing with a pandemic of sorts.*

The young ages of exposure will change the rules of sexual behavior.[4] With the average age of exposure being eleven,[5] pornography is becoming society's sex education tool. Many, if not most, teens are learning about and initiating sex earlier by watching adult actors have real or simulated sexual intercourse in pornographic movies.[6] At a time when the hippocampus is forming new neurons and the amygdala is forming new emotional sexual memories, it may be that pornography is imprinting the brain at such an early age that we may be facing a social epidemic of colossal proportion in the near future. A national study on this subject is sobering:

> Seekers of pornography, both online and offline, are significantly more likely to be male, with only 5% of self-identified seekers being female. The vast majority (87%) of youth who report looking for sexual images online are 14 years of

4   Elissa P. Benedek and Catherine F. Brown, "No Excuses: Televised Pornography Harms Children," *Harvard Review of Psychiatry.* 7(4), Nov-Dec 1999, 236-40.

5   Jennings Bryant, "Frequency of Exposure, Age of Initial Exposure, and Reactions to Initial Exposure to Pornography," Report presented to the Attorney General's Commission on Pornography, Houston, TX. In J Zillmann and. J Bryant, *Pornography: Research Advances and Policy Considerations,* Erlbaum, 1989, 25-55.

6   Rebecca L. Collins, Marc N. Elliott, Sandra H. Berry, David E. Kanouse, Dale Kunkel, Sarah B. Hunter, and Angela Miu, "Watching Sex on Television Predicts Adolescent Initiation of Sexual Behavior," *Pediatrics*, Vol.114, No. 3, September 2004, 280-289.

age or older, when it is developmentally appropriate to be sexually curious... *Those who report intentional exposure to pornography, irrespective of source, are significantly more likely to cross-sectionally report delinquent behavior and substance use in the previous year. Further, online seekers versus offline seekers are more likely to report clinical features associated with depression and lower levels of emotional bonding with their caregiver. Results of the current investigation raise important questions for further inquiry.* [7] (emphasis added)

Young males imprinted with pornography at an early age will continue to fuel the pandemic.[8] Indeed, all social bonding for them is affected by pornography.[9] A true Romanization of our culture will dovetail with Europe and Asia's declines as other less sexualized societies out-reproduce and out-perform us.

It appears that most of our young men are being exposed to pornography, and many are becoming addicted to various degrees depending on extent of exposure and on personal vulnerability. While many are able to abstain long enough to go on a mission, they are at risk upon returning to relapse, according to the *Church News*:

In the Church, many young men fill honorable missions during which they uphold high standards of chastity. At an age when hormonal drives are fully matured, these exemplary young men return to a world saturated with sex. *Many who completely avoided this temptation during their missions slip after returning. This has created a much greater problem than most people realize, say bishops.*[10] (emphasis added)

[7] Michael L. Ybarra, Kimberly J. Mitchell, "Exposure to Internet Pornography among Children and Adolescents: A National Survey," *CyberPsychology & Behavior.* 8(5), 2005, 473-486.

[8] Neil M. Malamuth, "Pornography's Impact on Male Adolescents," *Adolescent Medicine*, vol. 4, 1993, 563-576.

[9] S. Stack, I. Wasserman, R. Kern, "Adult Social Bonds and Use of Pornography," *Social Science Quarterly*, vol. 85, 2004, 75-88.

[10] "Young and Trapped," *Church News*, March 17, 2007, http://www.desnews.com/cn/view/1,1721,470005916,00.html.

With virtually 100 percent exposure as teens, men are at increased risk for slipping into addiction later in life unless they have proper protection, both spiritually and "technically." A common scenario bishops face is a young man coming in, usually caught viewing pornography or sometimes volunteering a clean, uncoerced confession. He may, with coaching and help, make it to the mission field and do well in this environment for two years. When returning home, however, an alarming number, likely the majority, relapse within weeks. A combination of relaxation of the mission standards with re-exposure to standard media, with its "intro-fare" of the scantily clad and sexually suggestive, kindles preoccupation and relapse. We haven't fully appreciated the risk that even slight exposure, much less heavier pre-mission viewing, has on the newly returned missionary.

EDUCATION AND INTERVENTION

Education on pornography and the vulnerability of youth would likely go a long way to preventing relapse, and global education on this subject would have a positive effect on all. For instance, many bishops would gain insight into the reasons for the recidivism of this problem. John Mark Haney, a counselor from Austin, writes about teenage pornography addiction:

> With pornography, professionals sometimes fail to understand the power of the compulsion youth are facing, and it is not uncommon for school, *religious,* or private-sector professionals to advocate a simple treatment plan that is based upon willpower or moral character. Since pornography can be an addiction, *these "just say no" types of approaches are likely to only create more frustration and self-defeating ideation in teenagers who do not have the willpower to stop.* For such young people who can no longer control their actions, the intervention and treatment modality must *recognize the problem as a full addiction,* and treat it with the *same consideration given to alcohol or chemical substances.*[11] (emphasis added)

---

[11]   John Mark Haney, Article 10, "Teenagers and Pornography Addiction: Treating the Silent Epidemic," http://counselingoutfitters.com/vistas/vistas06/vistas06.

It may be that we have emphasized the important, essential spiritual aspects of healing from this sin but have failed to fully realize the chemical power of the addiction in our young men and the risk that both young and old face. Haney continues to describe the problem:

> Today, however, the scene is very different. The Internet and cable television have ushered in an *age of unprecedented access* to hardcore pornographic images, and *teenagers are jumping in head first for the ride.* Once young people had to work to find pornography (often from the trash or a friend's father), but today children with rudimentary computer skills can find thousands of x-rated images with a couple of clicks of their computer mouse, and many youth are subsequently being inundated with sexual stimuli before they have the developmental capacity to integrate the material into their healthy sexual identity formation.
>
> Indeed, the amount of pornography available to young and old alike has roared into everyday life so overwhelmingly that *it has challenged the ability of social science to create models of treatment and outcomes to keep up with the pace of change. What is certain, however, is that for many young people, pornography is not a casual interest, but an addictive force that is leading to a quiet epidemic of young people who cannot control their online or television habits.* And because of their accessibility, the Internet and cable porn channels have become the *super fix for a new breed of addicts* who literally sacrifice health and happiness to indulge in the *magic images they quietly worship.*[12] (emphasis added)

THE MARRIED MAN

It seems the need has overwhelmed the numbers of experienced, effective counselors available in many areas. More global education and training will likely be required if we are to stem the tide of the problem among our own people. This education needs to be truly

---

[12] Ibid.

global, with parents, women, and girls all being educated in how this might affect their lives as well.

The risk of good men becoming addicted is likely much higher than we have realized and will escalate as our highly exposed young men become older and marry. A *Church News* article describes those who are married and struggle with pornography addiction:

> They are men with two relationships. One with family, the other with fantasy. They have learned to lie and hide and get by. Most justify their actions: "I'm not hurting anyone but myself." But eventually the lie and their life collide. Pornography hurts the people they love most — their wives and children.
>
> Tragically, said Todd Olson, a licensed clinical social worker and program director of the LifeSTAR network, which specializes in helping Latter-day Saints deal with sexual addictions, pornography draws a husband away from his family and entices him to connect with things that are not real. "There is so, so much pain," he said.[13]

How can a man live this double life? Rationalization is essential in this process. He tells himself that since it is a private sin, if no one knows, and the behavior is stopped, no one else need be harmed. This, of course, allows shame and guilt to drive the secrecy deeper and harden the deception. The soul cankering is thus a dual trauma from the damage of the sexual sin pornography is, in and of itself, and the deception and lie the person lives. Given the damage to the one in addiction, the spouse, and to the marital relationship, recovery is complicated but possible. The *Church News* article reports its seriousness:

> Rory Reid, a licensed therapist, author and program director for the Provo Counseling Center, said although nearly half of women who learn of their husbands' compulsive sex-

---

[13]   "Fight to Stop Porn," *Church News*, March 24, 2007,
       http://www.desnews.com/cn/view/1,1721,470006230,00.html.

ual behavior threaten divorce, less than 8 percent actually dissolve the marriage, and in those situations, the husband has shown no effort to change or continues to lie about his behavior.

Brother [Dan] Gray said he encourages his clients to not make any major decisions for one year. They feel pressure and anger. "They have to get to a place where the Atonement has meaning." Often, Brother Gray said, it is hard for a woman to forgive her husband. It is a process of rebuilding trust and should not be rushed. Some women, not ready to immediately forgive, live with tremendous guilt, he added. "They worry they are committing the bigger sin."

Brother Gray counsels bishops to regularly check on a spouse, many whose testimonies are shaken to the core. They wonder, "Why was I guided to marry this man?" Sister [Dorothy] Maryon said. However, she emphasizes, "Most of these relationships can be healed. It takes a huge toll on everybody involved. Believe it or not, couples come out of it stronger and healthier."[14]

We live a high standard, a temple standard. Many may feel trapped in an addiction with no way out. A man caught with a sexual addiction once told my father, who was serving as his priesthood leader, that he had planned on taking it with him to the grave. As we reach out in love, it is our hope that we can extend a loving hand to those embedded in secrecy to seek help, then "look to God and live."[15]

SETTING THE HOOK

One of my favorite places in the world is Alaska in July or August. This is because the coho (or silver, as we call them) salmon run the rivers. We will fish for a week, then dream about it for a year

---

[14] Ibid.
[15] Alma 37:47

while living down in the lower 48. It is "guy" heaven, where the fishing can only be described as amazing.

We typically use pixies with a triple hook and a lure that looks like salmon eggs. The fish are not actually feeding; they are swimming upriver to spawn and aggressively strike the lures to destroy what they think are other fishes' eggs. They are undoubtedly shocked when they hit the lure and find that a triple hook is attached. This hook has three razor sharp barbs that set quickly and deeply. Fight and struggle as the fish might, we are usually successful in first tiring the salmon out with the fight, then reeling it in. Sometimes the fish will succeed in spitting out the hook or in breaking the line, but this is the exception.

One year, my son had a hook fly back and bury two barbs in his face, one deep in his cheek and the other into the upper lip. Fortunately, there was a medical clinic about a forty-minute boat ride away, and I was allowed to use the clinic's equipment and medication to numb up his face and extract both hooks. It would have been impossible for him to remove the hooks without a doctor because they had set so deeply. He healed without scars but still remembers to be careful when pulling on a snagged line!

We are living in a world of hooks and are at risk of being "hooked" more quickly and deeply than we might imagine. Many rationalize that they can see the R-rated movie because they can handle it. They don't want to miss a highly acclaimed movie, especially one with excellent critical reviews. Even if nudity and sexuality are present in a PG-13 or even PG movie, they tell themselves that it's okay given the rating, and that it was a great movie, except for "that one part."

The above scenarios represent "intro-fare" material. These experiences plant seeds of thought which mature, sometimes years later on a business trip when the man is alone and stressed, into an initial curious peek at frank pornography. And that quick peek is like the salmon hitting the triple hook. The pornography hook sets almost instantly and deeply into the brain and spirit, particularly with the cyber-acceleration of the Internet. Extraction can never be done alone, and a weak moment is paid for with sometimes years of agony for the addicted one and those they love. The three hooks of pornography are pride, guilt, and shame. These hooks are deeply buried and allow the "fisherman" to pull on the line and lead the "fish" whenever and wherever he wishes, "according to his will."[16] The lures are omnipresent in our society and require vigilance to avoid.

Randall Wright, Ph.D., in his book *Why Good People See Bad Movies*, surveyed active LDS high school and college students by asking the question, "If you watch R-rated movies, please tell why you do. If you do not watch R-rated movies, please tell why not."[17] The responses are enlightening, and alternately disappointing or inspiring, depending on the response.

- "I think the reason I see R-rated movies is because I hear they are good and worth the money. I feel like I am missing out when I don't see these movies."[18]
- "When you have conversations with friends the subject of movies often comes up. Which ones are the best? Which had the coolest special effects? Most of the time it is R-rated movies that are discussed."[19]
- "I think it's because of what people say and the advertisements that go out. After I saw the appealing ads, I broke my streak of not watching R-rated movies and have watched them ever since."[20]
- "Immediately following General Conference or a really uplifting talk, I make the resolution to do everything right. It takes me about a week to forget!"[21]
- "The popularity of a movie makes it hard to resist. My boyfriend and I both agree that we shouldn't watch R-rated movies. But, if we are in a video store and we come across one

---

[16] Alma 12:17
[17] Randall A. Wright, *Why Good People See Bad Movies*, National Family Institute, 1993, 11.
[18] Ibid, 19.
[19] Ibid.
[20] Ibid.
[21] Ibid, 20.

that we heard a lot about, once in a while we slip and rent it. We use our own judgment."[22]

- "When movies are good, except for one bad part, I'll close my eyes and sing a hymn."[23]
- "Some movies are rated R for only a few bad things. Some really good movies may have a really violent shoot-out or a graphic sex scene achieving an R-rating. R-rated movies are actually clean, except for a few bad scenes."[24]
- "Lots of times the movie will look really good, except for maybe one or two scenes. It is entertaining and the bad scenes won't hurt us, and it will be worth it to see a good, entertaining movie."[25]
- "Some R-rated movies are not bad all the way through. They are usually only bad in one spot, and the rest is good. I can only watch R-rated shows if my parents are there anyway."[26]
- "I have many friends who say they just close their eyes when the bad parts come, or they just fast forward through those parts. I think most people do not realize how those things stay in your mind and desensitize you to vile and base things."[27]
- "I have seen so many films that were such good movies if only that one scene was taken out. Obviously, I have regretted going because of that one scene. I think I have become dulled to things like this over the years because I've made exceptions to the rule so many times."[28]
- "My roommate's father is a bishop in his home ward. The first movie that he saw when he came home from his mission was a rated R movie with his father. He continually uses this to justify seeing rated R movies."[29]

---

[22] Ibid.
[23] Ibid, 23.
[24] Ibid.
[25] Ibid.
[26] Ibid, 23-24.
[27] Ibid, 24.
[28] Ibid.
[29] Ibid, 51.

● "Our bishop back home goes to R-rated movies and my parents sometimes see them."[30]

This book was published in 1993. At that time, when the Internet was building momentum, it may still have been possible to have the casual attitude many of the young people expressed in these quotes and yet stay free from pornography addiction. Pornography was more difficult to access for most in the early 90's, although the Internet was already becoming a factor. Now, watching the soft porn in nearly *every* R and PG-13 movie will prep the mind for the easy slide, or click, into virtual cyber-oblivion. According to current peer-reviewed academic literature, almost 90 percent[31] of college age young men and 30 percent of the young women view pornography. It is sobering to consider that these numbers likely describe our own LDS people.[32] It is incumbent upon us all to address this pandemic with the same urgency we would any society-threatening disease, particularly in the Church. We must be careful that such widespread incursion among our own people does not relax our own cultural and spiritual mores against pornography, for the standard of the Lord will never change in this regard.

In summary, pornography has infiltrated in a "soft core" form into our media and prepared our culture to be widely addicted as the Internet has evaporated resistance. We must clearly understand that we deal with a hook that is not only widely disseminated, but also very difficult to treat and cure in each individual case. It will require our urgent attention and fastidious effort to combat and remedy this plague. Certainly filters are helpful and important to provide protective boundaries, particularly with youth, children, and those in recovery. One person in recovery from addiction said protective boundaries are like braces which stabilize recovery so healing can

---

[30]   Ibid, 52.

[31]   Jason S. Carroll, Laura M. Padilla-Walker, Larry J. Nelson, Chad D. Olson, Carolyn McNamara Barry, Stephanie D. Madsen, "Generation XXX: Pornography Acceptance and Use Among Emerging Adults," *Journal of Adolescent Research*, Vol. 23(1) 2008, 6-30.

[32]   "Defending the Home Against Pornography," *Church News*, April 21, 2007, http://www.desnews.com/cn/view/1,1721,470006290,00.html.

occur, much like bracing a broken bone. In the end, however, our de-sires must become our final filter as other filters will eventually fail.

Virtually every family has been or will be affected in some way. Let us remember that men and women, boys and girls who struggle with addiction are not "those people." They are your sons and daughters and their sweet companions. They are your husbands and wives. They are your grandchildren and their spouses. As Elder Bruce Hafen said, "I am the lost sheep. You are the lost sheep. All we like sheep have gone astray."[33] In our righteous desire to maintain an appropriate standard of complete avoidance of pornography, we should be careful not to use language that would only deepen the shame and guilt of our loved ones who may be secretly addicted and drive them deeper into deception and darkness. I hope that as we understand the physical and spiritual nature of pornography addiction, we can nurture an atmosphere of love for those so afflicted. We must maintain our standard of purity as Saints of the Most High, yet open our cultural and social arms so those privately suffering can have a safe place to emerge and to find peace.

---

[33]   Bruce C. Hafen, *The Broken Heart*, Deseret Book, 1989, 60.

Recovery Story 2

When I was around eleven years old an adult from the Sports Club where my family and I used to go swimming invited me to his house. There I saw for the first time images of hard core pornography. Those images have been embedded forever in the files of my mind, to be recalled thousands of times. I knew that what had happened was wrong, but I was too ashamed to tell anybody, including my parents. I was raised Catholic. I wanted immediately to go and confess to my priest, but he was gone that day. However, a few days later I found myself again at this man's door. I wanted to see those images again. And with a welcome smile he opened the door to me. Behind me was left my innocence, my peace.

Thus began my battle with lust, pornography, masturbation, and shame. This battle would last for many decades. What I didn't understand at the time was that lust was progressive.

At the age of fourteen, two young American men told me about a new religion. The word "Mormon" entered my vocabulary. A new light entered my life and I thought the darkness of my young past could be "washed away." But the battle with lust did not go away and it quickly became clear this was a battle with very few victories. I would sometimes go days, sometimes months, away from masturbation and lust. However, even though I would always promise myself that I would "never do this again," I was unable to stop. So I would ride the roller coaster of shame and guilt, followed by determination and repentance.

My bishops and I would quickly skip through the subject, as if we both knew that this happened but not much could be done about it. Petting was the big no-no and as long as I avoided it, I was ok. I fought my battles in order to be what I perceived clean enough for me to be able to go on a mission. While on a mission the spiritual growth helped me to stay out of trouble most of the time, but I still struggled at times. After my mission it seemed that the evil spirit came back to "my house seven times worse than at first," and for several years it was difficult to stay clean. Cycles of sin, guilt, shame-repentance and a new determination to do the right thing would repeat over and over. These cycles wore me out. At times I felt I was losing the battle—but I thought if I could just find the right girl and get married, then I could have the "real thing" and I wouldn't have to worry about this problem anymore.

I eventually found the right girl. She was a wonderful and beautiful person. I thought I would not have to resort to fantasy or imaginary sex anymore. I could leave that part of my life behind together with my lust. Six months into my marriage I found myself seeking the attention of other women. This became progressively worse and I eventually started to have relationships outside my marriage. I would adopt the excuse "I never had sex with that woman," but everything else was ok. And though pornography didn't have the pull it had once, I felt I had graduated to deeper levels of acting out my addiction to lust.

The cycle of sin, guilt, shame-repentance and determination to never do it again, repeated itself over and over again. I felt this cycle would never end and that the limits I had put for myself would soon be crossed. I did not know what to do to stop. I met with a wonderful Bishop, but I was too ashamed to disclose everything to him. He suggested more scripture reading and prayer. He even told me to run (exercise) more. Although these suggestions didn't cure my problem, my efforts to try to practice these suggestions had an impact in my future sobriety. However, at the time it felt like the Bishop's suggestions were like fighting the Dragon with a fork.

I struggled with this for many years and my wife and I worked together in trying to overcome this problem. There were periods of success but at other times my failure was too hard to bear. As the years went by, I started to feel more and more discouraged. I felt that no matter how long I would go without acting out, it was only a matter of time before I would eventually succumb to it again. I could repent, but I could not seem to forsake it. Why continue to try? I would imagine Satan sitting in a dark corner of my room with a smirk on his face thinking, "I have all the time in the world. All I have to do is wait. You apply all the little tools you have, all your little rituals . . . but in time you know: you'll eventually come back to it every time." AND IT WAS TRUE!!! I knew that even when I had changed my behavior, my heart had never changed.

I had given it my best, but it was now over. No matter how hard I'd tried in the past, I would eventually give in.

I lived a double life. I was tired of lying to myself. I could not live the Gospel. That was the bottom line. I had ruined my wife's future and my children's. I was no longer worthy of them. I needed to move on. I came up with a drastic plan to leave my wife, whom I really loved and considered my best friend, so that she could find someone worthy to take her to the Celestial kingdom. As I started to make arrangements for these changes in my life, I found myself in the deepest despair. In that darkest of moments, the Lord brought to my mind the story in John 5 of the man by the waters of Bethesda with an infirmity for thirty-eight years (that's how old I was at that time). The Savior asked him: "Wilt thou be made whole?" Those same words resonated that morning in my mind. "Will you allow me to heal you? Will you let me in? Rise, take up thy bed, and walk," were the words to the man in Bethesda. And the words that were directed to me were, "Get up, do your part, and I will do what you cannot do."

With apprehension, I determined to try once more. I met with a therapist who introduced me to a 12 Step program with LDS guidelines. He and I would meet every other week. I told my new bishop about my secret, and he and I met every other week, and I reported my progress to him. I followed this process of meeting with my bishop and my therapist every other week for almost two years. My wife and I became new partners in fighting this unseen force. I started to attend 12 Step support group meetings every week, even though they were forty minutes away. The gas and the extra time were a small price to pay when compared to what I had spent on my addiction. I started to see purpose to my healing, not only for my family and me, but also for the benefit of others who had gone down the same path that I had traveled. Then, slowly, prayerfully and painfully the healing began. I never prayed so many times in one day! There were times when I relapsed, but I wasn't fighting this alone any more. I had people in the group I could call, a loving bishop who was patient, and a sponsor who guided me through times of disappointments. A ray of brightness of hope began to illuminate my soul. Even though there were a few setbacks, my life had become so much better, my passions had been redirected, and I now saw a purpose even to my adversities and disappointments.

I now have more than six years of recovery. This is a miracle. But I also must never forget where I have been. I remind myself that after years of recovery I still "cannot take fire into my bosom and not get burned." That is my reality. The battle against lustful thoughts and actions will be a lifelong battle, but I now have the Savior as my source of strength and protection. If I do my small part, the healing hand of my Savior is ever present to help me do the things I cannot do on my own. His protection is like the air I cannot live without.

Today, I attend the 12 Step LDS meetings every week, sometimes twice a week. I look forward to seeing my old friends and meeting new ones. When I read the words "and how great shall be your joy with him in the kingdom of my father with the soul that repenteth," I experience a joy that my lust never gave me. As I listen to others whose hearts are ready to "come home," as I take a phone call from those who sit in front of a computer monitor ready to click the images that will bind them, as I see the countenances of men change as they themselves stand amazed at the grace that is transforming their lives, as I write to you, my friend, I can promise you that miracles have not ceased! He is at the door waiting for you to let Him in.

I love my Savior, for He has rescued my soul from Hell. I have learned to lean upon Him and rely upon His power every day. So, I take each day one at a time and I ask myself, "What can I do to feel His grace this day?" I only worry about doing His will today. Day by day, He is always there to do for me what I cannot do for myself. His love never faileth.

CHAPTER 6

IT *IS* A DRUG!

*With advent of the computer, the delivery system for this addictive
stimulus has become nearly resistance-free. It is as though we have devised a
form of heroin 100 times more powerful than before, usable in the privacy of
one's own home and injected directly to the brain through the eyes. It's now
available in unlimited supply via a self-replicating distribution network,
glorified as art and protected by the Constitution.*

Jeffery Satinover

In 1991 Sunderwirth and Milkman published a paper entitled "Behavioral and Neurochemical Commonalities in Addiction." They
hypothesized that all addiction, both drug and natural, is mediated by
"a deficit of dopamine in the reward system." This deficit produces
a craving which underlies all addiction. "In order to satiate these
feelings, they may engage in any number of activities or drugs which
temporarily restores dopamine neurotransmission."[1]

At the time, many therapists and neuroscientists disputed a physical basis for most "natural addictions" such as obesity, sex, and pathologic gambling. As we will see in this chapter, scientific evidence now
strongly supports an organic basis for all addiction, and similar
changes in the brain have been shown to occur with such diverse addictions as cocaine, overeating resulting in obesity, and sexual addiction (pedophilia). In 2001 Howard Shaffer, who was head of the
Division on Addictions at Harvard said, "I had great difficulty with
my own colleagues when I suggested that a lot of addiction is the re-

---

[1] Stanley G. Sunderwirth and Harvey Milkman, "Behavioral and Neurochemical
Commonalities in Addiction," *Contemporary Family Therapy*, 13(5), October 1991,
421-432

sult of experience…repetitive, high-emotion, high-frequency experience."[2] He went on to say that changes in neural circuitry occur in this context even in the absence of drug taking. Steven Grant of the National Institute on Drug Abuse said, "What is coming up fast as being the central core issue…is continued engagement in self-destructive behavior despite adverse consequences.[3]" Science is confirming these concepts, and we will review recent studies which confirm the addictive nature of natural processes such as uncontrolled sexuality.

All addictions appear to cause physical changes (shrinkage) in control and pleasure areas of the brain; this has been well demonstrated in both drug addictions (cocaine and methamphetamine), and in "natural" addictions (obesity and sexual addiction). Significantly, recent studies show that recovery with healing allows the brain to return to a more normal state in both drug (methamphetamine) and natural (obesity) addictions.

Dr. Satinover gave the quote in the chapter heading as testimony to the United States Senate in hearings on pornography,[4] and others have described pornography as a drug.[5] Subsequent research on addiction has vindicated this claim, and has closed the distinction between exogenous (from without) and endogenous (from within) brain "drugs." As a physician, it is interesting to me that we have no trouble calling methamphetamine and cocaine (which are stimulants) "drugs," yet we are remiss to call any stimulants our own brain makes "drugs." An example may help. When we saw the lion on the safari, everyone in the Land Rover agreed that they felt their hearts race. Adrenaline, also called epinephrine, which our own bodies produced, caused this. Is it a drug, a neurotransmitter, or both? As a doctor, I have ordered the drug epinephrine to be given to patients whose

---

2   Constance Holden, " 'Behavioral' Addictions: Do They Exist?," *Science*, 294, November 2, 2001, 980-982.
3   Ibid.
4   Jeffery Satinover, MS, MD, (Princeton University), Senate Committee on Commerce, Science, and Transportation; Subcommittee on Science Technology, and Space; Hearing on the Brain Science Behind Pornography Addiction and Effects of Addiction on Families and Communities, Thursday, November 18, 2004.
5   Mark Kastleman, *The Drug of the New Millennium; The Brain Science Behind Internet Pornography Use.* Power Think Publishing, 2007.

hearts were stopping. Indeed, it should be on the "crash cart" in every hall of every hospital. Doctors and pharmacists consider it to be a drug, as does the Federal Drug Administration, or FDA. What about dopamine? We will discuss this chemical later in the chapter. It is a close cousin of adrenaline, only differing by a carbon and a couple of hydrogen atoms. My father passed away from Parkinson's disease, which is caused by a deficiency of dopamine in a key motor part of the brain, or area important in allowing us to move our muscles. We gave him dopamine so he could move. It required a doctor's prescription, and we bought it at the pharmacy. We (patients), the doctors who prescribed it, and the pharmacists all recognized that dopamine was a drug, as did (and still does today) the FDA.

In his fascinating book, *The Brain That Changes Itself*, psychiatrist Norman Doidge of Columbia unequivocally includes pornography as a true addiction: "The addictiveness of Internet pornography is not a metaphor. Not all addictions are to drugs or alcohol…All addiction involves long-term, sometimes lifelong, neuroplastic change in the brain…Pornographers promise healthy pleasure and relief from sexual tension, but what they often deliver is an addiction, tolerance, and an eventual decrease in pleasure."[6] In describing how the endless variety of Internet pornography locks a person in, he says:

> Hardcore porn unmasks some of the early neural networks that formed in the critical periods of sexual development and brings all these early, forgotten, or repressed elements together to form a new network, in which all the features are wired together. Porn sites generate catalogs of common kinks and mix them together in images. Sooner or later the surfer finds a killer combination that presses a number of his sexual buttons at once. Then he reinforces the network by viewing the images repeatedly, masturbating, releasing dopamine and strengthening these networks. He has created a kind of "neosexuality," a rebuilt libido that has strong root in his buried sexual tendencies.[7]

---

[6]   Norman Doidge, *The Brain That Changes Itself*, Penguin Books, 2007, 106.
[7]   Ibid, 111-112.

ADDICTION:
A HYPOFRONTAL SYNDROME

As a neurosurgeon, I have operated on many people through the years who have suffered traumatic brain injury from motor vehicle and other accidents, from falls, and from assaults. Tumors and other brain problems such as aneurysms can also cause similar damage. Let us consider a motor vehicle accident. With the tremendous force of deceleration suddenly stopping the skull, the brain inside the skull keeps traveling into the frontal bone (the forehead). This produces a commonly seen finding on CT scans called a contusion, or "brain bruise." The frontal lobes of the brain swell, and the orbitofrontal, midfrontal, and other frontal areas involved in mediation and judgment of pleasure responses are damaged by the trauma and frequently become hemorrhagic (they bleed). Sometimes this produces severe, life threatening pressure on the rest of the brain, and we must operate and remove some of the damaged frontal lobe to prevent coma and death. Upon recovery, these patients can manifest what we in neurosurgery call a "frontal lobe syndrome," or "hypofrontality." On follow-up CT scans of the brain, the frontal lobes frequently show atrophy, or shrinkage.

Family members will comment that the loved one "just isn't the same." A formerly dignified and sophisticated person may by silly and may laugh or cry inappropriately and show other signs of impaired judgment. They usually manifest impulsivity, or inability to prevent themselves from doing things they normally would not have done. They also exhibit compulsivity, or repetition of certain behaviors they normally wouldn't be fixated on.

Addiction also produces a similar "hypofrontal syndrome." Prominent addiction neuroscientists describe the same behavioral findings of frontal damage in the addicted. Studies of individuals struggling with addiction show reduced "cellular activity in the orbitofrontal cortex, a brain area we rely on to make strategic, rather than impulsive, decisions. *Patients with traumatic injuries to this area of the brain display problems—aggressiveness, poor judgment of future consequences, inability to inhibit inappropriate responses that are similar to those observed in substance abusers.*"[8] (emphasis added) Another addiction researcher uses the term cortical "hypofrontality" to describe the impaired function of the frontal control areas in addiction.[9]

Later in this chapter we shall see that addiction actually causes visible shrinkage in these frontal control areas, not unlike traumatic brain injury. This has been found both in drug addictions and in natural addictions involving sexuality and overeating. Fortunately, with abstinence, there is evidence that the brain can heal and that these areas can regain their size with recovery (unlike traumatic brain injury, where the damage is more permanent). *Thus addiction is literally a "collision" with the adversary producing not only a spiritual wound, but also causing physical damage to the brain. In this sense, the phrase "He restoreth my soul"[10] has special relevance, as we consider that healing must address both the spirit and the body, which are the "soul of man."*[11]

BRAIN DRUGS

Pornography causes release of adrenaline from an area in the brain called the locus coeruleus, and this makes the heart race in those who view, or even anticipate, viewing pornography. The sexual pleasure of pornography may be partially caused by release of dopamine from the ventral tegmental area, and this stimulates the nucleus accumbens, one of the key pleasure centers of the brain.

Why is it that some consider adrenaline and dopamine to be drugs if drug companies produce them, yet they will not acknowledge these *same chemicals* to be drugs if pornography stimulates the brain to produce them? As we will see, they are powerful endogenous (meaning our body makes them) drugs, which can actually change the physical and chemical makeup of the brain in addiction, just as they are powerful exogenous (meaning we take them into our bod-

---

[8]   Joanna L. Fowler, Nora D. Volkow, Cheryl A. Kassed, and Linda Chang, "Imaging the Addicted Human Brain," *Science and Practice Perspectives*, April 2007, 4-16.
[9]   Eric J. Nestler, "Is There a Common Molecular Pathway for Addiction?" *Nature Neuroscience* 8(11), Nov 2005, 1445-9.
[10]   Psalms 23:3
[11]   Doctrine and Covenants 88:15

ies) drugs when prescribed by a doctor. The problem with pornography is that we are using adrenaline, dopamine, and other powerful
brain drugs *without a prescription*. Pornography is actually a form of
prescription drug abuse when viewed in this light.

As we become more computer literate, it may be easier for us to
understand the close similarities between our brains and computers.
A basic review of neuroanatomy and neurochemistry might be useful. Under the skull lies the cerebral cortex. This is the large structure with the bumps and grooves we think of when we picture the
brain. It contains the nerve cells, or neurons, where conscious and
unconscious thought takes place, and where movement, vision, hearing, sensation, and emotion are processed and blended. David Noonan, in his book *Neuro*, eloquently described the nervous system's
complexity:

> There is nothing in nature as perfect or as powerful as
> the human nervous system—not the seamless folding of the
> seasons one into the other; not the rolling, biogenetic mass
> of the oceans; not the great silent spin of the planets around
> the sun. The nervous system fires every human act, drives
> every human moment. It enables man to think and to move,
> to feel and to wonder, and makes him the dominant life form
> in the known universe. A charged web that hangs in every
> human body, its electrochemical circuits carry the elusive
> spark of life itself. *And if that which is human is also somehow
> divine, then nervous tissue is both the means of the miracle and
> the miracle itself. Complex beyond man's understanding, the
> human nervous system is the most sophisticated arrangement of
> cells that exists.*
>
> William Shakespeare at his desk, Albert Einstein at his
> blackboard, Brooks Robinson at third base, Pablo Casals in
> concert, Henri Matisse at his easel. These are examples of
> the human nervous system at work. The composition of
> Hamlet, the formulation of the theory of relativity, the flaw-
> less fielding of a line drive, and the rendering of order and
> beauty in music and painting are all products of the nervous

system. *Neurons fire in unknown patterns and the world is seen, the universe is understood, man's nature is explored, the ball game is saved.*[12] (emphasis added)

With such a complex instrument as the brain, it is interesting that we have been slow to recognize the role of neurochemistry in destructive, addictive behaviors. We are just now realizing that it appears ever more likely that all compulsive reward behaviors have a common final pathway in the same pleasure centers of the brain. I will review some of the basic chemicals involved in pleasure in the brain and discuss how pornography is *literally* substance abuse.

A fascinating paper published in *Nature Reviews Neuroscience* details physical changes in brain cells that occur in learning and memory.[13] No one seriously disputes that long-term memory physically changes neurons at the cellular level. Addiction is described by the authors as a sort of *learning-gone-awry*; they surmise "addiction represents a pathological, yet powerful, form of learning and memory."[14] If addiction is pathologic learning which has damaged neurons, then recovery is "healing learning" which reverses the changes, as much as possible, over time.

Dopamine is an excitatory neurotransmitter important in several systems in our brains, perhaps best know for its role in movement and by its absence in certain motor systems in Parkinson's disease. Dopamine is chemically closely related to epinephrine and norepinephrine, the three belonging to a class of chemicals known as catecholamines. Although dopamine's relationship to sexual function may be more peripheral physiologically,[15] the tie to the pleasure reward of sexuality is likely more direct. Epinephrine and norepinephrine are better known to many as adrenaline and noradrenaline

---

[12] David Noonan, *Neuro – Life on the Frontlines of Brain Surgery and Neurological Medicine*, Ballantine Books, 1989, 1-2.
[13] Julie A. Kauer, Robert C. Malenka, "Synaptic Plasticity and Addiction," *Nature Reviews Neuroscience,* 8, 8440858 November 2007, 844-858.
[14] Ibid.
[15] Raul G. Paredes and Anders Agmo, "Has Dopamine a Physiological Role in the Control of Sexual Behavior? A Critical Review of the Evidence," *Progress in Neurobiology*, 73(3) June 2004, 179-225.

and are also excitatory in nature. These are called "fight or flight" neurotransmitters and are important in the sympathetic nervous system. They become active during times of strong emotion such as fear, anger, or sexual response and arousal. *Dopamine is becoming better recognized in the peer-reviewed literature recently as a final pathway neurotransmitter in the key pleasure centers of the brain.*

Under the *cerebral cortex,* where conscious thought occurs, an area of the brain known as the *limbic system* is located. The limbic system of the brain is important in emotion, appetite, reproductive drive, and other reflexive functions important in survival. An analogy may help. Imagine the brain as a horse and rider. The horse is the limbic system, while the thinking part of the brain, the cerebral cortex, is the rider. The rider can learn to direct the horse, but sometimes this may be difficult if the rider is inexperienced and the horse is not well broken in. Our cortex, then, is a controlling bridle riding on the wild animal of the limbic system. In this metaphor, addiction is the limbic system running uncontrolled, with no bridle or restraint. Some primitive parts of the cortex are closely associated with and are considered part of the limbic system, such as the *parahippocampal and cingulate gyri,* and the *insular* cortex. These structures are important in pleasure pathways, probably in conscious thought associated with pleasure. Other key areas are the *amygdala,* located in the medial temporal lobes, the *medial forebrain bundle,* and the *nucleus accumbens* of the basal ganglia. There are others, but for our purposes these will serve as important representatives of the pleasure centers.

The amygdala is an area of the brain important in imprinting and probably in deep emotional memory. It may be that early sexual experiences may imprint this and other regions, setting a *pleasure thermostat memory* that may be very difficult to reset. The nucleus accumbens is a pea-sized area deep in the brain and is a primary pleasure center, and it will be a focus of our attention. *When dopamine activates the nucleus accumbens, pleasure is experienced.* This small structure is important in learning as related to reward.[16]

---

[16]   Jeremy J. Day, "The Nucleus Accumbens and Pavlovian Reward," *The Neuroscientist,* 13 (2), 2007, 148-159.

To reward the brain when a pleasurable stimulus is encountered and experienced, certain end-pathway neurotransmitters are activated in the pleasure centers. As a final pathway excitatory neurotransmitter, dopamine's release activates or excites key cells in these areas, which tells the brain, "I feel good." Depending on how strong the stimulus and what other neurotransmitters are released, various degrees of pleasure responses may be experienced, such as merely pleasant (feeling full after a meal) or extremely intense (sexual arousal and orgasm). Other transmitters such as the brain's natural opiates can provide euphoria, and adrenaline and noradrenaline can mediate excitement. Sexual pleasure is also associated with other hormones, such as oxytocin, from the posterior pituitary, which is connected to the hypothalamus. The drive for sexuality is mediated by testosterone, the primary male sex hormone, which also causes physical development, with estrogen and progesterone being crucial in developing these characteristics in women. Testosterone is produced in the testis in males, and in the ovaries and adrenal glands in females, and is controlled through production of brain hormones such as gonadotrophin-releasing hormone in the hypothalamus. The hypothalamus then releases luteinizing hormone and follicle-stimulating hormone, which travel to the testis and ovaries and mediate the changes in the body important in sexual function.

Oxytocin, the "Bonding" Hormone

Oxytocin is important in the production and release of breast milk and in producing uterine contractions necessary during childbirth. Oxytocin is increasingly recognized for its role as a "bonding" hormone. A recent study of small mammals called voles, which mate for life, is of interest here. When oxytocin is selectively blocked in these animals, they don't mate for life or bond.[17] Similarly, in hu-

---

[17] Karen L. Bales, Julie A. Westerhuyzen, Antoniah D. Lewis-Reese, Nathaniel D. Grotte, Jalene A. Lanter, C.Sue Carter, "Oxytocin has Dose-dependent Developmental Effects on Pair-bonding and Alloparental Care in Female Prairie Voles," *Hormones and Behavior* 52(2), August 2007, 274-279.

mans, oxytocin is released during sexual orgasm and causes uterine contractions during orgasm and also is involved in male sexual response.[18,19,20] "Vasopressin, released during sexual climax in males, may be important in male bonding."[21] Oxytocin has also been shown to increase trust in humans.[22] Bonding and love thus may have a strong neurochemical basis as well.[23]

The depression seen especially in women who are promiscuous with multiple partners may be related to vasopressin/oxytocin.[24] We will visit this in more detail later, but suffice it to say that the depression may be partially mediated by the neurochemical "promise" of bonding (mediated by oxytocin), yet unfulfilled by the subsequent detachment seen in the one night stand. Might oxytocin assist in "bonding" to pornography also, particularly when viewing is combined with the masturbation which typically accompanies it?

Patrick Carnes describes grief as one stage of recovery, where the addicted person actually feels emptiness when saying "goodbye" to his old friend, the addiction.[25] It may be a combination of craving for dopamine and yearning for oxytocin-bonded pornography, among other things, that pushes the person to act out and view pornography.

---

[18] Andrea Salonia, Rossella E. Nappi, Marina Pontillo, Rita Daverio, Antonella Smeraldi, Alberto Briganti, Fabio Fabbri, Giuseppe Zanni, Patrizio Rigatti, and Franscsco Montorsi, "Menstrual Cycle-related Changes in Plasma Oxytocin are Relevant to Normal Sexual Function in Healthy Women," *Hormones and Behavior*, 47(2) February 2005, 164-9.

[19] A. Argeolas, MR Melis, "The Neurophysiology of the Sexual Cycle," *Journal of Endocrinological Investigation*, 26 (3 Suppl.), 2003, 20-22.

[20] C. Sue Carter, "Oxtocin and Sexual Behavior," *Neuroscience. Biobehavioral Review*, 16, 1992, 131-144.

[21] Larry J. Young and Zuoxin Wang, "The neurobiology of pair bonding," *Nature Neuroscience 7*, 2004, 1048-1054.

[22] Michael Kosfeld, Markus Heinrichs, Paul J. Zak, Urs Fischbacher and Ernst Fehr, "Oxytocin Increases Trust in Humans," *Nature*, 435, 2 June 2005, 673-676.

[23] C. Sue Carter, "Neuroendocrine Perspectives on Social Attachment and Love," *Psychoneuroendocrinology*, 23, 1998, 779-818.

[24] Laura M. Bogart, Rebecca L. Collins, Phyllis L. Ellickson, David J. Klein, "Association of Sexual Abstinence in Adolescence with Mental Health in Adulthood," *Journal of Sex Research*, 44(3) August 2007, 290-8.

[25] Patrick Carnes, *Don't Call It Love*, Bantam Books, 1991, 195-198.

CONTROL STATION CENTRAL

How do nerve cells talk to each other? The neurochemicals are produced in the cell body of the neuron. The chemical is then transported down the long wire, or axon, to the end of the axon where there is an enlargement called the pre-synaptic terminal. Here the chemical is stored in small circular pockets called vesicles just inside the cell membrane. When the cell body is stimulated to fire, electricity travels down the axon (a process called depolarization) to the pre-synaptic terminal, where the electricity causes release of the chemical. The chemical then travels across the short space to the next nerve cell (the space is called a synapse). There the chemical binds to proteins floating in the cell membrane of the next cell. These proteins are called receptors and are specific to that particular chemical. When bound, this receptor/neurotransmitter complex causes the next nerve cell to depolarize, or "fire," when sufficient numbers of complexes are achieved, thus propagating the electrical impulse to the next nerve cell. In pornography addiction, this process occurs in the pleasure cell in the nucleus accumbens.

So what happens in the addicted brain? Most studies have focused on drug addiction, but that there are physical and biochemical changes to neurons in the pleasure centers in addiction is universally accepted. More relevant to our discussion is the fact that natural addictions appear to have the same final neurochemical pathways as drug addictions. For example, Eric Nestler, Director of the Brain Institute and Chairman of Neuroscience at Mount Sinai School of Medicine published an article in *Nature Neuroscience* in October of 2005 titled "Is There a Common Molecular Pathway for Addiction?" In it he states:

> Growing evidence indicates that the VTA-NAc pathway and the other limbic regions cited above similarly mediate, at least in part, the acute positive emotional effects of natural rewards, such as food, sex and social interactions. These same regions have also been implicated in the so-called "natural addictions" (that is, compulsive consumption of natural re-

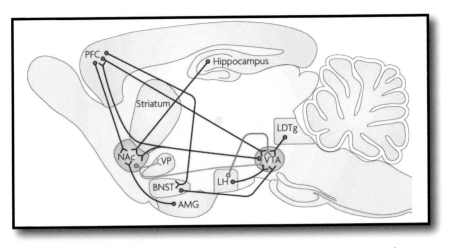

Figure 1: A basic diagram showing connections between important pleasure centers.[26] (Reprinted by permission from Macmillian Publishers, Ltd.)

wards) such as pathological overeating, pathological gambling and sexual addictions. *Preliminary findings suggest that shared pathways may be involved: two examples are cross-sensitization that occurs between natural rewards and drugs of abuse.*[27] (emphasis added)

The VTA-NAc pathway Nestler describes is the dopamine (VTA) stimulation of the nucleus accumbens (NAc). In other words, dopamine is produced by neurons in the ventral tegmental area in response to stimuli from cortical input (pornographic images, for our purposes). Dr. Doidge postulates that Delta Fos B, a chemical Dr. Nestler has shown is produced in addicted nerve cells,[28] contributes to sensitization or craving in pornography addiction.[29] The dopamine cells have wires (axons) that travel to the pleasure center of the brain, the nucleus accumbens, and stimulate it so the brain

[26]   Julie A. Kauer, Robert C. Malenka, "Synaptic Plasticity and Addiction," *Nature Reviews Neuroscience* 8, November 2007, 845.

[27]   Eric J. Nestler, "Is There a Common Molecular Pathway for Addiction?" *Nature Neuroscience.* 8(11), Nov 2005, 1445-9.

[28]   Eric J. Nestler, "Is there a Common Molecular Pathway for Addiction?" *Nature Neuroscience.* 8(11), Nov 2005, 1447.

[29]   Norman Doidge, *The Brain That Changes Itself,* Penguin Books, 2007, 107-108.

senses pleasure. Because pornography is a much more powerful stimulus than natural sexuality in the sensitized brain (addicted husbands
can prefer pornographic stimulation to marital sexuality), especially
with the cyber-acceleration of the Internet, the dopamine systems
are overused, and the dopamine is depleted. This causes cells in the
pleasure center (nucleus accumbens), which are used to a normal
amount of dopamine (normal pleasure response) to produce more
dendrites (receiving area on the neuron for axonal input from the
dopamine cells), and can cause dopamine producing cells to shrink.[30]
Dopamine may be important in "wanting" pleasure, and therefore
also important as a mediator of "craving in addiction."[31]

Let me say this another way. The nucleus accumbens is resting,
minding its own business, when pleasure stimulates the "thinking

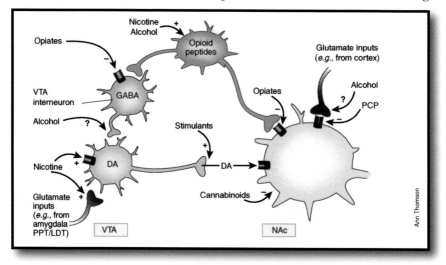

Figure 2: The figure from Nestler's paper shows the connections in Figure 1
on a cellular level. Note the pleasure center cell on the right receiving connections from the output cells on the left, with the regulatory GABA in-
terneurons interposed between the dopamine and endorphin "output" cells.[32]
(Reprinted by permission from Macmillian Publishers, Ltd.)

---

[30] Eric J. Nestler, "Is there a Common Molecular Pathway for Addiction?" *Nature Neuroscience*. 8(11), Nov 2005, 1446.

[31] Kent C. Berridge, "The Debate over Dopamine's Role in Reward: The Case for Incentive Salience," *Psychopharmacology*, 191(3) April 2007, 391-431.

[32] Eric J. Nestler, "Is There a Common Molecular Pathway for Addiction?" *Nature Neuroscience*. 8(11), Nov 2005, 1445-9.

parts" of the brain associated with the limbic system. These areas
have connections to the midbrain, in which lies the dopamine producing neurons in the ventral tegmental area, or VTA. The cortex
says to the VTA, "It's time to party!" The VTA then fires and releases dopamine from the end of its axons (wires connecting nerve
cells in different parts of the brain). The dopamine activates the
pleasure nerve cells in the nucleus accumbens, and "Bam!" the brain
says, "I feel good!" The extent of the response is in proportion to the
stimulus. Eating a good meal and normal sexual relations in marriage
are examples of appropriate pleasure responses that make life enjoyable. If we didn't have this system life would have no enjoyment.

The problem comes with addiction. In contrast, consider normal
marital sexuality. The experience is enjoyable and intense, ideally
with accompanying emotional bonding. Afterward, the person goes
about his life—goes to work, eats, sleeps, and lives. It is wonderful,
but in the proper perspective sex is a *part* of life, not the sole focus.
To the person addicted to pornography, sex does becomes the primary focus, and life is a distraction always trying to prevent him from
doing what he constantly wants to do, which is to view pornography.
At a cellular level, the VTA over-stimulates the nucleus accumbens
with excessive and repeated hits of dopamine, much more than the
normal pleasure response is designed to receive. There are "police"
nerve cells, which produce inhibitory neurotransmitters such as
gamma-amino-butyric acid, or GABA. These cells give feedback
from the nucleus accumbens back to the VTA and say, "Hey guys,
you're killing us! It was great, but enough is enough!" The dopamine
cells in the VTA get the message and after a while say, "OK, OK, I'll
stop!" Over time, the dopamine cells actually atrophy, or shrink.
Meanwhile, the pleasure cells in the nucleus accumbens, now in their
new baseline state, receive less dopamine than they did before the
addiction began. This produces craving! "I didn't mean it," the nucleus accumbens tells the VTA. "Could you send more dopamine,
please?" Finally, the urge becomes so strong the addicted person
views pornography again.

VISIBLE DAMAGE AND HEALING

When addiction causes shrinkage of certain nerve cells, the area of the brain containing these cells actually shrinks, and this can be seen and measured in drug addictions such as cocaine[33] and methamphetamine[34,35] and in natural addictions such as obesity[36] and, significant to our subject, sexual addiction[37] (see Table 1 next page)

With months of recovery, these damaged areas can regain their size, both in drug (methamphetamine)[38] and in natural (obesity) addictions.[39] It is significant that the visible changes of recovery from

[33] Teresa R. Franklin, Paul D. Acton, Joseph A Maldjian, Jason D. Gray, Jason R. Croft, Charles A. Dackis, Charles P. O'Brien, and Anna Rose Childress, "Decreased Gray Matter Concentration in the Insular, Orbitofrontal, Cingulate, and Temporal Cortices of Cocaine Patients," *Biological Psychiatry* (51)2, January 15, 2002, 134-142.

[34] Seog Ju Kim, In Kyoon Lyoo, Jaeuk Hwang, Ain Chung, Young Hoon Sung, Ji-hyun Kim, Do-Hoon Kwon, Kee Hyun Chang, and Perry Renshaw, "Prefrontal Grey-matter Changes in Short-term and Long-term Abstinent Methamphetamine Abusers," *The International Journal of Neuropsychopharmocology*, (2006), 9, 221-228.

[35] Paul M. Thompson, Kikralee M. Hayashi, Sara L. Simon, Jennifer A. Geaga, Michael S. Hong, Yihong Sui, Jessica Y. Lee, Arthur W. Toga, Walter Ling, and Edythe D. London, "Structural Abnormalities in the Brains of Human Subjects Who Use Methamphetamine," *The Journal of Neuroscience*, 24(26) June 30 2004;6028-6036.

[36] Nicola Pannacciulli, Angelo Del Parigi, Kewei Chen, Dec Son N.T. Le, Eric M. Reiman and Pietro A. Tataranni, "Brain abnormalities in human obesity: A voxel-based morphometry study." *Neuroimage* 31(4) July 15 2006, 1419-1425.

[37] Boris Schiffer, Thomas Peschel, Thomas Paul, Elke Gizewshi, Michael Forshing, Norbert Leygraf, Manfred Schedlowske, and Tillmann H.C. Krueger, "Structural Brain Abnormalities in the Frontostriatal System and Cerebellum in Pedophilia," *Journal of Psychiatric Research* (41)9, November 2007, 754-762.

[38] Seog Ju Kim, In Kyoon Lyoo, Jaeuk Hwang, Ain Chung, Young Hoon Sung, Ji-hyun Kim, Do-Hoon Kwon, Kee Hyun Chang, and Perry Renshaw, "Prefrontal Grey-matter Changes in Short-term and Long-term Abstinent Methamphetamine Abusers," *The International Journal of Neuropsychopharmocology*, (2006), 9, 221-228.

[39] Lauri T. Haltia, Antti Viljanen, Riitta Parkkola, Nina Kemppainen, Juha O. Rinne, Pirjo Nuutila and Valtteri Kaasinen, "Brain White Matter Expansion in Human Obesity and the Recovering Effect of Dieting,", *The Journal of Clinical Endocrinology & Metabolism*, 92(8) 2007, 3278-3284.

	Orbitofrontal Midfrontal	Insula Hippocampus Temporal	Nucleus Accumbens, Putamen	Cingulate	Cerebellum
Cocaine *BioPsy* 2002	X	X		X	
Methamphetamine *NeuPsyPhar* 2005 JNeurosc 2004	X	X		X	
Obesity *Neuroimage* 2006	X		X		
Sex (Pedophilia) *JPsycRes* 2007	X	X	X	X	X

Table 1: On the left four studies are listed. Two of these are 'drug' addictions (methamphetamine and cocaine), and two are 'natural' addictions (obesity and sexual addiction). Across the top are different areas of the brain important in control and pleasure.

addiction seen in brain scans correlated with the addicted person regaining control of their life through recovery. Dr. Doidge, in describing his treatment of men with severe pornography and sexual addictions, says... "even some of these men were able…to change…because the same laws of neuroplasticity that allow us to acquire problematic tastes also allow us, in intensive treatment, to acquire new, healthier ones and in some cases even to lose our older, troubling ones."[40]

Table 1 is a compilation of studies showing atrophy (shrinkage) of different areas of the brain associated with pleasure. Most of these areas are concerned with pleasure itself. The mid-frontal gyrus is involved with pleasure/control, and the cerebellum is a coordination center. Note that the sexual addiction study on the bottom row

---

[40]   Norman Doidge, *The Brain That Changes Itself,* Penguin Books, 2007, 131.

shows the most extensive atrophy. This is significant in that most recovering individuals I have spoken to who have dealt with both drug and sexual addictions say that the sexual addictions were more difficult to overcome than the drug addictions.

THE BRAIN "ALL LIT UP"

The pleasure center is thus physically altered. Nestler says, "This sensitization can last long after drug-taking ceases and may relate to drug craving and relapse."[41] For our discussion, substitute "pornography use" for "drug taking." Activation of certain "thinking parts" of the brain (the cerebral cortex) in drug addiction can be seen in brain scans. MRI scans of the brain can now look at which areas of the brain are less active after being damaged by addiction (this is called functional MRI, or fMRI). This has been well demonstrated in drug addiction[42,43] but is also seen in natural addictions such as obesity[44] and even pathological gambling.[45] It is interesting that extremely pleasurable foods such as chocolate stimulate these same pleasure centers.[46]

Recent studies have been done with people viewing pornography. The "thinking parts" of the brain which light up on the fMRI scans in these studies are very similar, and in many cases, identical to

---

[41]   Eric J. Nestler, "Is there a Common Molecular Pathway for Addiction?" *Nature Neuroscience*. 8(11), Nov 2005, 1446.

[42]   Bruce E. Wexler, Christopher H. Gottschalk, Robert K. Fulbright, Isak Prohovnik, Cheryl M. Lacadie, Bruce J. Rounsaville, and John C. Gore, "Functional Magnetic Resonance Imaging of Cocaine Craving," *American Journal of Psychiatry*, 158, 2001, 86-95.

[43]   Joanna L. Fowler, Nora D. Volkow, Cheryl A. Kassed, and Linda Chang, "Imaging the Addicted Human Brain," *Science and Practice Perspectives*, April 2007, 4-16.

[44]   Gene-Jack Wang, Nora D. Volkow, Jean Logan, Naomi R. Pappas, Christopher T. Wong, Wei Zhu, Noelwah Netusil, Joanna S Fowler, "Brain dopamine and obesity," *Lancet* 357(9253) February 3 2001, 354-357.

[45]   Jan Reuter, Thomas Raedler, Michael Rose, Iver Hand, Jan Glascher, and Christian Buchel, "Pathological Gambling is linked to reduced activation of the mesolimbic reward system," Nature Neuroscience 8, January 2005, 147-148.

[46]   Dana M. Small, Robert J. Zatorre, Alain Dagher, Alan C. Evans and Marilyn Jones-Gotman, "Changes in brain activity related to eating chocolate," *Brain* 124(9) September 2001, 1720-1733.

those in drug addiction fMRI scans.[47,48] Chronic changes in the
nerve cell transfer zones are likely responsible for relapse and craving.
Other neurotransmitters involved in regulating dopamine affect
the ability of the cortex (the "thinking part" of the brain) to control
the NAc (nucleus accumbens, or pleasure center). Multiple neurochemical systems are damaged by addiction. Nestler states this in
technical terms:

> Changes in postsynaptic responses could also be medi-
> ated by altered AMPA receptor trafficking or by adaptations
> in the neurons' postsynaptic densities (PSDs)... *These find-*
> *ings, along with the evidence of abnormal glutamatergic inner-*
> *vation of the NAc from frontal cortical regions would suggest a*
> *profound dysfunction in cortical control over the NAc, which could*
> *in turn relate to the impulsive and compulsive features of stimu-*
> *lant addiction.* (emphasis added)[49]

STARVING FOR DOPAMINE

Also supporting this common pathway are recent published reports of hypersexuality and compulsive gambling in Parkinson's disease patients treated with medication.[50,51,52,53] The defect in

47 Sherif Karama, Andre R. Lecours, Jean-Maxine Leroux,, Pierre Bourgouin, Gilles
    Beaudoin, Sven Joubert, and Mario Beauregard, "Areas of Brain Activation in
    Males and Females During Viewing of Erotic Film Excerpts," *Human Brain Map-*
    ping, 16, 2002, 1-13.
48 Nora D. Volkow, Joanna S. Fowler, Gene-Jack Wang, "The Addicted Human Brain
    Viewed in the Light of Imaging Studies: Brain Circuits and Treatment Strate-
    gies," *Neuropharmacology*, 47 Suppl 1, 2004, 3-13.
49 Eric J. Nestler, "Is there a Common Molecular Pathway for Addiction?" *Nature*
    Neuroscience, 8(11), Nov 2005, 1448.
50 Nir Giladi, Nina Weitzman, Shaul Schreiber, Herzel Shabtai, Chava Peretz, "New
    Onset Heightened Interest of Drive for Gambling, Shopping, Eating or Sexual
    activity in Patients with Parkinson's Disease: The Role of Dopamine Agonist
    Treatment and Age at Motor Symptoms Onset," *Journal of Psychopharmocology*,
    21(5), July 2007, 502-6.
51 Sui H. Wong, Zenita Cowen, Elizabeth Anne Allen, and Peter K. Newman, "In-
    ternet Gambling and Other Pathological Gambling in Parkinson's Disease: A Case
    Series," *Movement Disorders*, 22(4), March 15, 2007, 591-3.
52 Sui H. Wong, Malcolm J. Steiger, "Pathological Gambling in Parkinson's Disease,"
    British Medical Journal, 334(7598), April 21, 2007, 810-1.
53 Sean S. O'Sullivan, Andrew J. Lees, "Pathological Gambling in Parkinson's Dis-
    ease," *Lancet Neurology*. 6(5), May 2007, 384-6.

Parkinson's Disease is a deficiency of dopamine in the midbrain in an area that supplies areas of the brain concerned with motor function. The medication increases the amount of dopamine in the brain, but a side effect is that it can increase dopamine in the pleasure center, the nucleus accumbens.

This starvation for dopamine in the nucleus accumbens may be one of the central components of craving leading to relapse.[54] Another factor in craving leading to relapse may be endorphin mediated. Endorphins are natural chemicals that produce euphoria and a natural high. Opioids, such as morphine, act on neurons in the nucleus accumbens to mediate more euphoric effects of pleasure. Endorphins are produced in the arcuate nucleus, and this nucleus projects axons to the nucleus accumbens in much the same way the ventral tegmental area (VTa) projects to the nucleus accumbens and delivers dopamine. A rat model study demonstrated that cocaine administration increases endorphin release from the arcuate nucleus and endorphin delivery to the nucleus accumbens.[55] Of interest is the fact that after rats had been conditioned to receive cocaine, when the same cues were given indicating imminent cocaine delivery, the endorphin levels still went up even though no cocaine was delivered. *In other words, the anticipation of the cocaine still activated the pleasure center. This type of anticipation may be a component of craving and may indicate a "starvation" mode is operative in the natural opiate centers.*

Secondarily, several drugs have been shown to inhibit birth of new neurons in the hippocampus, an area of the brain important in learning and memory. Nestler says, "For example, might this effect contribute to common abnormalities in memory or other cognitive functions seen in many addicts?"[56] This may have a correlation in natural addictions such as pornography. Does this help explain why those in addiction become less focused at work or school?

[54] Nora D. Vokow and Joanna S. Fowler, "Addiction, a Disease of Compulsion and Drive: Involvement of the Orbitofrontal Cortex," *Cerebral Cortex*, 10:March 2000, 318-325.

[55] Falk Kiefer, Mirko Horntrich, Holger Jahn, Klaus Wiedemann, "Is Withdrawal-induced Anxiety in Alcoholism Based on B-endorphin Deficiency?" *Psycopharmacology*, 162, 2002, 433-437.

[56] Eric J. Nestler, "Is there a Common Molecular Pathway for Addiction?" *Nature Neuroscience*, 8(11), Nov 2005, 1448.

There are many other neurotransmitters operative in the reward/pleasure centers of the brain. Serotonin has complex, sometimes paradoxical effects, but seems to mediate well being. It may affect sexual function as well.[57] Depressed serotonin levels have been associated with depression, as have depression of adrenaline and noradrenaline, which are catecholamines produced in an area called the locus coeruleus). Drugs that treat depression may act to increase one or both of these systems, that is, the serotonin and catecholamine systems. Sexual side effects are not uncommon, such as inhibition of orgasm or impotence.

ADDICTION: PATHOLOGICAL LEARNING

When a person who has sensitized his brain to pornography enters the preoccupation phase, he begins to relive memories of past images *and* past highs from the "drug" itself. The amygdala, an area of the brain important in emotional memory, may cause the person to have a deep emotional memory of the past pornographic viewing experiences. This structure has significant connections to the orbitofrontal and cingulate gyri, "thinking areas" of the cortex important in judgment, control, and sexual arousal. These areas have direct projection to the ventral tegmental area (VTa) where dopamine is produced. Also these areas are associated with projections to the locus coeruleus (adrenaline and noradrenaline) and the arcuate nucleus (endorphins).

As the person moves into ritualization, he may tell himself that he won't do it this time, that he will resist, but powerful anticipatory cravings are already in motion, as is the confidence-shattering knowledge that he has relapsed so many times before. At this point, the heart rate will begin to increase (adrenaline from the locus coeruleus). It is likely as the occulofrontal and cingulate gyri (thinking parts of

---

[57]   PF Frohlich, CM Meston, "Evidence that Serotonin Affects Female Sexual Functioning Via Peripheral Mechanisms," *Physiology & Behavior*, Vol 71(3-4), 1 November – 15 November 2000, 383-393.

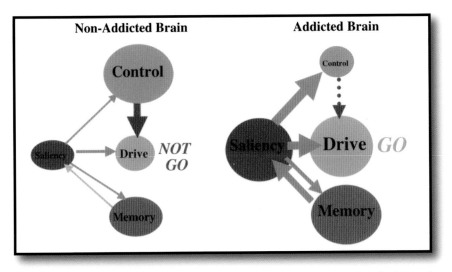

Figure 3: The interplay between control and pleasure in normal and addicted brains.[58] (Reprinted by permission from Elsevier Science and Technology Journals)

the brain associated with sexual arousal and control) interface with the amygdala (deep emotional memories imprinted with sexual learning), sexual images are recalled in addition to the memory of previous sexual pleasure from this growing mixture of brain chemicals. These areas interface with the ventral tegmental area of the midbrain and produce dopamine. Because those in addiction have sensitized this area, it now has a new normal low level of dopamine until stimulated. But when activated by the anticipation of pornography the response is more intense, and the dopamine is released from the presynaptic terminals to cross the synapse and bind to the dopamine receptors in the nucleus accumbens, which is starving for dopamine.

A similar process may be happening with endorphin delivered from the arcuate nucleus to the nucleus accumbens during the sati-

---

[58]   Nora D. Volkow, Joanna S. Fowler, Gene-Jack Wang, "The Addicted Human Brain Viewed in the Light of Imaging Studies: Brain Circuits and Treatment Strategies," *Neuropharmacology*, 47 Suppl 1, 2004, 3-13.

ating portions of acting out episodes.[59,60] *The effect of these brain chemicals is to induce and reward a relapse of viewing.* Dr. Judith Reisman terms this a "toxic" mixture of brain chemicals. In testimony to the US Senate, she called this chemical cocktail "erototoxins."[61] The cycle is deepened with each binge, and the cells in the brain continue to change in a process of addiction that cellular neuroscientists are calling long term potentiation (LTP), which is associated with long term depression (LTD). Addiction is being recognized more and more as physically plastic, or a changing process with regard to nerve cells.[62]

Previously, some argued that only true drug dependencies are addictions, while so-called natural addictions are actually forms of obsessive-compulsive disorder. As Dr. Nestler has written, however, the evidence is becoming convincing that all addictions affect the brain in the same way, whether induced by drugs or by natural addictions such as food and sexuality. Regardless of whether the addiction is alcoholism or pornography, behavioral patterns of deceit and cyclic acting out are similar. Likewise, the loved ones of those in addiction experience similar frustrations. In my opinion, when the scientific literature is reviewed there is no doubt that the final pathway of all addictions leads to the same pleasure centers and involves the same brain chemicals as we previously discussed.

Many report headache, irritability, restlessness, sleeplessness, anxiety, and other symptoms during the first few weeks of abstinence. These classic symptoms of withdrawal can be relentless and can lead the addicted person to relapse, with the brain drug fix bringing reliable relief. The despair and depression which follow, however, mean the relief is a temporary respite until the next episode. With each cycle, the neurochemistry of addiction is engrained even more deeply.

---

[59]   Anders Agmo, Raul G. Paredes, "Opioids and Sexual Behavior in the Male Rat," *Pharmacological Biochemical Behavior,* 30, 1988, 1021-1034.
[60]   Anders Agmo, R Berenfeld, "Reinforcing Properties of Ejaculation in the Male Rat: Role of Opioids and Dopamine. *Behavioral Neuroscience,* 104(I), 1990, 177-182.
[61]   Judith Reisman, "The Brain Science Behind Pornography Addiction and the Effects of Addiction of Families and Communities," Testimony to US Senate Subcommittee, Nov 18, 2004.
[62]   Julie A. Kauer, Robert C. Malenka, "Synaptic Plasticity and Addiction," *Nature Reviews Neuroscience* 8, 8440858, November 2007, 844-858.

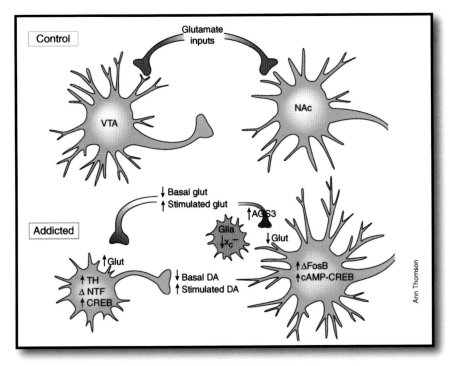

Figure 4: Illustration from Nestler's paper showing a normal sized dopamine producing neuron on the left (VTA area of the brain) with inputs to the pleasure center neuron in the nucleus accumbens on the right. Below, the addicted state is shown, with a shrunken dopamine producing cell on the left and an enlarged, "hypersensitive" pleasure center cell on the right.[63] (Reprinted by permission from Macmillian Publishers, Ltd.)

In summary, I believe there are at least three factors driving pornography and sexual addiction. The first two are common to all addiction, both drug and natural, and the third may be specific for sexual addiction.

1. Cortical hypofrontality, which increases impulsivity, compulsivity, judgment, and increased emotional lability. In a sense, the "brake pads" of the brain wear out, and the person runs through important "stop signs."

63   Eric J. Nestler, Is There a Common Molecular Pathway for Addiction?" *Nature Neuroscience*, 8(11), Nov 2005, 1446.

2. Dopamine depletion, which creates a state of pleasure craving. Endorphins, serotonin, and other neurotransmitters are
   involved, but the pleasure thermostat is reset in the mesolimbic dopaminergic pathways, creating a "new normal" in the
   addicted state. Simple pleasures aren't enough anymore, and
   the person must act out in addiction to get back to this "new
   normal" state.

3. Oxytocin/vasopressin mediated bonding, which is imprinted
   through masturbatory conditioning in concert with the
   amygdala and hippocampus. Thus the pornography experience becomes a virtual mistress, and provides another tether
   which must be addressed to heal.

CHAPTER 7

THE PERSONAL PRICE
OF ADDICTION

Lust not after her beauty in thine heart;
neither let her take thee with her eyelids.
For by means of a whorish woman
a man is brought to a piece of bread:
and the adulteress will hunt for the precious life.

Proverbs 6:24-26

I know of several professionals who have given away much for their addictions. One is a physician, a good man and an excellent doctor who was drawn into a fentanyl addiction. This drug is a strong relative of morphine and produces an extremely euphoric high. He described the addiction as feeling as if he wanted to strap a drum of the drug on his back, run an IV into his arm from the drum, open it up and let it run forever.

Another very talented doctor, a surgeon, allowed himself to become addicted sexually and acted out in adultery. He felt suicidal and was able to return to work only after counseling and monitoring.

A third surgeon, with an excellent reputation and well known in his community, allowed himself to devolve into child pornography. One day the FBI raided his home and took his computers. He went to prison for several years and lost his medical license.

Consider the power of pornography to isolate and captivate in the following example. Someone stopped by to check on a relative who had not called into work and they discovered he had died in his home several days previously. He had married early in life. The mar-

riage lasted briefly, then he lived alone in a home near his work. He
had no car and walked to work. When family members would stop
by, he would politely visit at the door, but had not allowed anyone
into his home in at least eighteen years. He had essentially no friends
and went home every day after work and stayed until the next morning. Although he had money in the bank, he had no running water
in the home.

When the home was cleaned, his relatives found stacks of pornographic magazines going back to the early 1970's, and around seventy
pornographic movies. It seemed his life was going home to this drug,
which seemed to save him from his isolation, but instead only deepened it. His tragic and sad life had funneled into complete dependence on this powerful brain drug and had crippled any other interest
or outlet.

When we undertake to alter or damage the pleasure centers of our
brains, to reset our thermostats for pleasure, we tread very dangerous
ground. Society has bought into the lie that the only constraint
against purely recreational sex is physical disease. The concept of sin
has largely disappeared in a "whatever turns you on" world. Safe sex
is the new religion. As long as there is no physical disease transmitted, any emotional, spiritual, or psychological trauma is discounted
with regard to sexual behavior if the individual is OK with it.

HANGING OUT, HOOKING UP, AND CHECKING OUT

A recent article in the *Wall Street Journal* by Jeff Zaslow entitled
"Some Date: How Homecoming Is Losing Out to Hanging Out,"
describes the new trend of hanging out. Basically, young men ask
girls out to prom, then don't take them to prom. They take the pictures, go out to eat, and then go hang out at someone's house. The
author surmises it is part of a larger problem. Hanging out is related
to hooking up, or sexual encounters with friends with no expecta-
tion on the male's part of any emotional connection. Zaslow's article explains hooking up:

Studies, of course, show more young people skipping romantic relationships in favor of 'hooking up.' As teens socialize in packs, forgo one-on-one dating and trade sex nonchalantly, it is no stretch to find that boys are asking girls to homecoming and not bothering to take them there. Many teens today prefer to gather in someone's basement because it's easier to pair off in dark corners. 'There aren't as many chaperones in basements as at dances,' says Ms. Caramanico.

Meanwhile, 60% of 125 college students in a new study by Michigan State University have had a sexual "friends with benefits" relationship. Nine out of 10 "hookups" didn't lead to dating relationships, the study found. More ominously, after casual sex, females are more likely than males to show symptoms of depression, according to a study reported last year in the *Journal of Sex Research*.

"Young women are longing for romance," says Laura Sessions Stepp, author of "Unhooked: How Young Women Pursue Sex, Delay Love and Lose at Both." She interviewed girls who considered it empowering to be dismissive of romance and casual about sex. Later, many were beset with regrets.

Obviously, boys no longer have to call girls on Wednesday for a Saturday date. Now, college boys seeking weekend hookups send girls "U busy?" text messages at 2 or 3 a.m., and girls routinely rouse themselves and go, according to Ms. Stepp's research. Many girls spend the next day clutching their cellphones, waiting in vain for the boy to call.[1]

Another study published in 2007 found that adolescent sexual abstinence resulted in better mental health in adulthood,[2] and in still another study unattached sexual behavior was more likely to result in

---

[1] Jeff Zaslow, "Some Date: How Homecoming is Losing Out to Hanging Out," *Wall Street Journal*, November 1, 2007.

[2] Laura M. Bogart, Rebecca L. Collins , Phyllis L. Ellickson, David J. Klein, "Association of Sexual Abstinence in Adolescence with Mental Health in Adulthood," The *Journal of Sex Research* 44(3), August 2007, 290-298.

depression.[3] How naïve we are to think we can disregard lessons
tested in the "laboratory of history,"[4] as Durant called it, and not be
harmed. How foolish to think we can allow the checks and balances
of the complex pleasure centers of the human brain to be casually
damaged and not face serious consequences. The "great and spacious
building"[5] of addiction is easy to enter, but extremely difficult to leave.
Indeed, those who successfully exit will find it to have been the most
difficult task they have ever accomplished.

Is hooking up related to pornography? Undoubtedly it is both a
cause and an effect. How many of the 2 a.m. phone calls described
in Zaslow's article were from boys viewing pornography at 2 a.m.
who then called a young woman to come and act out the images rag-
ing in his brain? She falsely assumes he cares about her as a person,
yet his perspective is merely appetitive.

THE LAW OF THE HARVEST

Pornography sells unattached sexuality. With its pervasiveness,
we are now seeing serious social and psychological consequences as
a result of society's buying into the "porn is safe recreation" lie. Safe
physically, but what about emotionally? Miriam Grossman, MD, a
psychiatrist at UCLA, has found that college women experience serious emotional trauma from "unattached sexuality."[6] She surmises
that oxytocin, the bonding hormone mentioned earlier, might be responsible, consistent with studies we have referenced. Some few in
the responsible press may be willing to recognize that there are other
dangers to unattached sexuality than infectious disease. For instance,
Kathleen Parker, writing for the *San Antonio Express News* on November 23, 2007 penned "Hookup's Physical, Emotional Scars Aren't

---

[3]   Catherine M. Grello, Melinda L. Harper, Deborah P. Welsh, "No Strings Attached:
     The Nature of Casual Sex in College Students," *The Journal of Sex Research*, 43(3)
     August 2006, 255-267.
[4]   Will and Ariel Durant, The Lessons of History, Simon and Schuster, 1968, 35-36.
[5]   1 Nephi 8:26
[6]   Grossman, Miriam, Unprotected: A Campus Psychiatrist Reveals How Political
     Correctness in Her Profession Endangers Every Student. Penguin Group 2006,
     published under the name Anonymous, MD. She finally revealed her identity on
     "Dr. Laura."

So Casual."[7] In it she refers to Grossman: "Grossman is most concerned that politically correct ideology has contaminated the health field at great cost to young lives. As Grossman sees it, when the scientific facts contradict what is being promoted as truth, then ideology has trumped reality."[8] I believe pornography is a silent partner in this social and emotional pathology.

As part of his recovery, I asked a young man to list all he had lost as a result of his pornography addiction. As he later did this, he told me he began to cry as he thought of all he had given up, and he realized it was not worth it to him. Inability to attend a church school and the delay or denial of an opportunity to serve a mission were immediate effects. Failure to see women as people instead of objects with the devastating effect of the inability to marry successfully, much less in the temple, is a loss we may see as more youth delay marriage and dating.

ISOLATED AGONY

One of the most insidious effects of a pornography addiction is isolation. Isolation is the prerequisite to acting out in an addiction. The person must isolate physically. He must find a place where he can be alone, where no one will disturb him as he shuts out the world so he can act out. He must then isolate socially. He must disconnect from others so he can be alone. As he prepares to act out he disconnects from other humans so he can be truly alone. Emotional isolation is essential. If he thinks about those he loves and what his acting out would do to them, he would be unable to act out. This is where the anesthesia of changing dopamine, endorphin, adrenaline, and serotonin levels may motivate and help numb the pain and ease those in addiction into the fog, as the world and everything he cares about recedes from his view. Once in the fog, firmly isolated, he can then descend into the world of acting out, view pornography, and masturbate. Here, in this world, he is truly alone. He is in a circular room

---

[7]   Kathleen Parker, "Hookup's Physical, Emotional Scars Aren't So Casual." San Antonio Express News, November 23, 2007.
[8]   Ibid.

of mirrors, where everywhere he turns he sees only the obsession in his own eyes. This has been magnified by the Internet, where whatever the brain can desire is realized with a click. The monitor screen becomes a mirror of compulsion and draws the mind and soul of the addicted person in. It provides whatever fantasy he wants as fast as he can type the key words in, further reinforcing the neurochemical rut in which he finds himself entrenched.

Guilt and shame reinforce isolation and cause the person trapped in addiction to live a double life, introducing deceit. This sin further corrodes the soul and confidence of the victim and keeps the addictive sin hidden. One man said he would take it to his grave rather than disappoint his loved ones. While this appears to be rational to the addicted person at the time, it is part of the "unmanageable"[9] life gone tragically awry.

Addiction is a door that leads to what Lehi called "wandering in strange roads."[10] Once lost, the person will yearn for life before addiction. He will imagine what life would be like without it, yet without recovery will be drawn back "like a tractor beam."[11] Stopping the addiction on one's own has been described as like "trying to stop a bad case of nausea with willpower alone."[12]

DATING AND MARRIAGE

If we consider the male perspective of hanging out in light of the growing pervasiveness of pornography we may better understand why more and more returned missionaries seem to show no interest in dating and marriage. In light of dopamine depletion and oxytocin-mediated bonding, consider the following from Dr. Victor Cline:

> In my experience as a sexual therapist, *any individual who regularly masturbates to pornography is at risk of becoming, in*

---

[9] Patrick Carnes, *In the Shadows of the Net: Breaking Free from Online Compulsive Sexual Behavior*, Hazelden, 2001, 48.

[10] 1 Nephi 8:32

[11] "Finding Recovery from Porn Addiction." *Church News*, March 31, 2007 http://www.desnews.com/cn/view/1,1721,470006074,00.html.

[12] Ibid.

time, a sexual addict, as well as conditioning himself into having a sexual deviancy and/or disturbing a bonded relationship with a spouse or girlfriend.

A frequent side effect is that it also dramatically reduces their capacity to love (e.g., it results in a marked dissociation of sex from friendship, affection, caring, and other normal healthy emotions and traits which help marital relationships). *Their sexual side becomes in a sense dehumanized. Many of them develop an "alien ego state" (or dark side), whose core is antisocial lust devoid of most values. In time, the "high" obtained from masturbating to pornography becomes more important than real life relationships.…*It makes no difference if one is an eminent physician, attorney, minister, athlete, corporate executive college president, unskilled laborer, or an average 15-year-old boy. All can be conditioned into deviancy. *The process of masturbatory conditioning is inexorable and does not spontaneously remiss. The course of this illness may be slow and is nearly always hidden from view. It is usually a secret part of the man's life, and like a cancer, it keeps growing and spreading. It rarely ever reverses itself, and it is also very difficult to treat and heal. Denial on the part of the male addict and refusal to confront the problem are typical and predictable,* and this almost always leads to marital or couple disharmony, sometimes divorce and sometimes the breaking up of other intimate relationships.[13](emphasis added)

"Hanging out" becomes a natural for socialization for the returned missionary who resumes a prior pornography addiction from before his mission. He prefers to be superficial in his relationships with young women because he knows marriage carries real relationship risk. With emphasis on temple worthiness, it is more comfortable to avoid commitment. Some mistakenly think marriage will be an outlet for their sexual urges and that they will be able to stop pornography after marriage. Cline relates the following from his experience:

---

[13]   Victor B. Cline, *Pornography's Effects on Adult and Child,* http://mentalhealthlibrary.info/library/porn/pornlds/pornldsauthor/links/victorcline/porneffect.htm.

Being married or being in a relationship with a willing sexual partner did not solve their problem. Their addiction and escalation were mainly due to the powerful sexual imagery in their minds, implanted there by the exposure to pornography. They often preferred this sexual imagery, accompanied by masturbation, to sexual intercourse itself. This nearly always diminished their capacity to love and express affection to their partner in their intimate relations. *The fantasy was all-powerful, much to the chagrin and disappointment of their partner. Their sex drive had been diverted to a degree away from their spouse. And the spouse could easily sense this, and often felt very lonely and rejected.* I have had a number of couple-clients where the wife tearfully reported that her husband preferred to masturbate to pornography than to make love to her.[14] (emphasis added)

The losses accumulate, and the person is immersed in mental pathology, social and emotional isolation, and spiritual death until he says "Enough!" As one man said after a long struggle, "It wasn't worth the pain in the end."

---

[14]   Ibid.

CHAPTER 8

THE PRICE OTHERS PAY

Many hearts died, pierced with deep wounds.

Jacob 2:35

A few years ago I visited with a man whom I had known in the past. He was well respected in his community, a professional who appeared to have achieved success in most areas of life. He did well financially, had a good reputation in his field, held important church positions, and appeared to be happily married with a large family. What wasn't known is that he secretly had struggled with sexual immorality for years, and cable TV with its introduction of pornography in pay channels in the 1980's provided him easier access to pornography. He had lost his family and had been married at least a couple of times since. He had also lost his professional license, and with it, his good income. He had suffered a series of serious health problems. He had been excommunicated from the Church twice. He told me he used to think that we had to die to experience hell in the next life, but he had found that hell could exist on this earth. His goal was to be able to enter the temple again someday.

I thought of others in his life who were affected by his addictions. His wife, who had trusted that he would support and love her so she could bear and raise his children. His children, who lived with secondary guilt and shame and with the loss of loving parental bonds. The community, who knew of his actions and that he was a member of the LDS Church. Although his addiction was experienced in isolation, the effects were generalized far and wide and involved many others. I felt compassion for this person whose addiction had ruined his life, but I realize that he has access to the healing power of the Atonement.

THE VIRTUAL MISTRESS

Perhaps most direct is the effect on the spouse. The unique, personal bond of sexuality has been betrayed with a virtual mistress. Many wives want to leave immediately, particularly when they discover the pornography, but most stay in the marriage. Many limp along, with the wife developing codependent behaviors as she tries to change her husband's behavior. For example, she may become a detective and constantly try to catch him in his acting out. She may change her own standards and perform sexually in a way that may be distasteful to her in an attempt to keep him from acting out with pornography. She believes that her happiness and peace of mind are dependent upon her husband's recovery. Note the following from the *Journal of Sex and Marital Therapy:*

> The vast majority of women in this study used words such as "betrayal," "cheating," and "affair" to describe the significance that their partner's involvement in pornography had for them. Although their partners were not in actual contact with other females, *these women clearly viewed the pornographic activities as a form of infidelity.* The theme that runs through their letters is that *the man has taken the most intimate aspect of the relationship, sexuality, which is supposed to express the bond of love between the couple and be confined exclusively to the relationship, and shared it with countless fantasy women.*[1] (emphasis added)

Another peer-reviewed paper describes the trauma to married women.[2] Married women in this study felt more distressed by their husband's pornography use than did those in dating relationships, and Internet pornography consumption was viewed as a threat to the marriage.

---

[1]   Raymond M. Bergner, Ana J. Bridges, "The Significance of Heavy Pornography Involvement for Romantic Partners: Research and Clinical Implications," *Journal of Sex and Marital Therapy*, Vol 28, 2002, 193-206.

[2]   Ana J. Bridges, Raymond M. Bergner, Matthew Hesson-McInnis, "Romantic Partner's Use of Pornography: Its Significance for Women," *Journal of Sex and Marital Therapy*, 29(1), January 2003, 1-14.

The extent of the pain to others this problem causes is illustrated in comments posted on the web site "Her Story Lives" sponsored by the Lighted Candle Society. Some examples are presented here:

9/7/07

I do not know one person whose life has not been seriously affected by pornography. Many of those that I know who have spent many nights crying themselves to sleep in heart-wrenching agony and the deepest of emotional pain as a result of pornography, are young mothers and wives of young men ages twenty to thirty addicted to that awful tragic substance tearing our very nation at its seams. Thank you, and God bless you for the work that you are doing.

9/7/07

I spent most of my adult years in denial knowing that my husband was sorely addicted with pornography. But was determined to somehow effect a change. We counseled together, read a lot, prayed together, and provided a path to overcome the serious plague in our lives. Our children could sense the tension, but we did not reveal the source to them. Eventually, my husband found his way back to me. Our love is stronger for overcoming this disease.

9/9/07

I woke up from a nap one day and caught my husband looking at pornography on the computer. That was over a year ago, and he hasn't looked at it on the Internet until this past week. My heart has been broken over and over again. Sometimes I wonder if this pain will ever go away and if my marriage will really last.

9/11/07

My husband has been addicted to porn for all of our three decades of marriage and many years prior to that. Countless times he has sworn to me that he has stopped the porn, but he just gets better at hiding it. I am done. I have given him so many second chances. Enough is enough. I am leaving him even though I love him and we have no other major problems. I am tired of his lies. He presents a false image to me and to everyone in his life. I want to be free of this poison at last.

10/27/07

About a year and a half ago I found out that my husband of seven years had been indulging in pornography off and on throughout our marriage, some years much more than others. It was a secret that he had kept very well hidden from me...I was devastated...We had two kids. What was I going to do? The titles of some of the web sites I found horrified me.

And not that long ago I had asked him directly about it since I knew that he had struggles as a youth and we had just found out about other family members being involved, he boldly denied that he had ever even looked since we had been married...A blatant and bold face lie...I was so naive.

But I can say a year later I know we are far from the end in this pornography riddled society, but things are so much better. HE is so much better! It took a lot of work, counselors, support groups, late night or all night "discussions," fights, daily inventory, prayers, and prayers, pain, and, I tell you what, I went through a whole range of emotions, feelings, even ideas that I would have NEVER anticipated which led to some situations that neither of us would ever have dreamt and hope to never repeat...But mostly it took a lot of love, forgiveness, and repentance.

It is very hard to forgive this, but it is also very hard to admit and to change so we have had to work together. I am grateful that I have a husband who recognizes it as bad and realizes it for the unsatisfiable demon that it is...I feel so bad for those who are suffering on both sides of not recognizing that. There are so many things that made so much more sense after I found out about this "little problem" of his. I remember times in our marriage where I really struggled with what I knew about his pornography issues from before we had gotten married. I thought it was just me and that I wasn't being forgiving enough, that it was my problem but as it turned out those were the times that he was indulging the most...Interesting...He was often very cold and apathetic, he had poor self esteem...However, now I can truly say for the first time in eight and ½ years that I love my husband, not just because I love everyone, but because I really love who he really is.

Once he took pornography out of his life he became a better person. He is more compassionate and sympathetic, he has more confidence, he is more pleasant to be around. His whole countenance has changed and not only do I love the change but he does too. And one of the most interesting things about it is that even our sex life is better. We are now a happier family on a more regular basis. I know that the battle is far from over but we are making progress and I am so grateful that my husband has been able to have a taste of life without pornography because it truly is better![3]

These heart-rending personal experiences are only the tip of the iceberg. I have known couples who are typical of this dual agony— the addicted man in his own misery and the wife tied to the misery by marriage. Just as Grossman found that it wasn't politically correct to discuss the depression she found among sexually promiscuous young college women at UCLA, it is similarly unpopular to recognize the misery pornography causes and the devastating toll it takes on individuals, relationships, families, and communities.

NIP AND TUCK: WHEN LOOKS CAN KILL

In testimony to the United States Senate on the harmful effects of pornography, Mary Anne Layden, Ph.D. discussed the effects of pornography on the wives of men addicted to pornography. She said, "Some wives will resort to plastic surgery, especially breast implants.

---

[3] http://herstorylives.com/list.asp.

Research indicates that women who get breast implants are four times as likely to commit suicide as other women are."[4] It is more than mere coincidence that this surgery is exploding at a time when pornography is increasing the sexual energy and thought underlying our culture. Cause and effect are a mute point; they reinforce and potentiate. In my operating room, a surgeon was talking about a popular R-rated movie and commented on a nude scene. I rather obviously changed the subject, but it occurred to me that this never would have occurred in 1959, the year I was born, when *Ben Hur* won Best Picture. Let us consider how this might relate to our subject and whether or not this surgery is as harmless as advertised.

A growing trend is the societal co-addictive behavior of the sexualization of women, particularly with breast implants. It is important to make a distinction between sexualization and feminization. Are all breast implants intended strictly to sexualize and not feminize? Of course not. Breast reconstruction has allowed millions of women to better face the physical and psychological trauma of recovery from breast cancer. Certainly not all strictly cosmetic implants are to sexualize, either. But it appears as if our society is making what should be the exception into the rule.

Recent peer-reviewed literature has cautioned that the effects of strictly cosmetic breast implants are not as innocuous as some might suppose. In May 2001, a study in *Epidemiology* found the risk of suicide to be twice that of other women, with marital difficulties, depression, emotional disorders, and low self-esteem being possible contributing factors.[5] In November of 2007, a study published in the *Annals of Plastic Surgery* concurred with other studies showing the increased rates of suicide and concluded, "Future studies are needed to determine whether the consistently observed excess of suicide among women with implants reflects underlying psychiatric illness

---

[4]   Senate Committee on Commerce, Science, and Transportation; Subcommittee on Science Technology, and Space; Hearing on the Brain Science Behind Pornography Addiction and Effects of Addiction on Families and Communities, Thursday, November 18, 2004.

[5]   Louse A. Brinton, Jay H. Lubin, Mary Cay Burich, Theodore Colton, and Robert N. Hoover, "Mortality among Augmentation Mammoplasty Patients," *Epidemiology* 2001, 12:321-326.

prior to breast augmentation surgery or other factors."[6] A study from August 2007 also published in the same journal reports the risk and says, "The excess of deaths from suicides, drug and alcohol abuse and dependence, and other related causes suggests significant underlying psychiatric morbidity among these women. Thus, screening for pre-implant psychiatric morbidity and post-implant monitoring among women seeking cosmetic breast implants may be warranted."[7] A recent article in the *American Journal of Psychiatry* recommends, "The higher-than-expected suicide rate among women with cosmetic breast implants warrants further research. In the absence of additional information on the relationship, women interested in breast augmentation who present with a history of psychopathology or those who are suspected by the plastic surgeon of having some form of psychopathology should undergo a mental health consultation before surgery."[8] A special report published in the journal *New Scientist* titled "When Looks Can Kill: The Nip and Tuck Generation Faces a Danger Far Worse Than the Operation Going Wrong" references four major studies all showing increased rates of suicide.[9] According to the August *Annals of Plastic Surgery*, study rates don't begin to rise until ten years after the surgery, but then rise steadily. The rate increases to a 4.5 fold increase between ten and nineteen years after surgery, and six times higher at twenty years.[10]

6 Joseph K.McLaughlin, Loren Lipworth, Diane K. Murphy, Patricia S. Walker, "The Safety of Silicone Gel-Filled Breast Implants: A Review of the Epidemiologic Evidence (Review Article)," *Annals of Plastic Surgery*,. 59(5), November 2007, 569-580.
7 Loren Lipworth, Olof Nyren, Ye Weimin, Jon P. Fryzek, Robert E. Tarone, Joseph I. McLaughlin, "Excess Mortality From Suicide and Other External Causes of Death Among Women With Cosmetic Breast Implants," *Annals of Plastic Surgery*. 59(2) August 2007, 119-123.
8 David B Sarwer, Gregory K.Brown, Dwight L. Evans, "Cosmetic Breast Augmentation and Suicide," *American Journal of Psychiatry*, 164, July 2007, 1006-1013.
9 Rachel Nowak, "Cosmetic Surgery Special: When Looks Can Kill," *New Scientist* 19(2574) October 2006, 18-21.
10 Loren Lipworth, Olof Nyren, Ye Weimin, Jon P. Fryzek, Robert E. Tarone, Joseph I. McLaughlin, "Excess Mortality From Suicide and Other External Causes of Death Among Women With Cosmetic Breast Implants," *Annals of Plastic Surgery*. 59(2) August 2007, 119-123.

These psychological risks are not the only concerns. Indeed, the official web site for the U.S. Food and Drug Administration warns women, "Breast implants do not last forever. If you decide to get breast implants, you will likely need additional surgeries on your breasts over your lifetime due to rupture, other complications (for example, capsular contracture, breast pain), or unacceptable cosmetic outcomes (for example, asymmetry, unsatisfactory style/size, wrinkling/rippling)."[11]

Women are bombarded constantly with what the perfect woman should look like. These social pressures are undoubtedly behind the implants that over 300,000 women a year get, and media pressures are surely a dominant factor. Mainstream women's magazines and most television shows foment the myth and socialize women to try to become "what he wants," to paraphrase the common title we all see at the grocery store check out displays. Pornography is "this big elephant in the middle of the room and no one talks about it."[12] It is undoubtedly a growing force in driving the "nip and tuck" generation forward.

CODEPENDENCY

As the addicted person's life unravels, those close to him are affected. Frequently, wives become codependent as they either try to control his behavior, thus becoming consumed in his addiction, or acquiesce and allow their own values to change. Carnes defines nine processes common in codependent behavior in his book *Don't Call It Love*.[13] In this book he presents his results from working with over one thousand sexually addicted people and their spouses or partners.

• Collusion. Many cover up for the addicted person by keeping secrets or lying.
• Obsessive preoccupation. It is difficult for them not to play detective and neglect others in focusing on fixing the addict.

---

[11] FDA site www.fda.gov/cdrh/breastimplants/qa2006.html
[12] Rory Reid, *LDS Church News*, March 10, 2007
[13] Patrick Carnes, *Don't Call It Love; Recovery from Sexual Addiction*, Bantam Books, 1991, 165-167.

- Denial. Ignoring the reality and keeping busy with other things can cause them to overextend in other areas.
- Emotional turmoil. Codependent behavior causes people to ride an emotional roller coaster and have a hard time stabilizing emotions.
- Manipulation. Some use sexuality as a tool to manipulate their spouse.
- Excessive responsibility. They are extremely tough on themselves and blame themselves for getting into the relationship in the first place and for not being able to stop the addictive behavior.
- Compromise or loss of self. They may find they are giving up their own interests and even their values or morals in their attempts to accommodate those who are addicted.
- Blame and punishment. Some have affairs or act out in other harmful ways; they may shame their spouse by telling intimate details of his current or past behavior to others.
- Sexual reactivity. The predominate impulse was to close down sexually, although some might become hypersexual to hold the addict in the relationship.

The intense, prolonged pain is illustrated in a story shared by the wife of an addicted person:

A month after her temple marriage to a returned missionary, she returned home from work in the middle of the day. Her husband, struggling to find employment, was on the computer viewing pornography. "I remember thinking, *'Do I stay or do I go?' I felt betrayed and deceived. I didn't know if this was serious enough to end a temple marriage.*" Instead of leaving, she determined to find help. She talked to her bishop and sought counseling, read books, and attended support groups. *"We jumped from one thing to the next, trying it for several sessions. Nothing was working."* Worse was the fact that she felt totally ignored in the process. *"I was really hurting,"* she said. "He had been dealing with this for many years of his life."

*She searched in vain for someone to validate her feelings, to un-
derstand the private and painful hurt of her heart.* Ultimately,
she started a *therapy journal.* She would cry and write, cry
and write, for pages and pages, hoping to understand her
thoughts. Finally, she came to one conclusion: *It is painful
when my husband looks at pornography and has a physical reaction to it because it feels like he is having a sexual relationship
with another woman. To her, she concluded, pornography was
akin to adultery.*[14] (emphasis added)

The sanctity of marriage and the betrayal of the sexual relationship is complex. In Carnes' book *In the Shadow of the Net* about
compulsive sexual Internet addictions, he explains this relationship:

Sex is "complicated with reverence" because it is, in fact,
the closest many people ever come to a mystical experience.
Indeed, this is why so many people chase after sex with such
desperate abandon. Whether or not they know it, they are
searching for God. The Internet and cybersex enable people
to chase all the more frantically and intensely.[15]

It is the relationship of the sexual experience to its God-given
creative power that makes it so binding for the happily married and
so destructive for those who abuse it. Misuse of this tremendous
power damages not only the addicted one, but also his wife, children,
and all who are in the circle of his influence. Fortunately, the healing power of the Atonement will heal all who will reach out and accept it.

---

[14] "Dual relationship with family, fantasy," *Church News*, March 24, 2007,
http://www.desnews.com/cn/view/1,1721,470005993,00.html.
[15] Patrick Carnes, *In the Shadows of the Net*, Hazeldon, 2001, 213.

RECOVERY STORY 3

My Name is (name withheld) and I'm now in recovery from a sexual addiction that lasted thirty-eight years. I grew up in a family that struggled with addiction. My parents always had some form of pornography available while I was growing up, and my first real exposure was at age four. My father is still a practicing alcoholic, but my mother is now in recovery and is serving as a facilitator in the Addiction Recovery Program.

At age five I began regular semi-active attendance in the LDS church activities, which continued on through age sixteen. However, my church attendance never could combat what I was exposed to at home. I learned to drink, use drugs, and look at pornography because it was normal in my family. Compounding the problem was the fact that in the neighborhood I grew up in, all the kids were sexually active. Pornography filled my needs that were lacking in the home, and as time went on, I began to fanaticize more and more about sex. Sexual thoughts and images constantly filled my mind. Through our local baby sitters I was shown how to act out my fantasies through masturbation, as I was introduced to their sexual habits.

At school I excelled in math and science, but my social skills were terrible. Emotionally I withdrew because of my addictions. Eating filled my needs for a while, but by age eight I was overweight. Overeating and pornography were the only ways I knew to cope with what was lacking in my life. Spirituality was not present in my home. Spending a lot of time out of the home, in activities like sports and hunting, helped me to keep my sanity.

When I moved out of that neighborhood at age twelve, my addiction slowed. I became more active in scouting and achieved the rank of Life scout. It was one of the happiest times in my life as I look back at adolescence. Most of my friends were active in church, so I went too. Then my family moved again, often because of my father's addictions. I always felt ashamed of my parents, and I never understood why until now.

At age fourteen we moved to a farming area; friends were miles away. The solitude and idleness I experienced on the farm led me back into my problems. Through some of my new friends I was given access to pornographic magazines. I hid these magazines in my house from age twelve to thirty two. Once again, masturbation became my way of coping with life.

I started drinking alcohol at age thirteen to combat the feelings of guilt and shame from my masturbation addiction. By age fourteen I began using drugs. Drinking and drugs helped me cope with my inadequacies. When I started dating, alcohol was always included because that was a way to get a girl drunk, thereby increasing my chances for sexual advancements.

I was married at age eighteen to a sixteen-year-old girl, who was living with an alcoholic father. She wanted out, so we got married. Three years later we had two little girls, but our marriage ended in divorce. Our youngest daughter died of SIDS, and I received custody of my eighteen-month-old daughter. My life spun out of control. My drinking, drugging, porn, and masturbation addictions were now full blown.

At age twenty-four I found sobriety through AA and quit using drugs and drinking. I married a woman I knew from high school that I met going to AA meetings. However, both my wife and I were struggling with pornography addiction and our marriage only lasted two years. Now, divorced for a second time my battle with pornography's evil twins (guilt and shame) became overwhelming. I started back to church several times between ages twenty-four to thirty, but the guilt and shame were too hard to bear. Once again, my sexual addiction became my way of coping with stress, boredom, frustrations, inadequacies, fear, anger, etc.

Marriage to my third wife seemed to give me a new beginning. We got active in church and planned a temple wedding. As I got stronger spiritually, pornography use was slowly disappearing from my life. I was considered active for the first time in my life. Then we moved into a home with a large satellite dish. Later I realized there was pornography on many different stations. I soon found myself returning to my sexual addiction as a night of darkness set in on my life. The words in Joel 2 were coming true. My food addiction also came back.

When I became involved in the church's 12 Step program, my problems started going away. But when the Internet became available, my addiction returned with a vengeance. I now had access to every kind of porn imaginable and then some. The battle was in full swing. I tried filters of every kind and some worked, as long as I let them. But still I was entrenched in the addiction. The daily habit was back. I was powerless. I needed help. I needed hope.

I attended education week at BYU in 2002 after seeing that they were offering classes about addiction. I wanted help. I went to every class available on the addiction processes. I also started attending PASG (Pornography Addiction Support Group) meetings, but I still continued to struggle with pornography. In an effort to do even more to overcome my porn addiction, I attended my first SA (Sexaholics Anonymous) meeting. I found the additional help and hope I needed when I asked someone to be my Sponsor (support person) and help me learn to apply the 12 Steps of recovery. Knowing the steps wasn't enough. I had to learn to live them.

In 2004 I was set apart as a missionary in the PASG meetings. Today my life is full of more peace than I have ever experienced in my entire life. I still battle this addiction every day, and some days are better than others. But I now have complete sobriety. I read, study, ponder, and pray about the words of Christ daily. My wife and I pray together every morning and night, in addition to my personal prayers. I continue to enjoy greater peace and happiness as I grow in recovery through the Atonement of the Savior. By His power I am healing.

My addiction was uncontrollable for thirty-eight years, but I now am enjoying four years of recovery and healing. I have learned through the 12 Step program how to turn to the Savior for strength to fight this battle on a daily basis. Through the power of the Atonement and the perfect love of Christ, I have received peace and happiness and the scars of the past thirty-eight years are being healed. In Alma 50:23 it says "there never was a happier time." That is the way I feel about my life now. Ether 12:27 has also come true in my life.

I pray that my story will give hope to others and inspire them to get help. It is never too late. You have never gone so far that the Savior cannot bring you back. My life is living proof of the love and healing power of Jesus Christ. This addiction does not sleep because Satan, the father of all lies, desires to destroy our souls so that we will be miserable like he is. But, Jesus Christ is our Hope, our Solution, and our Savior. We must find Him and follow Him. His power is greater than any addiction out there. His love has healed me, and His love can and will heal you if you will let Him.

CHAPTER 9

SPIRITUAL EFFECTS

*Unto the pure all things are pure: but unto them that are defiled and
unbelieving is nothing pure; but even their mind and conscience is defiled.*

Titus 1:15

Speaking of those who seduce others to desire sexual immorality,
Paul said, "They allure through the lusts of the flesh . . . while
they promise them liberty, they themselves are the servants of corruption: for of whom a man is overcome, of the same is he brought
into bondage."[1] Although speaking of ancients who had become unclean, he could not have described those who view the pornography
of today better: "Having eyes full of adultery, and that cannot cease
from sin."[2] Speaking of eyes, the Savior said, "Whosoever looketh on
a woman, to lust after her, hath committed adultery with her already
in his heart."[3] As addiction ensues, the "will of the flesh,"[4] mediated
by damaged pleasure centers in the brain, "giveth the spirit of the
devil power to captivate."[5]

FLAXEN CORDS

This addictive property of sin is also described in Proverbs: "His
own iniquities shall take the wicked himself, and he shall be holden
with the *cords* of his sins."[6] (emphasis added) Some of the most de-

---

[1] 2 Peter 2:18
[2] 2 Peter 2:14
[3] Matthew 5:28
[4] 2 Nephi 2:29
[5] Ibid.
[6] Proverbs 5:22

scriptive language regarding cords and the progressive nature of addiction was spoken by Nephi. He explains how Satan binds: "He is
the founder of all these things . . . and works of darkness, yea, and he
leadeth them by the neck with a flaxen cord, until he bindeth them
with his strong cords forever."[7] Does "leadeth" refer to initial curiosity, and "bindeth" refer to completed addiction?

I have considered this *flaxen* to *strong* cord progression and how
it might relate to physical changes in our brains. I have had some
personal, spiritual moments when doing brain surgery. One I will
always remember was a few years ago when I received a call from a
physician friend of mine who had climbed on a new CT scanner just
to check it out. It turns out he had a blueberry-sized tumor called a
colloid cyst in the center of his brain blocking the ventricles, or CSF
cavities in the brain. Although the tumor was benign, it was in a very
dangerous place, and the risk of obstruction and sudden death were
high. The next day I performed surgery on him to remove this tumor.
It was necessary to free it from the fornix, a delicate wire of nerves
carrying memory in each side of the brain. After removing the
tumor, I could look through the Foramen of Munroe into the floor
of the third ventricle. This area contains the hypothalamus where
emotion and hormones interplay. It is close to and connected to the
nucleus accumbens, the ventral tegmental area, the arcuate nucleus,
and locus coeruleus, and all the other integral areas involved in pleasure and emotion. I thought of Noonan's quote, long one of my fa-
vorites: "And if that which is human is also somehow divine, then
nervous tissue is both the means of the miracle and the miracle itself.
Complex beyond man's understanding, the human nervous system is
the most sophisticated arrangement of cells that exists."[8] *Somehow
these structures I was looking at and gently manipulating with curative
intent were ports through which the immortal spirit manifested itself to the
temporal world.* Although I have performed hundreds of brain surgeries, this one somehow helped me gain more insight into this
process than I previously had.

---

[7]   2 Nephi 26:22
[8]   David Noonan, *Neuro – Life on the Frontlines of Brain Surgery and Neurological Medicine*, Ballantine Books, 1989, 1-2.

In some way, this unique organ allows our spirit to punch through into this world. It is in the neuron that this transition occurs. That is why damaging the brain sexually is more than just a neurochemical addiction. Because the brain is the most tangible representative of the soul, the merging of the body and the spirit, pornographic damage to the brain literally damages the soul. *The chemical chains of addiction thus become the spiritual chains of sin.*

STRONG CORDS

These flaxen cords are earlier, more electrically mediated compulsions and curiosities, while the strong cords may represent the morphologic, physical changes we are now calling long term potentiation (LTP), dendritic arborization, receptor downgrading, ratio alteration, pre-synaptic depletion, and the atrophy and hypertrophy some addictive models describe. In other words, these terms are recognized scientific terms which detail the actual physical and chemical changes that addiction to drugs cause, whether the drug is produced by the brain or by the drug company. Repentance, or change from sin to righteousness, thus requires extra support, with terms like recovery, sobriety, and avoidance of relapse becoming more relevant. Otherwise, Nephi's warning of the strong cords binding forever are destined to become reality. Dopamine is synthesized in the body from an amino acid, phenylalanine. This chemical is one of the twenty amino acids that the proteins in our bodies are composed of. These amino acids, or building blocks, are held together in *chains* by peptide bonds. The carbon atoms in the dopamine molecule itself are held together by covalent *bonds* in a chain of carbon atoms. The metaphor could not be more direct: *Chemical and spiritual chains and bonds merge to bind the soul.*

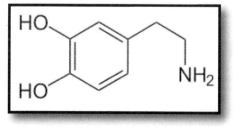

Figure 1. Chemical structure of Dopamine: Note the *chain*-like structure, with each angle or bend representing a carbon atom, and the line representing a covalent *bond*.

In April of 2006 President Thomas S. Monson described how Tongan fisherman value octopus meat and use a lure called a maka-feke to catch them. It is made from a round stone and large seashells. The octopus thinks it looks like an appealing meal and grabs the lure. The fisherman simply pulls the octopus into the boat, and the octopus is doomed. He then discusses the maka-feke of pornography: "Avoid any semblance of pornography. It will desensitize the spirit and erode the conscience. We are told in the *Doctrine and Covenants*, 'That which doth not edify is not of God, and is darkness' (*Doctrine and Covenants* 50:23). Such is pornography."[9]

After warning priesthood brethren about the dangers of pornography in the October 2004 Priesthood Session of General Conference, President Gordon B. Hinckley shared the tragic story of a man who hid a twenty-year addiction from his wife, then confessed it to her only when he learned he had terminal cancer. President Hinckley read her very sobering letter to the priesthood brethren, and then warned that those who did not repent would continue to face their addiction in the spirit world:

> Let any who may be in the grip of this vise get upon their knees in the privacy of their closet and *plead with the Lord* for help to free them from this evil monster. Otherwise, this vicious stain will *continue through life and even into eternity.* Jacob, the brother of Nephi, taught: "And it shall come to pass that when all men shall have passed from this first death unto life, insomuch as they have become immortal...*they who are righteous shall be righteous still, and they who are filthy shall be filthy still*" (2 Nephi 9: 15-16).[10] (emphasis added)

Elder Dallin H. Oaks lists several harmful spiritual effects of pornography in his conference talk of May 2005:

> The immediate spiritual consequences of such hypocrisy are devastating. Those who seek out and use pornography

---

[9]   Thomas S. Monson, "True to the Faith," *Ensign*, May 2006, 18-19.
[10] Gordon B. Hinckley, "A Tragic Evil Among Us," *Ensign*, November 2004, 59.

forfeit the power of their priesthood. The Lord declares: "When we undertake to cover our sins, ... behold, the heavens withdraw themselves; the Spirit of the Lord is grieved; and when it is withdrawn, Amen to the priesthood or the authority of that man" (D&C 121:37). Patrons of pornography also *lose the companionship of the Spirit.* Pornography produces fantasies that destroy spirituality. "To be carnally minded is death"—spiritual death (Rom. 8:6; see also 2 Ne. 9:39). The scriptures repeatedly teach that the Spirit of the Lord will not dwell in an unclean tabernacle. When we worthily partake of the sacrament, we are promised that we will "always have his Spirit to be with [us]." To qualify for that promise we covenant that we will "always remember him" (D&C 20:77). Those who seek out and use pornography for sexual stimulation obviously violate that covenant. They also violate a sacred covenant to refrain from unholy and impure practices. *They cannot have the Spirit of the Lord to be with them.* All such need to heed the Apostle Peter's plea: "Repent therefore of this thy wickedness, and pray God, if perhaps the thought of thine heart may be forgiven thee" (Acts 8:22). *"Brethren, you have noticed that I am not discussing the effects of pornography on mental health or criminal behavior. I am discussing its effects on spirituality—on our ability to have the companionship of the Spirit of the Lord and our capacity to exercise the power of the priesthood."*[11] (emphasis added)

To the one who is mired in this seemingly inextricable problem, know there is hope, healing and absolute freedom. Toni Handy, a missionary with the LDS Addiction Recovery program, described the pain those addicted and their loved ones feel as the "black tar pit of despair." Know that the Savior stands ready to lift all who seek Him out of the pit, even when damaged agency has left *asking God to rescue* as the only choice. Elder Jeffrey R. Holland explains the Savior's role:

---

[11]   Dallin H. Oaks, "Pornography," *Ensign*, May 2005, 87.

This reliance upon the merciful nature of God is at the
very center of the gospel Christ taught. I testify that the Savior's Atonement *lifts from us* not only the burden of our sins
but also the burden of our disappointments and sorrows, our
heartaches and our despair (Alma 7:11-12). From the beginning, trust in such help was to give us both a reason and
a way to improve, an incentive to lay down our burdens and
take up our salvation. There can and will be plenty of difficulties in life. *Nevertheless, the soul that comes unto Christ, who
knows His voice and strives to do as He did, finds a strength, as
the hymn says, "beyond [his] own."* ("Lord, I Would Follow
Thee," LDS Hymns, #220). The Savior reminds us that He
has "graven [us] upon the palms of [His] hands" (1 Nephi
21:6). Considering the incomprehensible cost of the Cruci-
fixion and Atonement, *I promise you He is not going to turn His
back on us now.* When He says to the poor in spirit, "Come
unto me," He means He knows the way out and He knows
the way up. He knows it because He has walked it. He
knows the way because He is the way. *Brothers and sisters,
whatever your distress, please don't give up and please don't yield
to fear.* (emphasis added)[12]

He lifts us when we cannot lift ourselves, whether we ourselves
are in the abyss of addiction or are the spouse or parent in the depths
of despair. We must not give up because He will come with strength
"beyond [our] own."[13] Elder Holland's apostolic promise is comforting and sure, "I promise you He is not going to turn His back on
us now."[14]

SEAL YOU HIS

In the end we will be bound to something, to some master. Elder
Neal A. Maxwell said, "Ironically, if the Master is a stranger to us,

12 Jeffrey R. Holland, "Broken Things to Mend," *Ensign*, May 2006, 70-71.
13 Lord, I Would Follow Thee," *LDS Hymns*, #220).
14 Jeffrey R. Holland, "Broken Things to Mend," *Ensign*, May 2006, 69-71.

then we will merely end up serving other masters. The sovereignty of these other masters is real, even if it sometimes is subtle, for they do call their cadence. Actually, 'we are all enlisted' (Hymns, 1985, no. 250), if only in the ranks of the indifferent."[15] We can choose to be bound with strong cords to Satan or to the Lord: "Ye shall bind yourselves to act in all holiness before me."[16] At some point, a time of sealing will come, when final choice will dictate to whom we are sealed. We usually think of sealing as in temple sealing, either in the context of conditional sealing of families together, or in sealing by the Holy Spirit of Promise.[17,18] King Benjamin admonished his followers and us to be "steadfast and immovable, always abounding in good works, that Christ, the Lord Omnipotent, may *seal you his.*"[19] (emphasis added)

The adversary, however, considers those bound by his strong cords his own: "If ye have procrastinated the day of your repentance even unto death, behold, ye have become subjected to the spirit of the devil, and he doth *seal you his.*"[20] (emphasis added) This is reminiscent of his original plan to destroy the agency of man, "that one soul shall not be lost."[21] He considers those who have not fully repented and recovered from this sin of pornography, who still live in secrecy, *his*, and feels he has claim upon them. He still does not want to lose any of those he now considers *his*. To break these strong cords it will require "all we can do,"[22] with the Atonement of the Savior making up the difference.

---

[15] Neal A. Maxwell, "Swallowed Up in the Will of the Father," *Ensign*, November 1995, 22.

[16] *Doctrine and Covenants* 43:9

[17] 2 Peter 1:10-11

[18] Bruce R. McConkie said, "If *we die in the faith*, that is the same thing as saying that our *calling and election has been made sure* and that we will go on to eternal reward hereafter." (emphasis added) Spoken at the funeral of S. Dilworth Young; quoted in *The Life Beyond*, by Joseph Fielding McConkie and Robert C. Millet, Bookcraft, 1986, 140.

[19] Mosiah 5:15

[20] Alma 34:35

[21] Moses 4:1

[22] 2 Nephi 25:23

CHAPTER 10

THE ISOLATION OF PRIDE

My Will, and not Thine

Ezra Taft Benson

At the very start of any sin, pride is always a prerequisite. In his definitive talk on pride, President Ezra Taft Benson defines the essence of pride:

> The central feature of pride is enmity—enmity toward God and enmity toward our fellowmen. Enmity means "hatred toward, hostility to, or a state of opposition." It is the power by which Satan wishes to reign over us. Pride is essentially competitive in nature. We pit our will against God's. When we direct our pride toward God, it is in the spirit of "my will and not thine be done." As Paul said, they "seek their own, not the things which are Jesus Christ's" (Philip. 2:21). Our will in competition to God's will allows desires, appetites, and passions to go unbridled (see Alma 38:12; 3 Ne. 12:30).[1]

To act out in pornography addiction, it is necessary to first place personal desire above all else. In essence, one makes the god of lust the most important focus in his life, and replaces loved ones, peace, and eventually all else with lust as loss accumulates on the altar of addiction. This leads to an immediate diminution of faith. As the person continues to view pornography, faith continues to decrease as the Spirit leaves and as God and His boundaries become more irrelevant and obstructional to acting out in addiction. Unfortunately,

---

[1] Ezra Taft Benson, "Pride, The Universal Sin," *Ensign*, May 1989, 4.

pornography and apostasy become eager companions on Internet search engines as the person searches out the sites of first the fringe believer, then the critic, and finally the apostate. Alexander Pope's poem describes this process:

> *Vice is a monster of such frightful mien*
> *That to be hated, needs but be seen.*
> *But if too long we gaze upon her face*
> *We first endure, then fondle, then embrace.*[2]

Many who initially wander the strange roads of the Internet out of boredom or curiosity find they "gaze upon her face" until they embrace addiction more quickly and deeply than they ever thought possible. Pride allows them to dissociate from God and all other important aspects of their lives as their own addictions become preeminent. As they lose more faith, the cycle only deepens. When we see those formerly strong in faith waver and question, it is almost a given that they are wandering in newly found pleasures as they discard protective spiritual boundaries. The Lord was speaking directly to us in our day when he warned that "he that looketh upon a woman to lust after her shall deny the faith, and shall not have the Spirit, and if he repents not he shall be cast out."[3] The association between lust and loss of faith is non-negotiable. In the end, sensation will win if that is the god chosen. He also warned that those who lust and "commit adultery in their hearts"[4] will "deny the faith, and shall fear."[5] Just as "perfect love casteth out fear,"[6] so can lust cast out perfect love, allowing fear to enter and produce "torment."[7] Charity, which is perfect love, or the pure love of Christ,[8] "thinketh no evil."[9] Fear of dis-

---

[2]   Alexander Pope, *Essay on Man*, Epistle 2, part v.
[3]   *Doctrine and Covenants* 42:23
[4]   *Doctrine and Covenants* 63:16
[5]   Ibid.
[6]   1 John 4:18
[7]   Ibid.
[8]   Moroni 7:47
[9]   1 Corinthians 13:5

covery, fear of loss of control, and fear of progressive and time-dependent impairment of agency is inherent in addiction. To be addicted is to lose boundaries, and the proud refuse to respect all boundaries not in accordance with their own will. Ironically, the addiction becomes the new master. The new companions, shame and guilt, tear openly at self-esteem, while actually bolstering pride. This illustrates the difference between self-esteem and pride: one is building, the other destructive.

THE HOLLOW SOUL

As addiction progresses, shame deepens secrecy, which is fed by fear, and the double life becomes established. Pride operates here, too. Pride causes the person to project false confidence, to convince the world that he really does have it all together. Meanwhile, guilt continues to eat away at self-esteem, and the person is like my father and mother-in-law's raspberry plants.

A few years ago my mother-in-law noticed the tips of the leaves didn't look quite right. She took them to a nursery and was told some unpleasant news. The plants had been infected with the raspberry crown borer, a clear-winged moth. These insects have a two-year life cycle. The larvae tunnel down the inside of the stem, leaving it looking relatively normal on the outside at first. The first sign of infestation and injury is wilting and dying of foliage in April through June. Later, infested canes become spindly and may actually break as the supporting structure of the cane is eaten from the inside out. To treat it, the entire cane must be rooted out, and chemical control must be used. Treatment must continue for two or more consecutive years to eradicate the crown borer. I examined an infected cane. Although it looked relatively normal on the outside, it was essentially hollow on the inside.

How like addiction! At first, only subtle "wilting" may be noticed by loved ones. Just as my mother-in-law knew something wasn't right when she first saw the wilted leaves of her raspberry plant, a spouse or parent may sense something isn't right. Maybe there is more anger, less spirituality, or even periods of hyper-spirituality to compensate. Inside, the addicted person is becoming hollow; emotionally, spiritually, and mentally. Some may continue hiding the larvae inside for years until they finally break off at the ground. One wife described her husband's behavior:

> She met her husband in college. He went on a mission and so did she. After a five-year courtship, they married in the temple. But in marriage there was an immediate disconnect. He worked longer and longer hours. She would wake up in the morning and discover he had been on the computer all night.
>
> *"It felt wrong,"* she said. *"Everything felt wrong."* Pregnant and insecure, she began obsessively checking the computer for pornography. On several occasions she found what she was looking for. She would cry. He would make excuses. Their bishop dealt with the problem by giving her husband simple advice: "Don't look anymore." She knew it wasn't that easy. "It was crazy making," she said. "I was obsessed with continually checking the computer." At night, she'd feign sleep until he dozed off. Then she would check his computer again and again. I would confront him. He would get angry and turn it on me…He said, *"I have it under control."* Maybe his problem was her fault, she finally concluded. Then one night she learned her husband had betrayed her again. Returning to bed she stopped on the stairs and prayed. "You have to let me know what to do," she pleaded. "I can't keep doing this." Instantly, she knew she had value. Anger filled her soul. She raced upstairs, turned on the lights, and yelled, "I won't accept this in my home! You are not going to do this to me! You are not going to do this to my family!" *For the first time in the marriage he broke down.* "I am addicted to pornography," he said, noting that he had been viewing it since he first saw it at a member friend's home *when he was eight years old.* "I need help." He felt better. The burden he had been carrying his entire life was lifted. *She felt nauseous.* She could barely get up in the morning. Now, she feared, the bur-

den was hers. "*I didn't know if I was strong for staying or weak for not leaving,*" she said.[10] (emphasis added)

What a coincidence that just as the raspberry crown borer required two or more years of treatment, Carnes found that it usually takes two years to reach the growth phase,[11] which he defines as someone in strong recovery.

WHITED SEPULCHERS

Another illustrative analogy may be drawn by considering the story told in the book *The Picture of Dorian Gray* by Oscar Wilde.[12] Dorian Gray is a wealthy, eligible bachelor who seems to have everything going for him. A friend paints his portrait when he is young, handsome, and rich. What no one else knows is that Dorian has a dark side. He lives the immoral life of the libertine privately, and although there are rumors, he keeps together the façade for the sake of his pride. As he grows older, though, everyone notices that he doesn't seem to age. Only Dorian knows the secret: his portrait not only ages, but shows the sinister lines of soul-canker. He hides the portrait because his pride demands that he deceive the world. With time, his face becomes a hideous monster. In the end, he plunges a knife into the painting to destroy it. He dies, and the painting reverts to its original, youthful, and innocent appearance.

How many "Dorian Grays" live their lives with corrupted paintings in their souls or hollow on the inside like the infected raspberry canes? The Savior described this hypocrisy as being "like unto whited sepulchers, which indeed appear beautiful outward, but are within full of dead men's bones, and all uncleanliness."[13] Pride is so much more than perceived arrogance or haughtiness. As President Benson explained, it is the enmity of pride that allows the person to isolate

---

[10] "Dual Relationship with Family, Fantasy," *Church News*, March 24, 2007, http://www.desnews.com/cn/view/1,1721,470005993,00.html.

[11] Patrick Carnes, *Don't Call It Love*, Bantam Books, 1991, 207.

[12] Oscar Wilde, *The Picture of Dorian Gray*, Random House, 1992; 1998 Modern Library Paperback Edition.

[13] Matthew 23:27

himself first from God in order to sin, then from everyone else as the addiction spirals downward.

By admitting powerlessness, the addicted one can leave pride behind and reach towards the Savior. Gratitude and humility provide fertile soil for healing, and self-esteem restores confidence. Many who formerly acted out in addiction are now humbly walking in the light, returning their miraculous gift to God by leading others to peace.

PART TWO

HEALING

He was afraid, and beginning to sink, he cried, saying, Lord, save me.
And immediately Jesus stretched forth his hand, and caught him.

Matthew 14:30-31

CHAPTER 11

SUPPORT IN RECOVERY

*To whom do we look, in days of grief and disaster, for help
and consolation?...They are men and women who have suffered,
and out of their experience in suffering they bring forth the riches of
their sympathy and condolences as a blessing to those now in need.
Could they do this had they not suffered themselves?*

Orson F. Whitney

The majority of successful addiction recovery programs, even secular ones, utilize the 12 Step program, or a form of it, according
to those in recovery I have visited with. It is fundamental that Step 2
requires individuals to believe in a Power greater than themselves, a
Power which can restore them to sanity and sobriety. It requires dependence on a Supreme Being to confront addiction successfully.
Originally modified from Alcoholics Anonymous, other organiza-
tions dealing with so-called natural addictions employ their own versions. The Church of Jesus Christ of Latter Day Saints has produced
"A Guide to Addiction Recovery and Healing" based on the 12 Step
program. This powerful guide was written by those who have "suffered from addiction and who have experienced the miracle of recovery through the Atonement of Jesus Christ."[1] This program allows
the addicted individual to interact with others so afflicted in the setting of missionaries and facilitators assisting the discussion. These
facilitators are those who have been addicted and who have at least
one year of recovery, defined as complete sobriety or abstinence from
acting out in addiction. The 12 Steps are nothing more or less than

---

[1] *A Guide to Addiction Recovery and Healing*, LDS Family Services Addiction Recovery Program.

the steps of repentance followed meticulously. With the loving guidance of a bishop, the Steps can lead the person to the scriptures, prayer, and the healing power of the Savior, who alone is "The Way"[2] out.

THE 12 STEPS

Step 1
Admit that you, of yourself, are powerless to overcome your addictions and that your life has become unmanageable.

Step 2
Come to believe that the power of God can restore you to complete spiritual health.

Step 3
Decide to turn your will and your life over to the care of God the Eternal Father and His Son, Jesus Christ.

Step 4
Make a searching and fearless written moral inventory of yourself.

Step 5
Admit to yourself, to your Heavenly Father in the name of Jesus Christ, to proper priesthood authority, and to another person the exact nature of your wrongs.

Step 6
Become entirely ready to have God remove all your character weaknesses.

Step 7
Humbly ask Heavenly Father to remove your shortcomings.

---

[2] John 14:6

Step 8
Make a written list of all persons you have harmed and become willing to make restitution to them.

Step 9
Wherever possible, make direct restitution to all persons you have harmed.

Step 10
Continue to take personal inventory, and when you are wrong promptly admit it.

Step 11
Seek through prayer and meditation to know the Lord's will and to have the power to carry it out.

Step 12
Having had a spiritual awakening as a result of the Atonement of Jesus Christ, share this message with others and practice these principles in all you do.

Note the action words in each of the 12 Steps: Admit, Come, Decide, Make, Become, Ask, Continue, Seek, Share. Recovery is an active process, which requires great mental and spiritual energy, especially early in the process, with continuing diligence for the rest of their life. The LDS Family Services Guidebook for addiction recovery is written as a workbook, in a *Preach My Gospel*[3] format. The purpose is to bring those in addiction out of darkness into the freedom of righteousness. In addition, there is a national organization called Sexaholics Anonymous (SA) based on the 12 Steps, which has provided strength and guidance for many. There are also several spouse support groups for the loved ones of those with sexual addiction.

---

[3]   *Preach My Gospel*, The Church of Jesus Christ of Latter-day Saints, 2004.

The book *Confronting Pornography*[4] is one resource, which may provide insight from various perspectives for the addicted, their families, bishops, and counselors. For instance, Chapter 1 by Victor Cline, Ph.D. provides excellent insight into what is required to overcome addiction. In 1975, Cline wrote "How the Mass Media Affects Our Values and Behavior"[5] and was visionary in anticipating the effect pornography would have in the future. Cline poignantly shares insights gained from his long and vast experience treating those struggling with pornography addiction and is positive in his prognosis for those who reach out for spiritual and professional help. Cline raised a strong, early warning voice on the emotional and behavioral consequences of pornography addiction. He summarizes:

> I have found that there are four major factors that most predict success in recovery. *First,* the individual must be personally motivated to be free of his addiction and possess a willingness to do whatever it takes to achieve success...You can never force a person to get well if he doesn't want to...*Second,* it is necessary to create a safe environment, which drastically reduces access to porn and other sexual triggers...*Third,* he should affiliate with a twelve-step support group...*Fourth,* the individual needs to select a counselor/ therapist who has had special training and success in treating sexual addictions.[6]

In another chapter, John Harmer shares his perspective gained in fighting pornography as Governor Ronald Reagan's Lieutenant Governor in California; his experience goes back to his first court battles with pornography in 1964. He has authored other excellent

---

4   Mark D. Chamberlain, Dan D. Gray, Rory C. Reid, *Confronting Pornography*, Deseret Book, 2005.

5   Victor Cline, "How the Mass Media Affects Our Values and Behavior," *Association of Mormon Counselors and Psychotherapists (AMCAP)*, Volume 1, No. 1, 1975.

6   Victor Cline, Brad Wilcox, "The Pornography Trap," *Marriage and Families Magazine*, September 2002, http://marriageandfamilies.byu.edu/issues/2002/September/trap.aspx.

works on this subject: *A War We Must Win*,[7] and more recently, *The Sex Industrial Complex*,[8] authored with James B. Smith.

Philip and Colleen Harrison, a married couple, each write chapters (11 and 19) on their experience with addiction (hers with food, his with pornography). These chapters are condensations of books they each wrote.[9,10] They provide much insight and are written from a "This is how I did it" perspective. Philip's book is a description of his thirty-year pornography addiction and recovery and is designed as a 12 Step workbook based on LDS scriptures. For insight into what it feels like to struggle through addiction and find the peace of the Savior, *The Perfect Brightness of Hope* by Phil S. is a personal story of one man's journey out of darkness and into light.[11] This compelling account will help those seeking recovery find hope and will help the loved ones of those who so struggle learn empathy and understanding.

Jill Manning's work, *What's the Big Deal about Pornography?*," is geared to youth, but useful for both old and young.[12] Dr. Manning is an excellent resource for any wishing to gain information useful in battling this problem for themselves or their loved ones.

A Brain Gone Wrong by Dr. W. Dean Belnap, is also most insightful with regard to brain mechanisms of addiction, and also sheds insight on imprinting and conditioning.[13]

The *Ensign* has published numerous articles on pornography addiction, including conference talks by General Authorities of the Church.

Since pornography has affected or will affect virtually every family more directly than most would admit or like to believe, everyone should become educated on this formerly taboo subject. Unless we

---

[7]   John L. Harmer, *A War We Must Win*, Bookcraft, 1999.
[8]   John L. Harmer, James B. Smith, *The Sex Industrial Complex*, The Lighted Candle Society, 2007.
[9]   Colleen Harrison, *He Did Deliver Me From Bondage: A Twelve Step Guide for LDS People*, Deseret Book, 2002.
[10] Philip Harrison, *Clean Hands, Pure Heart*, Windhaven Publishing, 2004.
[11] Phil S., *The Perfect Brightness of Hope*, Maasiai Publishing, 2002.
[12] Jill Manning, *What's the Big Deal about Pornography?*, Shadow Mountain, 2008.
[13] W. Dean Belnap, *A Brain Gone Wrong*, Meridian Publishing, 2008.

really come to understand that pornography is as real an addiction as any drug addiction and adequately address this problem, which "hundreds of bishops and stake presidents list . . . as their No. 1 concern for Church members,"[14] we are losing the battle. It is analogous to a person with cancer who decides to get into shape and hires a personal trainer. He then watches his diet carefully and exercises every day, taking care to get plenty of sleep. However, if he ignores the cancer and seeks no medical attention, the other efforts will have been in vain. As we seek to build the kingdom, let us not "leave the other undone"[15] in this essential matter.

---

[14]   "Protecting Homes from Pornography," *Church News*, March 10, 2007.
[15]   Matthew 23:23

CHAPTER 12

CONFESSION

For with the heart man believeth unto righteousness,
and with the mouth confession is made unto salvation.

Romans 9:10

Forsake means to abandon, to renounce and give up. With severely addictive sins this requires a much more extensive process than minor change. Ezekiel admonished Israel to "make you a new heart and a new spirit, for why will you die?"[1] The addictive heart is one which races with adrenaline and desire when preoccupation with pornography begins. Memories of past viewings merge with memories of sexual release accompanying them, and the one trapped in addiction moves into ritualization and prepares to act out. A new heart is a pure one, as King Lamoni's father said, "having this wicked spirit rooted out of my breast."[2] He then said, "I will give away all my sins that I may know thee."[3] The 12 Step program requires that the addiction be confessed to another human being. Some may rationalize that since no actual fornication or adultery has been committed, confession to God with abandonment will suffice. Some rationalize that since this is a private sin it can be privately worked out.

There are two problems with these rationalizations. First, this sin is serious enough in its own right that it must be confessed to gain spiritual forgiveness and to obtain the forgiveness of the Church. It is a breach of baptismal and temple covenants. Unless duly confessed, the adversary will continue to have claim upon the person for this sin. Second, given the nature of addiction, it will be impossible

---

[1] Ezekiel 18:31
[2] Alma 22:15
[3] Alma 22:18

to actually quit the behavior without the assistance of others. In secrecy, the person may think he can overcome the addiction by willpower alone and may go for extended periods of abstinence. At some point, however, when the stress is right, isolation returns, and old patterns are rekindled and acting out in the addiction is inevitable. *The addiction may lie dormant for months in some cases depending on the resistance, but it will return if the person is not in full recovery.* Confession is essential not only for spiritual healing and eventual forgiveness, but for mental and emotional healing and recovery as well.

To whom should the person confess? The single person might consider confessing to a parent if the relationship permits this. Parental support can be a crucial pillar of recovery for most. For those who are married, confession to the spouse is essential, however, the timing and actual disclosure should be undertaken after seeking the guidance of the Lord and counseling with those experienced in recovery. As the wife of a man in recovery said, "Pornography confession does not a perfect marriage make." Reactions from the wife may be varied. Depending on the marriage and relationship, she may be supportive and loving if she senses a serious desire to change. It is possible she may react with anger and may desire to separate and divorce.

The wife of one in recovery explained to me that in her experience, which is not unique, she was already feeling the pain of the damaged relationship, even though she didn't understand why at first. She said, "I felt the effects long before I *knew* about it." With regard to learning about the addiction she said, "Confession/disclosure strips away all of our false hopes and denial and rationalizations and delusions of control—the ways we have been trying to cope with the effects of sexaholism—and is very shocking and traumatic. It feels rather like the end of the world, but it can also be the beginning of a much better world." Note she said it "can be." The healing of the relationship depends on the eventual healing of each person, with each focusing on gaining personal peace through the Savior and not codependently trying to "fix" each other.

Even in the best of circumstances, the confession will transfer a great burden to her and instill in her a profound sense of loss. In the ideal situation the wife becomes a partner in recovery and learns to trust again as deceit is abandoned. Virtually all wives of those in recovery who have shared their stories with me have described a desire to know what is necessary, but not every detail. In other words, a man who struggles still with lustful thoughts may need someone to call frequently. Burdening his loving but traumatized spouse with the intimate details of his thought processes would be counterproductive and perhaps even damaging. He would be much better served calling a sponsor he had met in an addiction support group with such details. One wife told me her husband might call and say, "I'm struggling today, pray for me." For her, this helped her trust him, though she specifically said she didn't need to know the details of exactly what it was that was troubling him. This interplay of appropriate transparency is sensitive and probably different for each couple. If he relapsed or slipped, however, he would need to inform his wife, or trust would not be able to grow. By doing so, she would be confident that there would be no *significant* secrets, and the husband would know that any breach or relapse must be immediately reported, regardless of how painful to both it may be.

Free and voluntary confession is much better than discovery, particularly for rebuilding the trust that is damaged by the new knowledge of the betrayal and the double life. In *The Infinite Atonement*, Tad Callister quotes Mahatma Gandhi telling a personal experience in which as a youth he stole something. Fearing anger, Gandhi confessed to his father with a written confession. However, his father, who was ill and confined to his bed at the time, responded differently:

> He read it through, and pearl-drops trickled down his cheeks, wetting the paper. For a moment he closed his eyes in thought and then tore up the note…I could see my father's agony. If I were a painter I could draw a picture of the whole scene today. It is still so vivid in my mind. Those pearl-drops of love cleansed my heart, and washed my sin away. Only he who has experienced such love can know what it is…It transforms everything it touches. There is no limit to its power. This sort of sublime forgiveness was not natural to my father. I had thought that he would be angry, say hard things, and I

believe this was due to my clean confession. A clean confession, combined with a promise never to commit the sin again, when offered before one who has the right to receive it, is the purest type of repentance. I know that my confession made my father feel absolutely safe about me, and increased his affection for me.[4]

It will be easier for the wife to regain trust and feel safe about her husband again if the confession is free and clean, or in other words, uncoerced and completely voluntary. The words of the Lord are relevant here: "By this ye may know if a man repenteth of his sins; behold, he will confess them and forsake them."[5] Confession is prerequisite to forsaking and helps others know of their sincere repentance.

SHIFTING BURDENS

Even in the most optimal situation, this confession may be the most traumatic news the wife will ever have received. Although the sinner in the person feels relief of a great burden with a newfound spiritual beginning and the addict in the person senses an unfettering as newfound support can help to break chains, the burden has shifted to an innocent wife. She will be devastated by the betrayal. The realization that some of what she *thought* was real was not will be intense, even in otherwise good marriages. Healing in her own soul will take time, and the person confessing must understand that although the burden of helping her heal will be born by the Savior, he should ideally do all he can to help. She will go through her own recovery of sorts, a recovery from the trauma and hopefully, eventually a restoration of trust. She can find great strength in a support group of other women experiencing the same pain. Indeed, as she goes through her own 12 Step process of giving her pain to the Savior, instead of placing it on herself or her husband, she will find her own recovery from co-dependence facilitated.

Her husband would help her in this by assuming responsibility for

---

[4]   Tad Callister, *The Infinite Atonement*, Deseret Book, 2000, 191-192.
[5]   *Doctrine and Covenants* 58:43

the acute pain of the new knowledge and for the chronic pain as she processes this burden over time. However, several such spouses have shared with me that even if her husband is still experiencing difficulty in his recovery, she can experience her own healing independent of his action or inaction. If he is truly remorseful and understanding of her emotional trauma, his attitude will be one of complete humility and contrition. He will make no demands of her but rather encourage her to seek solace and support. She may find that formal counseling with an experienced therapist will help her to understand her emotions and to process the dual feelings of anger and empathy she may have toward her husband. The husband will understand that trust has been shattered and that the first step toward rebuilding trust ideally will be assisted by appropriate, yet discretionary, transparency. As he is able to heal and assume the attitude of one in true recovery, he will be concerned more for her recovery from this new knowledge than for his own reputation or needs. He will be solicitous of her thoughts and feelings through *her* own recovery from *his* problem. From her standpoint his attitude, perhaps more than any other single thing, will allow her to regain her trust in him. The Savior alone, however, will bring healing and peace to her soul.

Confession to others, after these essentials, should be on a need-to-know basis. Widely disseminating the information to others gratuitously would be unnecessary and potentially needlessly hurtful to others as is discussed in the next section.

DISCLOSURE:
THE DIFFERENCE BETWEEN CONFESSION AND RECOVERY SHARING

Disclosure is an important part of the repentance and recovery process. The important question to ask in regard to disclosure is based on the intent of the discloser. What is the motive? Is it to hurt or to heal? Let us consider several scenarios.

First, consider the person who is beginning the repentance and recovery process. He or she will begin the process with *confession*. In confession, the primary motive is to unburden the confessor by fully disclosing to the bishop, and to the spouse in the case of the married person. While the bishop and spouse must now bear the new burden, this is a necessary step in the healing process. Disclosure to others, even to other family members, should be done sensitively, particularly with regard to graphic details. Maturity, emotional stability, and age of children should be considered when disclosing sensitive issues regarding a parent. We must all be careful in disclosing other's struggles, and a guiding principle is to treat sensitive information about others as we would want sensitive details about our own lives to be treated.

Second, consider the person who has years of sobriety and strong recovery and is now temple worthy. When this person discloses in the setting of a 12 Step group or in an individual sharing with one new in recovery, it is not a confession. It may be more appropriately termed *recovery sharing*. The motive of this type of disclosure is not to confess to unburden and repent. For this person confession was previously accomplished with appropriate disclosure. In fact, we are counseled not to continue to confess our own sins or the past sins of others:

> Sin brings an uncleanliness before the Lord that must be reconciled. There is, however, a time and a place for confession and asking forgiveness... *It is not necessary, appropriate, nor healthy to expose our private or family mistakes and sins for public scrutiny.* The more widely a sin is known, the more difficult the repentance or change... Another side of exposing dirty linen is the carnal, insatiable appetite that some have to expose the faults of others....This can happen even in the family, when one, supposing he is protecting his *own* good name, *exposes in elaborate detail the faults and mistakes of his siblings, his children, or his parents in a form of self-justification designed to alleviate his personal pain...* Whenever we tell of others' sins or mistakes, we are in effect passing judgment on them.[6] (emphasis added)

---

[6]   Lynn A. Mickelsen, "The Atonement, Repentance, and Dirty Linen," *Ensign*, November 2003, 10-13.

The motive behind recovery sharing is to share the miracle of healing from sexual addiction with others in a safe and appropriate setting. It is not appropriate for anyone other than the person in recovery to decide when, with whom, and what to share. Recovery is a gift which those who have been healed may share with others who are earlier on the path of repentance and recovery. Recovery sharing is necessary for those still in darkness to be able to feel hope and believe that change is possible. It also strengthens the person sharing, as per Step 12, and thus edifies all.

TRANSPARENCY FOR LIFE

Confession opens the person's heart and eliminates a double life. It is, however, only the first step in recovery, even if the requirement from the sin standpoint has been satisfied. A strong force in recovery is the knowledge that nothing will be hidden. When disclosure is quickly made, it will help change the demand/reward payoff the person receives for acting out, even if more slip-ups or relapses occur as resistance is built. Remember, it takes time for the brain and spirit to heal. Even if the person seeking recovery is seeing a counselor and a bishop, it is essential that he have a transparency partner. This would ideally be a facilitator who is firm in recovery himself and knows the way. Experienced facilitators, missionaries, and spouses of those in recovery agree that in most circumstances the wife should not serve in this role. It would likely be too difficult for the wife not to become a "co-dependency partner." In other words, she might feel she must function in the role of a sort of "recovery policeman." It will be increasingly difficult for bishops to serve as the sole transparency partner given the increased numbers of those in recovery they will be faced with. Although the bishop holds keys of judgment for the person, a support person who is actually in recovery from addiction can also provide valuable strength and experience and *provide the credibility of one who knows.*

The beauty of the growing 12 Step programs such as the Pornography Addiction Support Groups (PASG) is that they allow those firm in recovery to help those emerging from addiction, pain, and deceit in a safe environment. One man in recovery told me that he developed trust and love for these individuals at this early, critical time in recovery. He felt that if these people could still love him after knowing his struggles, then maybe God could love him as well.

One of the main protections imparted by confession is the elimination of the deceit of the double life. However, some can go on for years continuing to relapse, with prompt confessions to the transparency partner or ecclesiastical leader. While preferable to deceit, the "sin and confess regularly" cycle can become an enabler itself. The addicted person views the pornography, promptly confesses, feels better about the confession, and then views again in short order. This can become another futile cycle in the "sorrowing of the damned"[7] if it continues without progress toward recovery.

No Secrets

Transparency is protective. It insulates the person from isolation and is a part of the healing process. Transparency allows the person to access the Atonement, to be justified and forgiven, and to lose "every desire for sin."[8] As the person continues to see "face to face" and not through "a glass darkly,"[9] he moves toward sanctification. In his talk about being sanctified, Elder David A. Bednar spoke of the parable of the pickle. He said, "The curing process gradually alters the composition of the cucumber and produces the transparent appearance and distinctive taste of a pickle."[10] Those who are in true recovery and have purified their minds and desires are transparent. They have no secrets. They live as if the veil is open to them, because they know it is. They are ready at any time to meet their Maker. Eventually, in the process of time, by putting the addiction on the altar the person offers "their whole soul as an offering."[11] This dual-

---

[7]   Mormon 2:13
[8]   Joseph Fielding Smith (compiler), *Teachings of the Prophet Joseph Smith*, Deseret Book, 51.
[9]   1 Corinthians 13:12
[10] David A. Bednar, "Ye Must Be Born Again," *Ensign*, May 2007, 19-22.
[11] Omni 1:26

ity of the *soul* is pertinent here: the addicted brain healed (*body*) and the wounded *spirit* restored. Thus the person becomes whole again, and when fully divested of every desire for his previous addiction, he becomes sanctified, "without spot."[12]

Joseph Smith described the process as follows: "The nearer man approaches perfection, the clearer are his views, and the greater his enjoyments, till he has overcome the evils of his life and lost every desire for sin; and like the ancients, arrives at that point of faith where he is wrapped in the power and glory of his Maker and is caught up to dwell with Him. But we consider that this is a station to which no man ever arrived in a moment."[13]

---

[12] Moroni 10:33
[13] Joseph Fielding Smith (compiler), *Teachings of the Prophet Joseph Smith*, Deseret Book, 51.

CHAPTER 13

CEREBRAL SOFTWARE

Bring into captivity every thought to the obedience of Christ.

2 Corinthians 10:5

But we have the mind of Christ.

1 Corinthians 2:16

When I was in my training as a neurosurgical resident, one of my neurosurgery professors would meet with us each morning at 6 a.m. for breakfast before beginning the day's surgery. He would share templates of knowledge about neurosurgery, which he called his "Rules of Three." He felt by organizing information into threes we could better remember the knowledge a neurosurgeon needs to know to pass boards and care for patients. He called this process writing "cerebral software" for our own computers, our brains.

Many in recovery have written "cerebral software" to protect themselves in this sexually saturated world we all live in. It is my hope that others will find these techniques helpful, not only as healing tools for the addicted, but also as protection against future addiction for all. *All of the information in this chapter comes from those in recovery who have shared.*

Actualization is a well-described process whereby a person pictures where he wants to be and what he wants to become. It may seem at first to be a positive fantasy, an unreachable goal. For example, when I was in college and medical school, I would imagine how great it would feel to make good grades at the end of the semester.

The thought of that possible, eventual, conditional goal would stay firmly in my mind as I studied throughout the term.

As I share these ideas I emphasize that they do not supplant the 12 Steps or the Addiction Recovery Program, the Pornography Addiction Support Groups (PASG), or any other support group, nor is it implied that those in recovery would not want to seek a competent professional therapist experienced in principles of addiction recovery. These suggestions should be viewed as supplementary and complementary to all of these programs, merely incorporating tools used in other venues and presenting them to the brain as a useable, functional instrument. These ideas are from those who have struggled and found peace or are striving for it.

CAN YOU SEE IT?

It appears that the majority of our returned missionaries and virtually all of our young men are being exposed. Pornography is so compelling that all who are not vigilant and aware are at risk. I feel this is a useful exercise for all men and boys and for women and girls who may feel a need to understand their loved ones, or even for themselves. Those in recovery will hopefully find healing, and those not addicted will use these principles to immunize themselves from the exposure they are certain to encounter at some point and to the risk of addiction that will apply to them as well. In sharing these principles and processes, I will speak directly to those struggling with addiction.

The first step is to imagine what life would be like without the addiction. Imagine how you would feel inside if there were no double life, no lies, and no compulsion to view pornography. Imagine if you were never hijacked by your addiction and could enjoy life without worrying about unclean, distasteful thoughts and desires. Imagine how you would feel if you were so pure inside that if you stood before your Savior today you would feel marvelous joy and peace instead of shame and guilt. This is the first step. Actualize in your mind your life free from all desire for pornography. Describe the person you would like to be in ten years from a spiritual and emotional perspective, and also describe the type of relationship with the opposite sex you would envision.

When you have gone through this exercise and have decided recovery is for you, you are ready for the three questions:
1. What do you want?
2. What are you willing to do?
3. How far are you willing to go?

These three questions form the essential backbone for successful recovery, defined not simply as abstinence from viewing pornography, but as having lost all desire for evil, and eventually becoming sanctified, holy without spot. Of course this goal is a process, not an event, and will occur over the process of time. Over the course of recovery, you can go back to these three questions during difficult moments when relapse may seem imminent.

WHAT DO YOU WANT?

Let's start with the first question: What do you want? The first step in deciding what you want is to actualize your future. Ask yourself: Do I want to be struggling with this problem in ten years, or do I want to look back at this as a painful learning experience which I haven't visited in ten years? Actualization is the first step: picture in your mind and in your emotional brain what you want to feel like and think about in the future.

An important exercise closely associated with the first question is to look at where you will be if you achieve this goal, and where you won't be if you don't. Answering these questions may help you understand what you have already lost.

- As a young LDS man or woman are you giving up serving a mission because of this problem?
- Are you unable to look at those of the opposite sex as human beings, objectifying them instead?
- Have you given up attending a Church school because you can't pass the ecclesiastical endorsement?

- If you have returned from a mission, do you prefer hanging out instead of dating because you dread a relationship leading to a temple marriage you feel you are not worthy of?
- If you are married, do you live with feelings of hypocrisy combined with feeling undeserving of a trusting spouse and children?
- Have you already lost a marriage or temple privileges or even your membership in the Church?
- Have your grades or work suffered because of your loss of focus?

Understand that to be addicted to pornography is to experience loss. The longer you are addicted, the more you will lose. The key is deciding now that you have lost enough today, that you don't want to lose any more. Take a moment and think about what you have lost in your life.

One young man told me he wept one night after I had asked him to do this. He realized it wasn't worth it to him and is now experiencing more success with recovery than he has previously had.

In surgery, when clipping a brain aneurysm, sometimes the vessel will rupture. The surgeon must put a temporary clip on the main vessel to stop the bleeding, while a permanent clip is placed on the aneurysm to prevent future bleeding. The key here is to *stop the bleeding.* Spiritual bleeding occurs with each relapse of pornography viewing. You must act now to prevent further damage by helping your "thinking brain" realize how much you have lost when you have allowed your "reflex brain" to control your life. If a relapse occurs, however, you must not give up but must use it as a learning experience to protect against future struggles.

WHAT ARE YOU WILLING TO DO?

After you have decided that recovery is for you, that you do want it, it is time for the next question, which is closely related to the first: What are you willing to do? When we desire something we could have if we were willing to pay the price, but we don't obtain it, we may not desire it deeply enough. Sterling W. Sill related the following story illustrating this principle:

A young man came to Socrates one time and said, "Mr. Socrates, I have come 1,600 miles to talk to you about wisdom and learning." He said, "You are a man of wisdom and learning, and I would like to be a man of wisdom and learning, and I would like to have you teach me how to be a man of wisdom and learning."

Socrates said, "Come follow me," and he led the way down to the seashore. They waded out into the water up to their waists, and then Socrates turned on his friend and held his head under the water. His friend struggled and kicked and bucked and tried to get away, but Socrates held him down. Now if you hold someone's head under the water long enough, he will eventually become fairly peaceable. And after this man had stopped struggling, Socrates laid him out on the bank to dry, and he went back to the market place.

After the young man had dried out a little bit, he came back to Socrates to find the reason for this rather unusual behavior. Socrates said to him, "When your head was under the water what was the one thing you wanted more than anything else?" And the man said, "More than anything else, I wanted air." Socrates said, "All right, *when you want wisdom and learning like you wanted air, you won't have to ask anybody to give it to you.*"[1] (emphasis added)

Some may be blessed with this level of desire early in recovery. One who is now a powerful facilitator in a 12 Step recovery group told me that he didn't want recovery this bad at first. He said it was a process of increasing desire for him as he "soaked in the group," much as we place dirty dishes in the soapy water to sit until the hardened food softens and is ready for the scrub brush. Another said that those who helped him work the 12 Steps "brought God to me." They

[1] Sterling W. Sill, *BYU Speeches*, February 9, 1965, 9.

became a "hand of the Savior" holding his hand and leading him out of the darkness into the loving arms of Jesus Christ. Of the continuing process of having the images removed from his mind, he said, "I put it on the altar, and He takes it away. He will not rip it out of my hands." This beautiful description of the Lord assisting but not mandating recovery is enlightening. At some point, one must want recovery more than addiction to successfully heal. Elder Bruce Hafen speaks about that desire:

> Some people want to keep one hand on the wall of the temple while touching the world's "unclean things" with the other hand. We must put both hands on the temple and hold on for dear life. One hand is not even almost enough. The rich young man had given almost everything. When the Savior told him he must sell all his possessions, that wasn't just a story about riches. We can have eternal life if we want it, but only if there is nothing else we want more. [2] (emphasis added)

As we "press forward with a steadfastness in Christ" (2 Nephi 31:20), we will find that our desires change. As our faith in the Savior increases we become more like Him in thought and deed. This process requires patience, and should be considered a process more than an event.

What are you willing to do? This question seems easy at first glance, but as the cliché goes, the devil really is in the details. Carnes speaks of first order and second order changes in *Don't call It Love*.[3] First order changes are to stop the immediate bleeding, whereas second order changes involve changing desire, motivation, and perspective.

- What is it that causes you to become preoccupied with sexual thoughts? Are you willing to give this up?
- When do you act out?
- When are you most vulnerable?
- What kind of Internet access do you have?

[2] Bruce C. Hafen, "The Atonement: All for All," *Ensign*, May 2004, 97.
[3] Patrick Carnes, *Don't Call It Love*, Bantam Books, 1991, 227.

- Do you have a filter, and if so, do you know how to get around it?
- When is your "isolation risk time" when you are most at risk?
- Do you access pornography at mainstream bookstores just wandering around "in strange roads?"
- Do you get on the Internet alone at night just to check email?
- Do you have access to pay channels which contain pornography?
- If so, do you flip channels, telling yourself you will not actually view, thus ritualizing and setting yourself up for relapse?
- Do you view mainstream television and flip channels or watch movies which may not contain frank nudity, but are still suggestive and kindle fires of desire?

What are you willing to give up so you won't ritualize? Remember the addiction cycle progression described by Carnes: Preoccupation, Ritualization, Acting Out, and Despair. What are you willing to do to prevent preoccupation?

First, list the situations and times when you usually view pornography or feel you are at risk to do so. Now look at this list and decide what you will change or give up to prevent purposefully doing activities which cause you to become preoccupied and ritualize. Write down specific actions you will take to address what you have listed to change what you do on a day-to-day basis. This requires complete honesty since you know exactly what your weaknesses are.

HOW FAR ARE YOU WILLING TO GO?

This question, how far are you willing to go, is related to the first two. Some are ready to answer this fully only after experiencing failure when they initially tried to address the first two questions. After *thinking* they had answered Question 2, they find that the changes were not deep enough to prevent relapse. It is in answering this question that we come to the fundamental question at hand: How does one change from being "deeply soiled in sin"[4] to a person firm in recovery with years of sobriety who has become spiritually pure?

---

[4] Dallin H. Oaks, "Pornography," *Ensign* 2005, 87.

In 1974 Elder Boyd K. Packer shared a concept, which has blessed the lives of many youths and adults since. He talked about how he dug trenches when he was a boy irrigating. A neighbor told him why trenches were needed: "If you want the water to stay in its course, you'll have to make a place for it to go." He then likened water to our thoughts, admonishing us to make a place for them to go. He recommended using hymns to fill gaps in our thoughts. Especially relevant to our discussion is his next analogy:

> The mind is like a stage—the curtain is always up except when we are asleep. There is always some act being performed on that stage. It may be a comedy, a tragedy, interesting or dull, good or bad; but always there is some act playing on the stage of the mind. Have you noticed that without any real intent on your part, in the middle of almost any performance, a shady little thought may creep in from the wings and attract your attention? These delinquent thoughts will try to upstage everybody. If you permit them to go on, all thoughts of any virtue will leave the stage. You will be left, because you consented to it, to the influence of unrighteous thoughts. If you yield to them, they will enact for you on the stage of your mind anything to the limits of your toleration. They may enact a theme of bitterness, jealousy, or hatred. They may be vulgar, immoral, or even depraved.[5]

Elder Packer's analogy is very descriptive of how our brains work. There is an area in the brainstem near the ventral tegmental area we spoke of earlier called the reticular activating formation. The neurons of this area support consciousness. When the area is damaged the patient is in a coma. Activation of this area allows the thinking part of the brain, the cerebral cortex, to function. Think of this area as the monitor or screen. When the reticular activating formation is "on," the cortex will then fill "the screen" with thoughts. I say "will" because *something* will occupy the screen. The conscious thought is what is

---

[5]   Boyd K. Packer, "Worthy Music, Worthy Thoughts," *Ensign*, January 1974, 25.

on the screen at the time, what we call our train of thought. We may have several programs running at once, but only one image will be on the monitor, just as Elder Packer said in 1974. So the key is that we can keep bad programs off the monitor by making sure we always have a good program to run. It is not enough to avoid thinking about pornography. In fact, for some, thinking about *not* thinking about it may actually paradoxically cause a person to think about it! We must therefore write *deflection* programs for our brains. We must reflexively bounce our thoughts to another program. For many, hymns work, as Elder Packer wisely suggested. For those entrenched in neurochemical ruts, with memories of previous images running in virus-like programs, it will require extreme effort, particularly early on as the brain faces withdrawal and craving.

OFF LIMITS

A key concept is sexual thoughts are drugs, and like a doctor's prescription, must be used "only as directed." Indeed, we should look to the Savior, who is the Great Physician, for guidance and sanction when sexuality is invoked. Those who are married must learn not to create fantasies that will enter into the sacred marriage relationship. This may seem impossible to the severely entrenched. The Lord will assist in this. He expects this level of purity from us. He has asked us to "let virtue garnish our thoughts unceasingly,"[6] and in doing so we "bring into captivity every thought to the obedience of Christ."[7] As we let "all [our] thoughts be directed unto the Lord,"[8] we learn to follow His counsel to "look to me in every thought."[9]

Early on, it may be helpful to use *blocking*, which is similar to deflection. Blocking requires the brain to compartmentalize what we think about at different times and simply refuse to go there. For instance, would you want a brain surgeon who likes to ski think about skiing instead of brain surgery if he were operating on your brain? Or

---

6 *Doctrine and Covenants* 121:45
7 2 Corinthians 10:5
8 Alma 37:36
9 *Doctrine and Covenants* 6:36

would you want your airplane pilot to think seriously about anything but landing the plane when you are in a thunderstorm? Is it any different for sexuality? Even for the married there is a time and place to think about sexuality and a time *not* to think about it. Ancient words of wisdom say, "To every thing there is a season, and a time to every purpose under heaven . . . a time to embrace and a time to refrain from embracing."[10] To remain safe in this over-sexualized world, avoidance of sexual thoughts is placing us firmly in the "arms of safety."[11] For the younger or older man or woman entrenched in sexualized thoughts it will be necessary to go back to question 3: How far are you willing to go? Don't give up if failure occurs at first.

List several things that you will use as deflection, diversion, or blocking programs when needed.

THE PERFECT DAY

Consider another concept, *time slotting*. A nanosecond is a billionth of a second. Do you think it is possible for virtually anyone to think good thoughts for a nanosecond? Probably so. What about a microsecond, which is a millionth of a second? A millisecond, or thousandth of a second? One second? I think it is possible for anyone to be completely pure for one second, and most would agree. What about sixty seconds? Can we extend it to two minutes? At first it may seem too work intensive. But it isn't necessary to look at the struggle a day at a time, just minute to minute at first.

We must actualize one moment at a time. When I ran my first marathon I had the advantage of training with someone who was an experienced marathon runner. I remember 26.2 miles seemed overwhelming to me. I still remember when I first ran ten miles, then twelve, and so on, until I ran a twenty-mile training run. The way I was able to bear it mentally was to run from mile to mile. I would not stop, but walked for one minute and drank water and sports drinks. At first it seemed unnecessary to walk, but especially after the halfway point, walking for a minute allowed recovery. During the

---

10 Ecclesiastes 3:1, 5
11 Alma 34:16

race, I would run from mile marker to mile marker, looking forward to a drink and a brief walking rest from the pounding of constant running. I had to increase my speed after the walking to maintain my desired pace, but it was definitely worth it to me as an older runner. I crossed the line at four hours and three minutes. Finishing that first marathon was almost a religious experience. It felt so good to stop!

I believe this principle applies well in the context of addiction recovery. To use the mile-to-mile concept, we invoke a minute-to-minute application. One young man told me he felt as if he couldn't resist one night, but decided to make it one hour, so he picked up a safe book to read, and at the end of the hour the compulsion was bearable. Elder M. Russell Ballard spoke of enduring to the end "until we are *safely dead* with our testimony still burning very brightly."[12] (emphasis added) The goal for one in recovery is to make it *safely to sleep* each day. We don't have to worry about running a marathon all at once; we don't have to live a lifetime of pure thoughts all at once, just one moment at a time. Minute to minute, hour to hour, until the day is over and you are safely asleep. One pure day is thus placed on the altar, and you will worry about tomorrow the next day. One pure day after another as "the light groweth brighter and brighter until *the perfect day.*"[13] (emphasis added)

At first it will require tremendous effort, sometimes reverting to minute-to-minute deflection and blocking. As time passes, however, the deflection programs become the norm, and finally virtually no effort is expended to remain pure and sober. One in recovery said to me wryly, "The 12 Step group ruined my addiction. You never enjoy the addiction the same again." Of course, he was describing the process of losing wrong desires. If the occasional unsolicited trigger is thrown at you, even after years of sobriety, these old "software programs" reflexively are instantly activated to achieve the perfect day. As time passes, resistance is increased and sobriety becomes the norm. Blocking and deflecting are replaced with peace as the inner strug-

---

[12] M. Russell Ballard, "Keep the Commandments – Beginning Right Now!" BYU Fireside. September 6, 1987.
[13] *Doctrine and Covenants* 50:24

gle lessens and leaves the soul. The person is then ready for the spiritual process of sanctification. In the process of time one so sanctified can say, as did the Prophet Joseph Smith, "I never think any evil."[14] Elder D. Todd Christofferson describes this process:

> Most importantly, we may look to Jesus to help restore the inner unity of our soul when we have succumbed to sin and destroyed our peace. Soon after His intercessory plea that we might become "perfect in one," Jesus suffered and gave His life to atone for sin. The power of His Atonement can erase the effects of sin in us. When we repent, His atoning grace justifies and cleanses us (see 3 Nephi 27:16–20). *It is as if we had not succumbed, as if we had not yielded to temptation.*
>
> *As we endeavor day by day and week by week to follow the path of Christ, our spirit asserts its preeminence, the battle within subsides, and temptations cease to trouble.* There is greater and greater harmony between the spiritual and the physical until our physical bodies are transformed, in Paul's words, from "instruments of unrighteousness unto sin" to "instruments of righteousness unto God" (see Romans 6:13).[15] (emphasis added)

One young man shared the experience of growth in his recovery process. He had six weeks of complete abstinence after four years of never making it past a week. He was severely tempted with craving one night, so he knelt down and prayed that God would take the temptation away. He did and was able to go to sleep safely. A few days later he was on an elliptical machine at the gym, and the TV in the room began to show immodestly dressed models. He said, "A couple of years ago I would have died to watch that, but I stared down at the monitor on the machine which said '90 revolutions per minute'

14 Joseph Fielding Smith (compiler), *Teachings of the Prophet Joseph Smith*, King Follet Discourse, Deseret Book, 1968, 361-362.
15 D. Todd Christofferson, "That They May Be One in Us," *Ensign*, November 2002, 71.

and never looked up." As Elder Maxwell said, "Time works for us when our desires do likewise!"[16]

One in recovery said, "Relapse is only a detour, not a head on collision," if the person promptly confesses, then continues to see longer and longer periods of sobriety. Abstinence is not recovery, however. The real problem is lust, and as lust disappears, many find that even their dreams become peaceful and pure.

A word about withdrawal. As craving sets in because of the dopamine dearth and the spiritual onslaught, physical signs of brain drug withdrawal can ensue. Headache, restlessness, anxiety, irritability, and other physical signs may occur as the brain tries to withdraw from the addicted state, and the stress can cause relapse. Breaking through to three months is a milestone, but continued vigilance cannot be overemphasized. Six months and one year are progressive anniversaries of sobriety, with two or more years moving into long term sobriety, what Dr. Carnes calls "growth phase."[17]

Those in recovery from addiction say learning is essential. Reading books about recovery and talking to those experienced in addiction recovery are helpful. A knowledgeable therapist is an important ally in helping you learn about why you act out and can teach mechanisms to build resistance. Some geographical areas, however, do not have enough experienced therapists who understand pornography addiction to whom those in recovery can relate. Therapists who are not LDS may not share our values; for example, one told an LDS young man struggling with pornography addiction to masturbate more to compensate. It is hoped that the concepts of 12 Step recovery might be used at the ward level by bishops and fathers. Additionally, those currently not addicted might use these same principles to tighten and protect their thoughts in an increasingly sexualized world so that they don't face addiction later in life.

Carnes describes several stages of recovery. The final phase he describes is *growth phase*, as was mentioned earlier. The person in

---

[16] Neal A. Maxwell, "According to the Desire of Our Hearts," *Ensign*, November 1996, 21.
[17] Patrick Carnes, *Don't Call It Love*, Bantam Books, 1991, 204-6.

this phase has usually been sober for at least one and a half to two years. Carnes describes a person in this phase as follows:

> Another characteristic of this growth stage is a deep ab-
> horrence of one's old behavior. Once people in recovery have
> enough distance from their old problematic behaviors, they
> often have extremely visceral reactions when they think about
> them. Many say they look back almost in disbelief at some
> of the things they've done. By the time recovery reaches the
> growth stage, it no longer involves false starts. Conscious-
> ness of sobriety and of richer relationships has brought the
> person to a new level of being. And it's at this stage that peo-
> ple in recovery often talk about the compulsion of addictive
> behavior as a gift. They have experienced a depth of hu-
> manity that many people never achieve. Their compulsive or
> addictive behaviors and subsequent recovery have given them
> a greater perception, compassion, and presence. Not only do
> they serve as models for other recovering people who follow
> them, but they are literally helping our whole society heal.[18]

Step 12 calls for reaching out to others. Those in the growth stage do so not only to help others, but they also reinforce and pro-tect themselves. These sensitive and insightful souls have gone through the refiner's fire and have emerged from darkness. Not will-ing to leave others to suffer, they turn and reach back into the dark-ness and take the hands of others who cry out in agony, usually silently, and lead them to the peace and wholeness only the Savior provides.

By admitting powerlessness and "turning it over to God," we allow Him to enter and restore agency and allow our brains to nor-malize and our spirits to re-assert themselves. Physically, the dam-aged pleasure systems and frontal lobe control areas must have time

---

[18]   Patrick Carnes, *In the Shadows of the Net*, Hazelton Foundation, 2001, 142.

to heal. In a sense, by turning it over to the Savior we allow Him and His assistants, namely bishops, facilitators, others in recovery from addiction, therapists, appropriate loved ones, and others to become our "frontal lobes" until agency has become operative again.

RECOVERY STORY 4

I was married to my husband, J. for twenty-three years when I discovered he had a sexual addiction. I will not go into details, but I was completely devastated. I had been faithful to him. He had lied to me from the beginning. I prepared to divorce him. A dear friend of mine who is a sex-addiction therapist, told me to wait a bit. Because I respected her opinion, I listened.

My husband and I had a real love affair early on in our marriage. We fell in love at a young age and had many similar interests and talents. We were religious and began having a family. We moved to California so my husband could go to graduate school. It was at this point that my husband stopped believing, and I followed him. Unbeknownst to me, he also began acting out sexually. We continued to participate outwardly in our faith.

Throughout the years of our marriage, I would accidentally discover incidents of sexual indiscretion by my husband. These incidents did not fit my perception of him or our marriage and they hurt me deeply. My husband denied them or claimed he was just curious and promised never to do it again. His lack of disclosure and unwillingness to discuss these incidents led to a deep rift in our emotional intimacy.

While I had many good characteristics, my character defects began to play a dominant role in my life and helped to make me feel miserable and had negative ramifications for my family also. One strong characteristic defect was my desire to control my husband's sexuality. While I believed what my husband told me about the incidents, something inside of me was worried, and so I tried to control him and his sexuality by telling him how much I despised men who were sexually disloyal or promiscuous. I began to suspect most men of wanting only one thing, sex.

I became an angry woman. I was married to a man who was affectionate, (although his affection was mostly a prelude to sex) who loved having sex with me, (which I erroneously assumed meant everything in that sector was fine and that I was loved), who helped around the house, who supported the family and was witty, charming and talented. People told me how lucky I was to have him as a husband. I knew I was. I just couldn't figure out why I didn't feel close to him. The emotional intimacy we had early in our marriage was gone.

I let my anger spill out to my children at times and began to feel crazy and horrible about myself. My self worth plummeted. Occasionally I thought about divorcing J. because I no longer loved him. However, I felt financially trapped because I imagined that I had no viable skills even though I had graduated from college with a degree in music education, had been a professional accompanist, taught gymnastics, and played in several professional dance bands.

I worried excessively about our children and about other things in life. The more I worried the less J. seemed to. Fighting and being critical became a way of life. I fought almost everything, thinking my way was best. I did not fight with J., however. I wondered why he would never, ever confront me when I nagged or was disrespectful of him. I also developed the characteristic of blame, blaming him essentially for the fact that I wasn't happy.

As the years passed, I began to accidentally come upon him sexually acting out. I tried to act cool but was very shocked. I even tried to act like it was sexy and participate in it. One time I had erotic pictures of myself developed, thinking that he might like that sort of thing. It was a pretty big step for me but apparently small change for him. He acted uncomfortable when I gave it to him as a gift. A therapist later told me I was a perfect example of what it means to be co-dependent! Yep, I was trying to control his sexuality through sex and was completely unsuccessful at it. I also felt that I must be ugly if he had to look elsewhere.

When our daughter discovered porn on J's computer, I was so shocked and angry I decided to pray although I hadn't done so for years. While not a believer, I had continued to grieve over the loss of my faith. As I prayed, I surprised myself by making a request for J. I said, "I think J. has a real problem. What can I do to help him?"

I heard an answer in my mind which surprised me. "Listen."

So I confronted him and for once shut up about how I felt. I listened to what he had to say. He had a sexual addiction and had continued his addiction in the face of potential loss of job and family. He was out of control.

He decided to get help. He began going to SA and introduced me to S-Anon by saying that it was a support group for the partners or families of those struggling with sexual addiction. I certainly needed support.

As I began to go to S-Anon meetings and read through the 12 Step program, I laughed inside. The steps suggested that perhaps I had some problems and that there was a way to recover. No one understood. I was fine. J. had the sexual addiction that had ruined our lives. I continued to go to meetings though because there was much relief in being around others who understood my situation.

Although I had stopped believing in God, I felt that my prayer had been answered upon learning of J.'s sexual problems. I decided to imagine a Higher Power who loved J. and who accepted him as he was. This helped me to imagine this Being as loving me also. As I began reading through the steps and imaging a Higher Power, I became willing to look at myself more closely.

Step One says, "our lives had become unmanageable." At first I did not see how my life was unmanageable. J.'s life was. He had the addiction, and this made my life unmanageable. It was his fault. As I continued reading and going to meetings I began to understand how my character defects of anger, blame, controlling attitudes, excessive worry, subtle put-downs of J. to my children, and not liking and taking care of myself were all symptoms of unmanageability. The most humbling and freeing aspect of Step One was to admit that I had never been able to manage my husband's sexual acting out and to learn that his sexual sobriety or lack thereof, while certainly affecting our marriage, was not my job to manage. In fact, while I had not caused and was not responsible for his sexual addiction, I had certainly helped create an atmosphere where it could flourish. After a long struggle with this step, I let go, and I felt great relief and serenity. At this point I decided to experiment and "Let go and let God" to see what happened with our relationship.

With a new willingness to imagine a higher power, I began to have hope. I worked Step Three and then turned to Step Four. It was difficult for me to take responsibility for what was mine but I did it. I began to accept and love myself even though I wasn't perfect. I began to love J.

I became willing to make amends where I could. It is hard for me not to live in regret about my part of our families past. The children have suffered, but Step Two gave me hope and so I press on, doing what I can through therapy and 12 Step work to make living amends to my family.

While not perfect at working the steps, the progress in my life is miraculous. I continue to forgive my husband, and I love him now in a more mature way than I ever did when we were younger. I accept his faults and recognize and accept my own and have seen progress in letting go of character defects. We enjoy each other and our family. While I do not know what the future will bring, I live every day in gratitude for what I have rather than for what I do not have. I have a newfound self-confidence and courage. As I turn my will over to my Higher Power and work the steps, I am better focused on MY job, which is keeping my side of the street clean and not worrying about J's side. Herein lies the miracle. J has had five years of recovery that, while not perfect, have given him a new happiness and serenity he never expected to have. I have a full time job that I enjoy. I love the phrase in the AA book that says "We no longer fight anything." I am no longer the angry, unhappy woman I was, and I sincerely thank my Higher Power and the 12 Steps for that.

CHAPTER 14

BINDING UP THE BROKEN HEART

*But He knoweth the way that I take, and
when He hath tried me, I shall come forth as gold.*

Job 23:10

In listening and learning as I have visited with the spouses of those in recovery, it is clear that many find peace and recovery from the pain of betrayal through the Savior. While ideally this would parallel their husband's recovery from the actual addiction, they all feel that it is essential to seek the healing of the Atonement independent of their husband's paths. Thus, the wives find that the Savior bears "their grief and their sorrows"[1] and allow the Savior also to bear the burden of their husband's recovery. I have been humbled as I have heard these brave women share their difficult and private paths. When I think of them, the words of a favorite hymn come to mind: "In the quiet heart is hidden sorrow that the eye can't see."[2]

One wife who now serves as a facilitator in a 12 Step support group described how difficult it was to attend the first meeting. Many are not ready to hear words such as "forgiveness," and the acute trauma of the sense of betrayal brings confusion, anger, and profound loss, especially if her husband may be only reluctantly compliant in his own recovery efforts.

---

[1] Isaiah 53:4
[2] "Lord, I Would Follow Thee," *LDS Hymns*, #220.

CO-DEPENDENCE

Virtually every spouse and mother, at least initially, felt the need to "fix the problem" for her loved one. She may be the computer policeman and may become, as one man said, "addicted to my recovery." Her well-meaning desire to help, however, may actually cause more harm than good if not guided by the principles of charity so clearly outlined in the 12 Steps. She may become codependent and find that by invoking the same 12 Step process of accessing the Savior's healing power she can also find recovery from her pain of betrayal and loss. This will help her to heal and allow her husband to access the Savior for healing also.

Love can be unconditional. Consider the love of a mother for her child. Even if the child betrays her and she experiences frustration, anger, and embarrassment, she will still love the child. This pure form of parental love is perhaps the closest we come in this life to experience the pure love of Christ. In learning to love this deeply, we learn to love as God loves us. As we become like Him, we learn to see first friends, then strangers, and finally enemies with empathy and understanding. We can then learn to love them first, as He did,[3] with charity, the pure love of Christ.[4]

Nevertheless, the same mother who loves her child unconditionally would be foolish indeed to continue to trust the child in the face of continued betrayals. The child could only regain trust through painstakingly demonstrating continued good behavior *over time.* Trust, as opposed to unconditional parental love, must be earned.

Marital love is not unconditional and involves trust as an integral component. Thus, even in the context of outward repentance with regard to Church sanction, and even with the tactical approval of a counselor, to eventually experience healing in the relationship, the formerly addicted must *at some point* regain the trust of the betrayed spouse, independent of ecclesiastical or therapeutic parameters. She would ideally seek her path of healing independent of his, and even if divorce eventually occurs, would allow time and the Savior to re-

---

[3] 1 John 4:19
[4] Moroni 7:47

store her peace. The husband must be willing to let her heal on her terms and in her own time. Just as he wants her to be understanding of his struggles, he must be understanding of the severe trauma he has brought into her life. A spouse of one in recovery said, "Because I was deceived in this, my confidence was shaken in how well I was able to not be deceived in other areas. Am I being paranoid or is it a real prompting when I can't trust?" The one in recovery from addiction must be willing to undergo extra scrutiny and perhaps unjust (at least from his perspective) criticism. He might ask her, "Do you still struggle with trust?" and "How do you feel?" and be solicitous of where she is with trusting him. Does she feel guilty for his problem? One wife asked herself, "Why couldn't I prevent this? Why would he choose something vile over something pure?"

We are a covenant people, and it is a loss for a wife to accept the fact that she is married to a spouse who has broken covenants. However, this higher standard of living may paradoxically feed the guilt of the addicted one and shame in both. There may be guilt in the spouse also, with thoughts such as "Why can't I trust or forgive?" Consider the experience of one wife in trying to forgive when faced with betrayal:

> I felt guilty and miserable. But as I looked honestly into my heart, I knew very well that full-grown forgiveness was not there. What more could I do? Was I going to lose my own soul to this horrible mess? Again, some advice from my bishop proved crucial. As we discussed the struggle to forgive one day, he said, *"Well, keep a place in your heart for forgiveness, and when it comes, welcome it in."* That seemed like weak advice in a way, but the Spirit etched it into my memory, and it became a golden rule to me. On bad days when I was angry, I could at least say to myself, "I want to forgive, and I will hang on to that as a goal and desire it and welcome it when it comes." [5] (emphasis added)

---

[5]   Name Withheld, "My Journey to Forgiving," *Ensign*, February 1997, 40.

Women who have attended support groups based on the 12 Step program have found great strength in the companionship of others experiencing this trial. They learn from others who have gone before them and understand that they are not alone, nor are they the first. They are able to avoid the burden of codependence and allow their husbands to find peace with themselves and with the Lord without feeling as if they are responsible for either their husbands' successes or failures.

BUILDING AND GAINING TRUST

The newly confessed sin, especially if a free and uncoerced confession is given, will leave the confessor lighter. He would come to understand, however, that he has transferred the burden to a previously uninitiated spouse who now must bear the burden of deceit and the realization that what she thought was real was an illusion. He should never demand trust; it will only occur in the process of time as she sees change in his spirit, demeanor, and attitude. One man, after a powerful spiritual experience, confessed in tears to his wife, then called his bishop that night and took his wife with him to confess to his priesthood leader. This story is unusual, and in fact *The White Book* of Sexaholics Anonymous recommends caution in disclosing addiction to a spouse without first counseling with one experienced in sexual addiction.[6] His sole concern was that she would have all of the support mechanisms she would need. He put any concern about his own reputation aside in consideration of her need for support. The marriage not only continued, but also thrived. He is now in his third year of complete sobriety and full recovery. This is not typical, however, and most roads to recovery are much more twisted and steep. It is well to avoid comparisons with others. Each path will be different.

So what might one in recovery do to begin to rebuild trust? First, a clean confession followed by complete *appropriate* transparency for the rest of his life. Second, full commitment to recovery, which includes ecclesiastical and therapeutic support, and 12 Step group sup-

---

[6]   *The White Book*, Sexaholics Anonymous Publications, 127-128.

port. Third, a visible change in attitude, with humility, gratitude, and self-esteem replacing shame, guilt, and pride.

The betrayed spouse may be aided in her recovery from betrayal by the successful recovery of her husband, but she must not depend on it. Her eye must remain firmly on the Savior, for to Him we all can "turn for peace."[7] As she is then able to first heal herself, then forgive, and finally trust, both may move towards a truly sacramental marriage as he finds his own path to the Savior. We usually think of *Doctrine and Covenants* 121:34-46 in the context of priesthood leadership, but it is also applicable in the context of marriage. Applying these principles to the marriage relationship, many "cover their sins"[8] and "gratify their pride"[9] in pornography, and in doing so invoke "amen to the priesthood or authority of that man."[10] Sadly, many involved in the pride of addiction manifest anger and sarcasm in their treatment of their spouse and children. They "exercise unrighteous dominion."[11] He may "act in," or overcompensate for addiction with periods or hyper-religiosity or anorexic intervals with appetites such as food and sexuality. These will cease as the person truly recovers and a spirit of submissive confidence emerges.

Those "called and chosen" influence "by persuasion, by long-suffering, by gentleness and meekness, and by love unfeigned."[12] There is no deceit or compulsion, only loving solicitude. There is only "kindness, and pure knowledge, which shall greatly enlarge the soul without hypocrisy and without guile."[13] Note the relevance to our subject: pure knowledge, which enlarges the *soul* (the brain, both spirit and body), and the elimination of hypocrisy and guile, as opposed to the "pathologic"[14] learning of addiction. It is interesting that *enlargement of the soul* parallels *enlargement of the damaged areas*

---

[7] "Where Can I Turn for Peace?" *LDS Hymns*, 129.
[8] *Doctrine and Covenants* 121:37
[9] Ibid.
[10] Ibid.
[11] Ibid, verse 39.
[12] Ibid, verse 41.
[13] *Doctrine and Covenants* 121:42
[14] Julie A. Kauer, Robert C. Malenka, "Synaptic Plasticity and Addiction," *Nature Reviews Neuroscience* 8, 8440858, November 2007, 844-858.

of the brain as discussed earlier. *Thus soul healing, in this sense, truly allows the Savior to make both body and spirit whole.*

"Many are called, but few are chosen, . . . because they set their hearts upon the things of this world."[15] Called and chosen to what? To "glory and virtue,"[16] whereby we may receive "exceedingly great and precious promises, and thus be partakers of the divine nature, having escaped the corruption that is in the world through lust."[17]

---

[15] *Doctrine and Covenants* 121:35
[16] 1 Peter 1:3
[17] 1 Peter 1:4

CHAPTER 15

PARENTAL PAIN

*A voice was heard in Ramah, and bitter weeping; Rachel weeping
for her children refused to be comforted…for they were not…Thus
saith the Lord; Refrain thy voice from weeping, and thine eyes from
tears: for thy work shall be rewarded, saith the Lord, and they
shall come again from the land of the enemy.*

Jeremiah 31:15, 16

The bond between mother and child is a precious one. From the
time she holds and feeds her infant she imagines what kind of
man or woman the child will become. She frets and agonizes over
her child's character, and the child in turn idolizes and adores her.
On Iwo Jima very few Japanese were taken alive, as they gave their
lives in battle to avoid capture. James Bradley's description of this is
poignant:

> Since their youth they had been told how true Japanese
> heroes always "died with the Emperor's name on their lips."
> Death on the battlefield was glorified for the home front, but
> the veterans knew the last word of a boy dying in battle was
> someone else's name, not the Emperor's. It was the same
> name all troops throughout history had cried out with their
> last breath. It was rendered in different tongues, but the
> meaning was universal. His last word was invariably
> "Okasan!" The German would cry "Mutter!" The English
> and American "Mother!," "Mom!," or "Mommy!"[1]

---

[1] James Bradley, *Flags of Our Fathers*, Bantam, 2000, 137.

Consider the significant trauma to the small town of Bedford, Virginia. The small town sent its sons to Europe to fight, and the majority of them were among the first waves to hit Omaha Beach in the D-Day invasion. Nineteen died that day, with three more following shortly thereafter, more than from any other town in America. The town was devastated, and the families never recovered. An example of the pain is seen in the lives of eighteen-year-old Raymond Hoback. He came from a small farm outside Bedford. He was likely killed on the beach since his Bible was found in the sand and returned to his family. His sister Lucille said, "My mother always treasured the Bible so much. She said that, next to her son, she would have wanted to have his Bible."[2] A few days after receiving the Bible, Mrs. Hoback published the following in the *Bedford Bulletin:*[3]

MEMORIAM

Do not say my sons are dead;
They only sleepest . . .
They loved each other, stayed together
And with their comrades crossed together
To that great beyond;
So weep not, mothers;
Your sons are happy and free . . .

Mrs. J.S. Hoback

In *The Bedford Boys* Alex Dershaw describes the trauma: "But the Hobacks did weep. Things were never the same. Her mother spent hours alone and rarely left the house. Every evening felt like a wake...Families grieved behind closed doors, sharing their pain with relatives and God...In a matter of minutes, a couple of German machine gunners had broken the town's heart."[4]

---

2   Alex Kershaw, *The Bedford Boys*, Da Capo Press, 2003, 207.
3   Ibid.
4   Ibid, 208.

The millions of mothers and fathers who have lost sons in war represent a great weight of silent agony, which will only be recognized in the next phase of our existence. What of the mother who loses her son to the war for the souls of men? She thinks of the babe in her arms and of reading to the innocent little boy. Now he thinks of women as objects, and she feels crushing failure as the primary formative woman in his life. It is a sort of living death where she remembers the innocence but sees the canker. A young woman we know recently fell in love with a young man who had returned from a mission. After the engagement, she learned he struggled with pornography addiction. She continued to try to understand, but finally he came to her and said in effect, "This is a problem that most struggle with. It's not that big of a deal. When we are married it won't be a problem." The young woman called off the engagement. The mother of the young man was a wonderful and faithful parent who had done her best to raise a righteous son. She was depressed and devastated and felt like a failure as a mother.

In visiting with mothers of young men who are addicted to pornography, it is apparent that they simply don't understand how their sons could want to view pornography. Although the father at least recognizes the powerful urges his son is fighting, the mother just doesn't understand it. One faithful mother admonished her daughter-in-law to see her son, who struggled with pornography addiction, as a child of God, as the mother did, in order to understand and empathize. As a mother, faithful though she was, she was unable to comprehend that the wife had to view her relationship conditionally, whereas the mother's love was unconditional. Her unconditional love is perhaps the most tangible portion of Divine love that still has the power to reach her addicted son, however. She must hold on to him with her love. For a time, she may be the one woman he can still see as a person and not as an object. Her role is explained by Orson F. Whitney:

> You parents of the wilful and the wayward! Don't give them up. Don't cast them off. They are not utterly lost. The Shepherd will find his sheep. They were his before they were

yours—long before he entrusted them to your care; and you
cannot begin to love them as he loves them. *They have but
strayed in ignorance from the Path of Right, and God is merciful
to ignorance.* Only the fulness of knowledge brings the fulness
of accountability. Our Heavenly Father is far more merciful,
infinitely more charitable, than even the best of his servants,
and the Everlasting Gospel is mightier in power to save than
our narrow finite minds can comprehend.

The Prophet Joseph Smith declared—and he never
taught more comforting doctrine—that the eternal sealings of
faithful parents and the divine promises made to them for
valiant service in the Cause of Truth, would save not only
themselves, but likewise their posterity. *Though some of the
sheep may wander, the eye of the Shepherd is upon them, and
sooner or later they will feel the tentacles of Divine Providence
reaching out after them and drawing them back to the fold. Either in this life or in the life to come, they will return.* They will
have to pay their debt to justice; they will suffer for their sins;
and may tread a thorny path; but if it leads them at last, like
the penitent Prodigal, to a loving and forgiving father's heart
and home, the painful experience will not have been in vain.
Pray for your careless and disobedient children; hold on to
them with your faith. Hope on, trust on, till you see the salvation of God.[5] (emphasis added)

This salvation of severely struggling children may not refer to exaltation but does require the sealing of the parents by the Holy Spirit
of Promise, either in this life or the next. Nevertheless, the Lord is
more merciful and understanding than we are, and He is able to comprehend and understands how agency suspended early in life will be
rectified. Boyd K. Packer taught the following:

It is a great challenge to raise a family in the darkening
mists of our moral environment. We emphasize that the

---

[5]   Orson F. Whitney, *Conference Report*, Apr. 1929, 110.

greatest work you will do will be within the walls of your home (see Harold B. Lee, in Conference Report, April 1973, p. 130), and that "no other success can compensate for failure in the home" (see David O. McKay, in Conference Report, April 1935, p. 116). *The measure of our success as parents, however, will not rest solely on how our children turn out. That judgment would be just only if we could raise our families in a perfectly moral environment, and that now is not possible. It is not uncommon for responsible parents to lose one of their children, for a time, to influences over which they have no control.* They agonize over rebellious sons and daughters. They are puzzled over why they are so helpless when they have tried so hard to do what they should. *It is my conviction that those wicked influences one day will be overruled...* We cannot overemphasize the value of temple marriage, the binding ties of the sealing ordinance, and the standards of worthiness required of them. When parents keep the covenants they have made at the altar of the temple, their children will be forever bound to them. [6] (emphasis added)

In 1989 Elder Packer made this pertinent statement regarding addiction: "At present the adversary has an unfair advantage. Addiction has the capacity to disconnect the human will and nullify moral agency. It can rob one of the power to decide. Agency is too fundamental a doctrine to be left in such jeopardy."[7] Robert Millet wrote, "As Elder Packer suggested, it may be that the power of evil in these last days is so oppressive that it chokes or restrains the proper exercise of agency. One day that will change."[8]

One nine-year-old child was at a friend's house. The friend's parents were divorced, and the child was living with the father. The boys found the father's pornography and viewed it, and the nine-year-old was hooked. He still struggles several years later. We must ask ourselves how, in fairness, can he be judged in the same light as

---

[6] Boyd K. Packer, "Our Moral Environment," *Ensign*, May 1992, 66.
[7] Boyd K. Packer, "Revelation in a Changing World," *Ensign*, May 1989, 14.
[8] Robert L. Millet, *When a Child Wanders*, Deseret Book, 1996, 119.

a young man never so exposed? The merciful Father in Heaven of this young man knew him before we did and knows that his agency was largely suspended at this young age. Somehow the Lord will view the moment of the suspension of the child's agency in the light of perfect understanding, and perhaps events from that time on will be viewed from a more enlightened perspective.

Can the Lord accept such a one into exaltation as a sanctified being? No, but consider the following example. Alvin Smith, older brother of the Prophet Joseph Smith passed away, as have millions of others, without receiving the fulness of the ordinances of exaltation in this life. Of him we read in Joseph's vision: "I beheld the celestial kingdom of God...I saw...my brother Alvin, that has long since slept; and marveled how it was that he had obtained an inheritance in that kingdom, seeing that he had departed this life before the Lord had set his hand to gather Israel the second time, and had not been baptized for the remission of sins. Thus came the voice of the Lord unto me, saying: All who have died without a knowledge of this gospel, *who would have received it if they had been permitted to tarry*, shall be heirs of the celestial kingdom of God; Also all that shall die henceforth without a knowledge of it, *who would have received it with all their hearts*, shall be heirs of that kingdom; For I, the Lord, will judge all men according to their works, according to the desire of their hearts. *And I also beheld that all children who die before they arrive at the years of accountability are saved in the celestial kingdom of heaven.*"[9] (emphasis added)

AGENCY SUSPENDED

What of those little ones abused and addicted before they even understood the future implication of these evil experiences? Would they "have received it with all their hearts"[10] had their agency not been suspended? What of children who die a soul death through sexual scarring and die spiritually? Might not the merciful Lord see them as having "died before they arrive at the years of accountabil-

---

[9]   *Doctrine and Covenants* 137:1, 5-10
[10] Ibid, verse 8.

ity,"[11] even if such death is spiritual? After being so scarred and having had agency severely affected, it is much more difficult for them to gain a "knowledge of this gospel."[12] Having died spiritually at such a young age, will they have a period of purification and sanctification in the world of spirits before becoming "heirs in the celestial kingdom"[13] because they "would have received it if they had been permitted to tarry"[14] *unaddicted?*

Orson F. Whitney said, "Only the fulness of knowledge brings the fulness of accountability."[15] Note also that Joseph Smith described "years"[16] of accountability as opposed to a single year. Certainly a nine or even fourteen-year-old who is addicted will have a different understanding and accountability than an adult who more willingly *decides* to stumble. Even the adult will be judged in accordance with gradations of understanding. In the end, however, only the sanctified can dwell with God. Only He who sees all knows how He will reclaim his little ones who have been abused and addicted before they began to understand the implications of their actions. We only know that "all things have been (and will be) done in the wisdom of him who knoweth all things."[17]

Consider the obvious question. What of one who says, "I was addicted as a child or as a young teen, and my agency was suspended. If the above is true, then I need not break the addiction, as all will be restored in the next life, and I will have a free pass." The key is again found in *Doctrine and Covenants* Section 137: "For I, the Lord, will judge all men according to their works, according to the desire of their hearts."[18] Any who resign themselves to addiction without maximum, consecrative effort *based on their ability* will consign themselves to judgment based on these desires.

---

[11] Ibid, verse 10.
[12] Ibid, verse 7.
[13] Ibid.
[14] Ibid.
[15] Orson F. Whitney, *Conference Report*, Apr. 1929, 110.
[16] *Doctrine and Covenants* 137: 8
[17] 2 Nephi 2:24
[18] *Doctrine and Covenants* 137:9

Why does it appear that agency is suspended for some, and others seem to get through with choice intact? We only know that God does not restrict agency and that the adversary's plan is to destroy it. Indeed, He sent us here "to prove [us] herewith, to see if [we] will do all things whatsoever the Lord [our] God shall command [us]."[19] Satan was rejected because he "sought to destroy the agency of man."[20] It is difficult to think of a tool more craftily designed to destroy agency than pornography addiction. He is still concerned that "one soul shall not be lost." Lost to his captivity, that is! He can then "deceive . . . and blind men"[21] and lead them "captive at his will,"[22] using his matchless "subtlety."[23] We must not underestimate the power of this tool in the hands of the adversary. Brigham Young expounded on the power of Satan:

> It requires all the care and faithfulness which we can exercise in order to keep the faith of the Lord Jesus; for there are invisible agencies around us in sufficient numbers to encourage the slightest disposition they may discover in us to forsake the true way, and fan into a flame the slightest spark of discontent and unbelief. . . . (These) spirits are watching us continually for an opportunity to influence us to do evil, or to make us decline in the performance of our duties. *And I will defy any man on earth to be more gentlemanly and bland in his manners than the master spirit of all evil. We call him the devil; a gentleman so smooth and so oily, that he can deceive the very elect.*[24] (emphasis added)

The adversary is using sexual temptation to deceive many of the elect today. As the children of the promise are deceived and addicted, it is excruciating for their parents to understand how this could hap-

---

19 Abraham 3:25
20 Moses 4:3
21 Moses 4:4
22 Ibid.
23 Ibid, verse 5.
24 Brigham Young, *Journal of Discourses*, Volume 12, 128.

pen. They feel that the failure of their child to understand is somehow their failure as a parent and take it personally. My father once told a sorrowful father with a rebellious son that sometimes all we can do is pray for the Lord to send divine assistance to help, thus "finding strength beyond our own."[25] An angel told Alma the Younger that he was sent because of the "prayers of . . . thy father; for he has prayed with much faith concerning thee that thou mightest be brought to the knowledge of the truth . . . that the prayers of his servants might be answered according to their faith."[26]

If you are the parent of one who struggles with pornography addiction, know that your prayers and struggles are your offerings placed on the altar of consecration and that the Lord "shall consecrate thine afflictions for thy gain."[27] Elder Bruce C. Hafen said, "Consider others who . . . have consecrated themselves so fully that, for them, *almost* is enough: A father who reached his outermost limits but still couldn't influence his daughter's choices: he could only crawl toward the Lord, pleading like Alma for his child. A wife who encouraged her husband despite his years of weakness, until the seeds of repentance finally spouted in his heart. She said, "I tried to look at him the way Christ would look at me."[28]

Sometimes all we can do is "crawl to the Lord"[29] pleading for assistance, never giving up. Know that there is consolation. Never stop loving, pleading, praying, hoping. You are not alone; unseen helping hands and loving hearts are eager to assist and love with you. In 1853, the Willie and Martin Handcart companies were caught in the Wyoming mountains in a snowstorm. Many died, and the suffering was immense. President Young dismissed the afternoon session of Sunday conference, telling the Saints, "Go and bring in those people now on the plains."[30] Years later, in a Sunday School class, criticism was directed at those who had allowed the handcart com-

[25] "Lord, I Would Follow Thee," *Hymns*, Deseret Book Company, 1985, 220.
[26] Mosiah 27:14
[27] 2 Nephi 2:2
[28] Bruce C. Hafen, "The Atonement: All for All," *Ensign*, May 2004, 97.
[29] Ibid.
[30] Brigham Young, *Journal of Discourses* 4, 113.

pany to leave so late. A survivor stood and reprimanded them for the criticism:

> I have pulled my handcart when I was so weak and weary from illness and lack of food that I could hardly put one foot ahead of the other. I have looked ahead and seen a patch of sand or hill slope and I have said, I can go only that far and there I must give up, for I cannot pull the load through it.
>
> I have gone on to that sand and when I reached it, *the cart began pushing me. I have looked back many times to see who was pushing my cart, but my eyes saw no one. I knew then that the angels of God were there.*
>
> Was I sorry that I chose to come by handcart? No. Neither then or any minute of my life since. The price we paid to become acquainted with God was a privilege to pay, and I am thankful that I was privileged to come in the Martin Handcart Company.[31] (emphasis added)

Who pushed his handcart? President James E. Faust spoke about assistance that comes to us from beyond the veil:

> Perhaps in this life we are not given to fully understand how enduring the sealing cords of righteous parents are to their children. It may very well be that there are more helpful sources at work than we know. *I believe there is a strong familial pull as the influence of beloved ancestors continues with us from the other side of the veil...*As we get older, the pull from our parents and grandparents on the other side of the veil becomes stronger. It is a sweet experience when they visit us in our dreams.[32] (emphasis added)

Regarding this subject, Joseph F. Smith spoke about heavenly ministrations:

[31]   *Relief Society Magazine,* January 1948, 8.
[32]   James E. Faust, "Dear to the Heart of the Shepherd," *Ensign,* May 2003, 61.

When messengers are sent to minister to the inhabitants of the earth, *they are not strangers*, but from the ranks of our kindred, friends, and fellowbeings and fellowservants. *In like manner our fathers and mothers, brothers, sisters and friends who have passed away from this earth, having been faithful, and worthy to enjoy these rights and privileges, may have a mission given them to visit their relatives and friends upon the earth again, bringing from the divine Presence messages of love, of warning, of reproof and instruction to those whom they had learned to love in the flesh.*[33] (emphasis added)

On another occasion he continued on this theme:

We are closely related to our kindred, to our ancestors, to our friends and associates and co-laborers who have preceded us into the spirit world. We can not forget them; we do not cease to love them; we always hold them in our hearts, in memory, and thus we are associated and united to them by ties that we can not break, that we can not dissolve or free ourselves from. *I claim that we live in their presence, they see us, they are solicitous for our welfare, they love us now more than ever. For now they see the dangers that beset us; they can comprehend, better than ever before, the weaknesses that are liable to mislead us into dark and forbidden paths. They see the temptations and the evils that beset us in life and the proneness of mortal beings to yield to temptation and to wrong doing; hence their solicitude for us, and their love for us, and their desire for our well being, must be greater than that which we feel for ourselves.*[34] (emphasis added)

GATHERED INTO OUR PLACE

We are all out on the plains in the spiritual snowstorms with howling winds struggling up a Rocky Ridge like the severely tested

---

[33] Joseph F. Smith, address given at the funeral of Elizabeth Cannon, January 29, 1882, *Journal of Discourses*, Volume 22, 350-351.

[34] Joseph F. Smith, "In the Presence of the Divine," April Conference, *Improvement Era* 19:646-652, May 1916.

handcart company. Many are freezing as their hearts "wax cold"[35] in iniquity. It is agony to see one's own child suffering spiritually. The Lord gave these comforting words:

> They shall not be beaten down by the storm at the last day; yea, neither shall they be harrowed up by the whirlwinds; *but when the storm cometh they shall be gathered together in their place, that the storm cannot penetrate to them; yea, neither shall they be driven with fierce winds withersoever the enemy listeth to carry them.* But behold, *they are in the hands of the Lord of the harvest, and they are his, and he will raise them up at the last day.*[36] (emphasis added)

It may be that the reclamation occurs "at the last day"[37] for some. The Savior said, "It must needs be that offenses come," knowing that although He Himself did not cause the offense, it would be a painful but necessary adversity to educate and eventually enlarge. Empathy could then be felt and imparted to others later in a way not possible for the uninitiated. We can be protected from the storm so it cannot destroy our families. We can be gathered into our place for we are His, and he will raise us up, if we will let Him. He will heal. He will redeem. He will forgive. He will atone.

When we have given Him our will as a freely offered gift and done "all we can do,"[38] He will come with "healing in His wings"[39] to lift us and our loved one out of pits of sin, despair, grief, and pain. Sometimes "all we can do" is plead for Him to rescue our loved one and us. To all who wander the strange roads of the addiction and pain, know that He knows the way back to peace. "I am the way,"[40] He said, because He understands the path of pain better than any, even the pain of the yearning parent. James E. Faust comforts:

---

35   Matthew 24:12
36   Alma 26:6-7
37   John 6:54
38   2 Nephi 25:23
39   Malachi 4:2
40   John 14:6

To those brokenhearted parents who have been righteous, diligent, and prayerful in the teaching of their disobedient children, we say to you, the Good Shepherd is watching over them. God knows and understands your deep sorrow. There is hope. Take comfort in the words of Jeremiah, "Thy work shall be rewarded" and your children can "come again from the land of the enemy (Jeremiah 31:16)."[41]

[41]   James E. Faust, "Dear to the Heart of the Shepherd," *Ensign*, May 2003, 61.

RECOVERY STORY 5

After years and years of battling addiction and attempting recovery, I was at the lowest point of my life. I had known better; I had been rescued from addiction, prison, and death earlier in my life and had even served a mission. Yet I had succumbed once again and was living on the streets, deep into addiction and crime. One night I committed a robbery and was hiding in the bushes a couple of blocks away. Watching and waiting for the police to clear the area, I was suddenly confronted with the awfulness of my situation and the enormity of the lie that I was living. My walls of denial were now down, and I could not deny that these were real people I was scaring and hurting, not faceless, unfeeling beings protected by insurance. Nor could I deny that I had thrown my life away and had violated virtually every principle I had believed in and covenant I had made. My mind was flooded with an overwhelming awareness of my sins, and I felt that I could be a son of perdition. It was more than I could bear.

I got the gun out, figured out how to get the safety off and a bullet in the chamber, then placed it in my mouth and began to pull the trigger. I actually felt the trigger begin to yield, when suddenly something happened. The street in front of me and the world around me went quiet, and I heard and felt a very soft yet clear voice say these words: "I'm still here." I knew that it was the voice of God. I was stunned, and started to say, "How could You be? After all that I've done?" But before I could even get those words out, I was wrapped for a moment in His unconditional love. My heart softened, and after a few moments I asked humbly, "So what do I do now?" The answer came clearly, "Start by being honest. Take my hand, and I'll show you the rest of the way."

I put the gun down, walked out of the bushes and up to some police officers on the sidewalk, and told them I was the person they were looking for. I went to prison for quite a few years. But I need-n't explain all of those details at this time. What I want to share is that with God's help, I walked out of death and back into life, and I now have a life far more wonderful and abundant than anything I could have imagined. Do you believe in miracles? Do you believe that the same God who transformed Alma the Younger and Ammon and the other sons of Mosiah still works miracles today? I testify that this is truly the case. I have been redeemed through Jesus Christ. As Ammon said, "I will not boast about myself, but I will boast of my God." Today, I have a beautiful wife, a sweet son who was born on Christmas morning, and a vibrant, living testimony that keeps the Spirit in my life on a daily basis. I attend the temple and have served in a variety of Church callings over the years. After being a facilitator for more than nine years, I am currently serving as a missionary in the LDS 12 Step Addiction Recovery Program. I have much joy in my life and am especially passionate about seeing people change for the better through Jesus Christ.

CHAPTER 16

REPENTANCE
AND RECOVERY

*And the servant of the Lord must not strive; but be gentle unto all
men, apt to teach, patient, In meekness instructing those that oppose
themselves; if God peradventure will give them repentance to the
acknowledging of the truth; And that they may recover themselves out
of the snare of the devil, who are taken captive by him at his will.*

2 Timothy 2:24-26

In working with those in recovery, my wife and I have been impressed with the great blessing many bishops are to those who struggle. We frequently hear those now in strong recovery express love and gratitude for loving and supportive ecclesiastical leaders. These dedicated servants of the Lord put personal time aside to be available to those in need, and do so even when it is not convenient.

In the past, many leaders have perceived pornography and sexual addiction to be a sin only, not understanding that it is also a serious addiction. Focusing on the necessary steps of repentance from the sin, they may not have known how to address the necessary concepts of recovery from the addiction.

TO CHANGE OUR MIND,
KNOWLEDGE, SPIRIT, AND BREATH

Those seeking repentance understand the need to confess serious sins to priesthood leaders. We work with our bishop to reconcile with the Church so we can again partake of the full blessings of fellowship. Individual forgiveness from the Lord is something we will privately sense as we change. Repentance involves change, as described by Elder Russell M. Nelson:

> The doctrine of repentance is much broader than a dictionary's definition. When Jesus said "repent," His disciples recorded that command in the Greek language with the verb *metanoeo.* This powerful word has great significance. In this word, the prefix *meta* means "change." The suffix relates to four important Greek terms: *nous,* meaning "the mind"; *gnosis,* meaning "knowledge"; *pneuma,* meaning "spirit"; and *pnoe,* meaning "breath." Thus, when Jesus said "repent," He asked us to change—to change our mind, knowledge, and spirit— even our breath.[1]

This comprehensive definition describes more than a minor change, and when we consider an addiction as powerful as that caused by pornography, this description of the level of change necessary is pertinent. An example of what happened to a young man now in recovery may help illustrate how much effort is required to change mind, knowledge, spirit, and breath in one who is addicted.

His mother noticed an unfamiliar icon on the family computer. She found it to be a pornographic site. On questioning her son, who was 16 at the time, he admitted having accessed the site. The son and his father went to the bishop, and after a careful interview, the bishop told the young man to refrain from taking and blessing the sacrament for a week, then to resume. The young man resumed his usual church activity, and served a mission. After his mission, he confessed to his father that he had been unable to stop as a young man, and although he had abstained from pornography while a missionary, he had started to view it again shortly after his mission. He is now involved in an LDS 12 Step recovery group, and has worked with an LDS therapist as well. He is now in recovery and is gaining sobriety.

---

[1] Russell M. Nelson, "Repentance and Conversion," *Ensign,* May 2007, 103.

As we consider this all-to-common story, several points come to mind. The bishop and the parents sincerely felt that the young man had changed, and although he was asked how he was doing several times, their assumption that full repentance *and recovery* had taken place was incorrect. It is becoming increasingly clear that with regard to pornography addiction, full *repentance* will require an ongoing program and attitude of *recovery* for the rest of the person's life. Whereas it is the bishop's stewardship to assess *repentance* and worthiness, he will need outside assistance to manage *recovery* from the addiction. The Lord has provided this help in several ways. One of the wonderful tools for recovery are the 12 Step programs, which allow the person to learn from those who have come out of addiction themselves. A returned missionary struggling with addiction wept when he heard one who has three years of sobriety share his miracle. They were then able to share phone numbers, with the one more grounded in recovery becoming a support person for the newcomer. In this way, the person providing support strengthens his recovery by living Step 12, and the person receiving support gains hope by learning from one who has come out of addiction. He sees, listens to, and learns from one who knows the way in a safe and confidential environment. Recovery groups specific to pornographic and sexual addiction have the extra power of specificity in the sharing portion, just as Alcoholics Anonymous (AA) has become the most well-known and recognized program for the alcoholic.

The Lord has revealed much to His children to help them with addiction. We in the Church can learn from our brothers and sisters outside of the Church who have gained knowledge from the crucible of years of experience in the trenches. We seem to have been spared widespread addiction in the past, in large part thanks to the Word of Wisdom, but pornography seems to have changed that. This largely silent addiction is changing many in the Church, and we are starting to see the result in early divorce and delayed marriage. Ignoring or underestimating the problem will only worsen it; now is the time to act. Most leaders are painfully aware of the prevalence and difficulty of dealing with pornography addiction. They are anxious to learn all they can about the nature of addiction, and are equally eager to bring every tool available to assist their members.

Elder Nelson's definition of repentance as a total change incorporates recovery with all its facets. It is a greater change than the confess/repent/repeat cycle that so many of the addicted experience. Many of those in meetings I attend have gone through multiple bishops, and as they move follow-up is tenuous. True *repentance* from pornography addiction, to be permanent, requires full *recovery*. Bishops who refer afflicted members to 12 Step support will do them a great service. As leaders are educated about the nature of addiction, they will be less likely to try to handle all the aspects of recovery without outside assistance, and less likely to underestimate the addictive, recurrent nature of pornography.

Another aspect of this problem is the marital trauma inflicted on the relationship, and the anguish the spouse experiences. While the bishop can provide understanding and spiritual guidance in his stewardship as shepherd of his flock, he would do well to make sure she has access to a spouse support group where she can associate with other women who have experienced this trauma. One leader was concerned that these meetings might encourage the women to emphasize the weaknesses of their spouse. True 12 Step-based spouse support groups are anything but this, and are focused on individual recovery. The woman is taught to depend on the Savior for personal support, whether or not her spouse heals, and whether or not the marriage survives.

Women who suffer from pornography addiction may attend general Addiction Recovery Meetings, where specific addictions are not shared. Hopefully with time, gender-specific PASG groups will form to help the addicted woman. There are community support groups for sexual addictions also; these are available in most large cities, and may even supplement Church-sponsored groups where needed.

Whether a bishop, facilitator, missionary, group leader, family member or support person we would do well to remember the words of Paul in 2 Timothy 2:24-26 (quoted in the chapter heading). We are admonished not to strive, or argue. He reminds us to be gentle and patient, and apt, or ready, to teach. Teaching is to be done with humility and meekness. Note the powerful relationship in verses 25 and 26 between repentance, which God grants, and recovery, which one must seek first on his own, in order to be freed from the snare of addiction, and the captivity of being led by the will of the adversary. God grants us repentance and we recover ourselves with His assistance, after "all we can do."[2]

---

[2] 2 Nephi 25:23

CHAPTER 17

AND MY SOUL HUNGERED

And I kneeled before my Maker.

Enos 4

We have considered mental exercises to buy time so healing can occur. Long term, or second order changes, are fundamental changes in the way one thinks, according to Carnes.[1] Scripturally, this is the mighty change, after which the person has no more disposition to do evil. The person repairs the faulty belief systems that allowed him to believe that there was a life in addiction.

One young man returned from a mission and fell into viewing pornography and masturbation, a resumption for him of a prior addiction dating back to when he was fourteen years old. He had participated in 12 Step ARP groups, had seen a counselor, and yet had continued to struggle with the same frequency cycle of relapse. In considering the three questions, he realized he could choose to experience more loss before deciding enough was enough. He realized he had not assigned this problem a high enough priority in his mind and life. He understood that for him to overcome this, it would have to be Priority #1 in his life. Like the man who seeks after the harlot described in Proverbs, he had sought pornography "as a bird hasteth to the snare, and knoweth not that it is for his life."[2]

SERIOUS BUSINESS

I learned about the word "serious" during my days training to be a neurosurgeon. One of the last months of my internship, I was

[1] Patrick Carnes, *Don't Call It Love*, Bantam Books, 1991, 227.
[2] Proverbs 7:23

assigned to rotate on the Chief of Neurosurgery's service; we'll change his name to Dr. Jones here. He was soon to be president of the American Association of Neurosurgeons and was brilliant and gifted. I will never forget my first one-on-one encounter with him. He was performing surgery on a posterior fossa craniectomy (a very sensitive brain surgery). Dr. Jones was intense anytime he was in the operating room; the intensity was logarithmically increased in a brain case. As he started, he began asking me questions, "What's that?"

He was removing the skull and I could see the dura mater, or covering of the brain coming into view. I saw a blue structure and knew it was a blood channel called a sinus, but couldn't recall exactly which one.

"It's a sinus."

"Of course it is! Which one?"

I couldn't recall if it was the transverse or the sigmoid, as I had only seen one or two other brain surgeries at that point. I answered, "It's the sigmoid."

He paused, then said with obvious disgust, "It's the transverse."

A few minutes later, he had the microscope in the field with me looking through the observer port. The brainstem came into view, and I could see cranial nerves. Sure enough, he asked which nerve we were seeing.

I knew it was either the 7,8 complex, or 9,10,11.

"I think it's 9,10,11."

Again the disgusted pause. "You need to read. It's 7,8."

Strike two. About that time I was looking for a hole in the floor, but it would get worse before it was over. He positioned the brain retractor deep in the brain and told me to tighten the "snake." I didn't know what a snake was, but figured out that it must be the arm holding the retractor in the brain. It was like a string of beads, and when locked it would hold whatever shape it was in. I tightened it and thought it was tight when he told me to move my hand away. I did, and it wasn't tight. The retractor fell out of the brain! Fortunately there was no harm to the patient.

At that point he stopped the operation and turned around to face me with his now very intense eyes. He said, in a stern and deliberate voice, "Son, this is serious business. Now, when I tell you to tighten the snake, YOU BETTER TIGHTEN THE SNAKE!"

I then felt the now familiar click as the snake tightened and locked. I honestly don't know how I survived that day. I went home and told my wife that I didn't think I could go through five years of training with this guy. It seemed an impossible task at that point. She patiently listened and told me I needed to get some sleep, as I had to go back the next day. I don't think I would have continued then or during later moments of agony without Jana's gentle but firm support. Somehow, I did keep going back the next day and all of the next days until I finished my residency six years later. I owe my career to Dr. Jones and his training and support and for choosing me to train in his program and giving me the chance to become a neurosurgeon.

I would repeat his words to me during that brain surgery to any who question how important this issue of pornography is in regard to peace and happiness: *"Son, this is serious business."* Just as I was too timid with "tightening the snake," we also may be too timid about turning off the TV or computer? Our boldness in righteousness becomes our retractor, enabling us to see clearly to successfully complete the *operations of life here necessary to qualify for eternal life.*

THE THREE QUESTIONS REVISITED

In Chapter 10 we discussed three questions. We addressed them primarily from a technical, mind control angle. Let us consider them now with a spiritual perspective in mind. "What do you want?" relates, of course, to desire. Elder Neal A. Maxwell gave us a masterpiece on desire in the October General Conference of 1996. He said, "Desires thus become real determinants, even when, with pitiful naiveté, we do not really want the consequences of our desires."[3] Who really wants to experience the misery and loss that accompany pornography addiction? Yet the misery is inevitable the instant the

---

[3] Neal A. Maxwell, "According to the Desire of Our Hearts," *Ensign*, November 1996, 22.

finger clicks with lustful intent. Elder Maxwell continues, "There-fore, what we insistently desire, over time, is what we will eventually become and what we will receive in eternity."[4] Unfortunately this works against those who will not pay the price for repentance and recovery. Note that we have discussed the dual nature of this "soul" malady; the spirit aspect (sin – repentance), and the body/brain qual-ity (addiction – recovery). Just as a soul can hunger lustfully for evil, Enos hungered *in his soul* for righteousness.[5]

This requires commitment, as Elder Maxwell emphasizes: "Righteous desires need to be relentless, therefore, because, said President Brigham Young, the men and women, who desire to obtain seats in the celestial kingdom, will find that they must battle every day (in *Journal of Discourses*, 11:14). Therefore, true Christian soldiers are more than weekend warriors."[6] Never was this more true than in maintaining purity in today's world, or in overcoming or avoiding pornography addiction. While the concepts of deflection and blocking of sinful thoughts spoken of previously are important in initially climbing out of the pit of addiction and sin, eventually the "new heart and new spirit"[7] will no longer desire evil, and the struggle will cease. Elder Maxwell describes this process: "What we are speaking about is so much more than merely deflect-ing temptations for which we somehow do not feel responsible. Re-member, brothers and sisters, it is our own desires which determine the sizing and the attractiveness of various temptations. We set our thermostats as to temptations."[8] In the end, we must simply decide and follow through in desiring righteousness by "ceasing to be un-clean."[9] He summarizes powerfully: "It is up to us. Therein lies life's greatest and most persistent challenge. Thus when people are

4 Ibid.
5 Enos 4
6 Neal A. Maxwell, "According to the Desire of Our Hearts," *Ensign*, November 1996, 23.
7 Ezekiel 18:31
8 Neal A. Maxwell, "According to the Desire of Our Hearts," *Ensign*, November 1996, 23.
9 *Doctrine and Covenants* 88:124

described as 'having lost their desire for sin,' it is they, and they only, who *deliberately decided to lose those wrong desires* by being willing to 'give away all [their] sins' in order to know God (Alma 22:18)."[10] (emphasis added)

We have considered the spiritual application of the first question, what do we *desire?* The next question adds the concept of action to the desire: What are we willing to do? Are we willing to make and keep covenants? Are we willing to "have the mind of Christ?"[11] We must understand that in the end full repentance requires us to cease from sin. Are we willing to make that mighty change now? True desire will result in action. In the end, to repent even from deep-rooted addiction, desire will draw us to the Savior for healing if we are relentless, as Brigham Young counseled.

CONSECRATION

"How far are you willing to go" relates to a consecrative level of commitment. In overcoming this problem and becoming sanctified, nothing less than this level of commitment will suffice. It may be that this is the Abrahamic test for the formerly addicted—becoming completely pure in thought, desire, and motive. That it is a severe test is not surprising. John Taylor said the Lord might "wrench your very heartstrings."[12] Speaking of Abraham's test he quoted Joseph Smith saying: "If God could in any other way more keenly have tried Abraham than by calling upon him to offer up his son Isaac, he would have done it."[13] That we are sent to the earth at a time of such severe testing is actually an opportunity to consecrate ourselves in righteousness.

Our test must be at least as severe as the physical tests placed on our forefathers. The Lord expects us to pass our tests, even if we suffer. Elder Maxwell said, "If our hearts are set too much upon the

[10] Neal A. Maxwell, "According to the Desire of Our Hearts," *Ensign*, November 1996, 23.
[11] 2 Corinthians 2:16
[12] John Taylor, *Journal of Discourses*, Volume 24, June 24, 1883, 264.
[13] Ibid.

things of this world, they may need to be wrenched, or broken, or undergo a mighty change."[14] The more set on the world our hearts and souls are, the more wrenching and breaking we may need to endure to undergo the change necessary for recovery from sin. We may arrive at the stage where we, like the high priests in Alma's day, are made pure to the point where we may enter into the rest of the Lord: "Now they, after being sanctified by the Holy Ghost, having their garments made white, being pure and spotless before God, could not look upon sin save it were with abhorrence; and there were many, exceedingly great many, who were made pure and entered into the rest of the Lord their God."[15] This mighty change is reminiscent of Carnes' description of those in the recovery phase of addiction: They look back at their former actions in disbelief. Our covenants, however, give us the opportunity not just to overcome sin but also to become sanctified. Moroni described this progression from the avoidance of the telestial to the consecration of the celestial: "Come unto Christ, and lay hold upon every good gift, and touch not the evil gift, nor the unclean thing . . . come unto Christ, and be perfected in him, and deny yourselves of all ungodliness, and love God with all your might, mind, and strength."[16] How pertinent to our discussion, to not touch anything with evil intent and to deny ourselves any evil pleasure. Moroni continues, "Then is his grace sufficient for you, that by his grace ye may be perfect in Christ . . . then are ye sanctified in Christ, that ye become holy, without spot."[17] As one who has been spiritually scarred heals and strengthens, he has the opportunity to understand human sexuality for the sacrament it is intended to be. Elder Jeffery R. Holland describes this in his talk "Of Souls, Symbols, and Sacraments":

> In this latter sense, human intimacy is a sacrament, a very special kind of symbol...sexual union is also, in its own pro-

---

[14] Neal A. Maxwell, "Swallowed up in the Will of the Father," *Ensign*, November 1995, 22.

[15] Alma 13:12

[16] Moroni 10:30, 32, 33

[17] Moroni 10:33

found way, a genuine sacrament of the highest order, a union not only of a man and a woman but also very much the union of that man and woman with God...I know of nothing so earth-shatteringly powerful and yet so universally and unstintingly given to us as the God-given power available in every one of us from our early teen years on to create a human body, that wonder of all wonders, a genetically and spiritually unique being never seen before in the history of the world and never to be duplicated again in all the ages of eternity— a child, *your* child—with eyes and ears and fingers and toes and a future of unspeakable grandeur.[18]

To consecrate this most holy sacrament to the Lord is to become like He is in creation and control. *How far are you willing to go?* As we give our will to Him in this most important way, we give Him "the only thing that is truly ours to give,"[19] and He gives us all in return: "All that my Father hath shall be given unto him."[20]

---

[18] Jeffrey R. Holland, "Of Soul, Symbols, and Sacraments," BYU Devotional, 12 Jan. 1988.

[19] Neal A. Maxwell, "Swallowed Up in the Will of the Father," *Ensign*, November 1995, 24.

[20] *Doctrine and Covenants* 84:38

CHAPTER 18

FIRM AND STEADFAST IN HUMILITY

And if men come unto me I will show unto them their weakness.
I give unto men weakness that they may be humble; and my grace is
sufficient for all men that humble themselves before me; for if they
humble themselves before me, and have faith in me, then will I make
weak things become strong unto them.

Ether 12:27

Finally, my brethren, be strong in the Lord,
and in the power of his might.

Ephesians 6:10

Early in my training as a neurosurgical resident I was assigned to do research in the lab. Although I would help with some night calls, it was largely a protected time where the resident could focus on writing papers and learning to contribute to the knowledge base of medicine. It was a valuable time, and I still enjoy writing book chapters and peer-reviewed journal articles for my specialty. I would try to play basketball at the church gym once a week if my schedule permitted, and I noticed that I felt particularly tired after an evening of ball. I then noticed my usually vigorous energy level wasn't there, and then began to feel a "rub" in my chest when I breathed. It wasn't painful, but it felt like I could feel my lung move with inspiration of air. I began to have the slight sensation I needed to cough, and that's when I asked one of the doctors at the hospital what he thought about it. He had me come by the office, listened to my lungs, and got a chest X-ray. On the initial X-ray we saw a tangerine sized area of consolidation in the upper left lobe, and he thought it might be a viral "walking pneumonia." I took some oral antibiotics, but the coughing was getting worse a few days later.

My chairman, although a neurosurgeon, was an excellent all-around physician, and while discussing my symptoms with him he wondered aloud if it was tuberculosis (TB). I was shocked at the suggestion, but then thought back a year and a half to my intern year just out of medical school. I had worked for a couple of months in the emergency room treating "all comers" and had gained valuable knowledge and experience treating general medical problems. Tuberculosis was becoming much more common, and I had seen it in the ER and treated it. Of course, as a young doctor I felt virtually invincible; illness was for patients, not me! I was more concerned, however, when I found I had lost twelve pounds.

That day I called the pharmacist and had my wife stop and pick up a TB test. I injected it under the skin of my forearm, and we went to sleep that night. The next morning I remember awakening and noticing my arm was sore. Suddenly the realization of the truth hit me, and I sat up and looked at my forearm. A large, angry, silver dollar sized welt had developed at the injection site, and I knew I had tuberculosis. I got out of bed and started to pack for the hospital. My wife woke up and asked what I was doing. When I told her, she asked if, being a doctor, I couldn't be treated at home. I knew that would be impossible given the contagiousness of the disease.

I was admitted, examined, and placed in isolation for a week. This meant I had to wear a mask, as did any who came into my room. I felt something of what the leper felt who had to cry "Unclean" when others approached to protect them. I had few visitors, not unsurprisingly! I will always remember with deep gratitude two of my fellow LDS residents, both of whom are now practicing orthopedic surgeons, who came to my room when few dared and gave me a priesthood blessing.

I couldn't start the medication, which would save my life, until I had produced a sputum specimen so an accurate culture of my organism could be obtained. I remember feeling unclean that first night, knowing that the TB germs were actively killing me and that I had done nothing to stop them. I will always remember when the medication I would take for the next year was brought in to me, three different TB drugs that would save my life. I felt an overwhelming sense of gratitude for the medication when the nurse brought it each day. I had little else to do, so one of my doctor friends brought me a stack of medical books I had requested, and I proceeded to read everything written about tuberculosis. I read about the discovery of isoniazid, one of the first drugs that allowed a person with TB to live, and felt so grateful to those who discovered and tested this drug. Human testing began in the early 1950's, just a few years before my birth.

Before this discovery, TB was the nation's number one cause of death. A diagnosis was a death sentence, although some could linger for years. Three drug companies, two in the United States and one in Germany independently began testing the drug at the same time. The press in New York got word that hopeless TB cases were being treated and saved with a secret "miracle drug" at Sea View Hospital. The New York Post ran the headline "Wonder Drug Fights TB." One paper "carried color pictures of patients actually dancing with joy in the wards of Sea View Hospital."[1] Shortly afterwards, the *American Review of Tuberculosis* published a twenty-seven page article,[2] and the word was really out. The first patients who received the drug were those who were end-stage and dying. They had tried all known treatments to no avail. I now understood how one of these patients felt: "Like the other forty-three patients who had received that first batch of isoniazid treatment, she had been dying from a fulminating case of tuberculosis pneumonia. Like all the others, she had tried every other known method of treatment, including streptomycin and PAS, but all such treatments had failed to cure her. Mrs. Hall was well aware that she had looked death in the face. She returned to

---

[1] Frank Ryan, *Tuberculosis: The Greatest Story Never Told*, Swift Publishers, 1992, 354.
[2] Edward H Robitzek, Irving Selikoff. Hydrazine Derivatives of Isonicotinic Acid (Rimifon, Marsilid) in the Treatment of Active Progressive Caseous-pneumonic Tuberculosis. *American Review of Tuberculosis*; 1952, 65:402-428.

the bosom of her family firmly convinced that she owed her life to a miracle drug called isoniazid."[3]

I remember waiting for the nurse to bring the medication for the first time. I took isoniazid, which is still the pillar of TB treatment today, with two other medications, rifampin and pyrazinamide. I clearly remember seeing the pills for the first time, the pills that would allow me to live. I still feel a wave of deep gratitude for the medication, and I still have the empty containers as a reminder.

It is said that doctors make the worst patients and that they have all the unusual complications. This was my case, and indeed a CT scan of my chest revealed a cavity, a "hole" in the upper part of my lung. The radiology department reviewed my films to find there was also fluid in my chest cavity from the inflammation and an area of infection in my chest wall. The disease was fairly advanced in my lung. I gained a new perspective on what it was like to be "the interesting case." They wanted to put a needle into the abscess in my chest wall, so I found an older chest specialist who had treated TB for years and reviewed my case with him.

He gave me some interesting advice. He told me to *not* let them needle it because this would cause a fistula which might not heal. He then told me to take my medications exactly as prescribed and that he thought I would recover if I did so. He also told me to exercise as I recovered my strength, so as to rebuild strength in my lungs. I took his advice, and a few weeks later my wife asked what I was doing when I walked outside in my running clothes, telling me it was too soon. I told her I was going to run my usual three or four miles, but only made it around the block once before I nearly crawled home in exhaustion. I had learned why TB was called "consumption."

Rather than quit running, however, I only became more determined. I walked and ran further and further distances, and eventually began playing basketball again. I have now run four marathons, and my chest X-ray has returned virtually to normal. I have much to be grateful for, and I know the experience has helped me be a more compassionate physician.

---

[3]   Frank Ryan, *Tuberculosis: The Greatest Story Never Told*, Swift Publishers, 1992, 357.

SPIRITUAL DISEASE

Pornography is a sort of spiritual TB. Just as TB was the leading cause of death 100 years ago, so Internet pornography is infecting and killing the souls of our people, both collectively and individually. Like TB, it travels through the air, and enters the body painlessly. It then begins to multiply. At first, the signs of disease are subtle and may not be easily seen. Later, though, the person's ability to breathe spiritually is affected as it destroys the soul.

Just as I was able to take powerful medication to treat the disease, so can those afflicted with pornography addiction feel the healing touch of the Savior and be restored to spiritual health. It is a fact that a person is not ever "cured" of tuberculosis. Although not active, the germs are walled off in the lungs, usually without any further problem. However, re-activation TB can occur if the immune system is stressed or weakened or if the person becomes overly debilitated. On the other hand, a person who has had TB is less likely to be infected by a new infection because their immune system has learned resistance to the organism.

So it is with pornography addiction. We use the term "in recovery" rather than "recovered" to remind the person that he must always be cautious to avoid "re-activation" of pornography addiction. It is important not to let spiritual defenses weaken. It may be that the person firmly in recovery with several years of sobriety may be less likely to wander into pornography than one who has never been addicted yet is casual about media consumption in today's sexually-saturated world.

The germ that causes TB is *mycobacterium tuberculosis* and is a close genus relative to *mycobacterium leprae*, the germ that causes Hansen's disease, or leprosy. Both are slow growing and contagious and still carry a social stigma of "Unclean!" My grandmother told me in the 1930's or 40's there was a woman on her street who was diagnosed with leprosy. At the time, like TB, there was no treatment, so lifelong isolation was the only protection. Grandma remembers the state health workers coming to the woman's home and taking her, kicking and screaming, from her children and family to live at the

Public Health Service Hospital in Carville, Louisiana, for the rest of her life. This hospital was only closed in 1998, along with a similar facility on the Hawaiian Island of Molokai. Rachel Pendleton, sixty-eight, who was still at the hospital when it closed was fourteen years old when mysterious bumps appeared on her legs. When state health workers came to take her away from her home in Corpus Christi, Texas she wasn't even allowed to hug her parents goodbye. She spent the next fifty-four years at Carville. "I want to go out and live a normal life," she says. "I spent the best years of my life in here. I do not wish to spend the last years of my life in this place."[4]

Another resident, Johnny Harmon, entered Carville in 1935. "The bottom seems to fall out, and you know darn well you've passed through a door that you're never going to come back out of," says Mr. Harmon, who was struck with Hansen's disease in 1935. "I'd get so lonesome," he says. "You can't ask [a] girl to marry you. You've got leprosy."[5]   Residents of Carville frequently changed their names to avoid embarrassing their families. They couldn't vote, marry, or co-mingle with the opposite sex.[6]   It was a modern "Valley of the Lepers," right out of the movie *Ben Hur.*

The spiritual parallels with pornography are profound. The stigma, which caused patients to change their names, is still there. A family may reluctantly talk about a child struggling with an alcohol, meth, or cocaine addiction, but they will keep pornography addiction deeply buried given the social damage. When stigma leads to shame, addiction is actually worsened as the person becomes more hopeless and resigned to his fate. Also, the isolation of addiction is seen spiritually and emotionally. Those in addiction can be living in the same home with other family members, yet be in another universe mentally, thus living in a self-imposed Carville of sorts. Just as heart-rending separations occurred in leprosy, so do these separations of formerly loving husbands and fathers occur as pornography separates partners emotionally, spiritually, and finally physically in divorce.

---

4   U.S. NEWS Story Page, CNN Interactive, "Leprosy Hospital's Closure Means New Start for Patients," April 24, 1998, http://www.cnn.com/US/9804/24/last. lepers/.
5   Ibid.
6   Ibid.

Just as leprosy prevented young people from marrying, pornography is also causing an epidemic of what we might call "pre-divorce," or the prevention of marriage. As young men learn to use pornography for their sexual fulfillment, they are not as interested in real relationships. They "bond" to the electrons on the screen through masturbatory climax and seal the deal with oxytocin and dopamine craving to boot. This modern social and spiritual "Valley of the Addicted" is a wasteland of true love, belonging, and caring. It is an obsessive world where the only reality is the next fix, which technology assures is only a comforting click away.

GRATITUDE AND HUMILITY, THE SANCTIFYING CYCLE

If selfishness and pride are the seedbeds and daily diet in the Valley of the Addicted, the antidote is gratitude and humility.[7] Just as I felt, and still feel, profound gratitude for the TB medicine and for those who developed it, one emerging from addiction will feel this gratitude towards the Savior for the rescuing miracle of His Atonement. This continuing gratitude will be an important part of his ongoing recovery and will insulate him against pride, shame, and guilt, the harbingers of relapse. Gratitude remembered daily will protect him against each day's challenges and will allow him to endure difficult moments. Indeed, gratitude roots us all in righteousness, as Paul said: "As ye have therefore received Christ…so walk ye in him: Rooted and built up in him…abounding therein with thanksgiving."[8] When faced with the world, one who has fully emerged from addiction will be so grateful he will constantly look to the Lord for continuing strength. Those thus rooted on the "rock of our Redeemer, who is Christ,"[9] are able to stand the "mighty winds"[10] and the "shafts in the whirlwind"[11] of this world. When the "hail and mighty storm

7   Ezra Taft Benson, "Pride, The Universal Sin," *Ensign*, May 1989, 4-7.
8   Colossians 2:6-7
9   Helaman 5:12
10   Ibid.
11   Ibid.

shall beat upon [them],"[12] it will "have no power over [them], to drag [them] down"[13] to the Valley of the Addicted, which is but one of the scenic tours available in the "gulf of misery and endless woe."[14] Those so protected have a miraculous promise given, that if they indeed root themselves by building upon this "sure foundation...*they cannot fall.*"[15] (emphasis added)

My mother owns a beautiful property in East Texas on the site of the original ranch where her great-grandfather accepted the Gospel in 1900. There are many beautiful trees on the land, including a magnificent live oak estimated to be at least 600 years old. In 2005, Hurricane Rita hit the Texas/Louisiana coast. My mother's property lay directly in the path of the eye of the storm. Thousands of homes were destroyed, and she was not able to return to her home for a month until power was restored to the area. We drove in with her and witnessed a scene of destruction. We saw hundreds of buildings that had been destroyed. We are thankful her home was not seriously damaged, but when we got out of the car we were all saddened by the scene of devastation we beheld. At least half of her beautiful trees were down, including one oak that had been a favorite. But the magnificent live oak was still standing. It was almost hard to see it well because of all the fallen trees around it, and it had been wounded, having lost two large branches. Even so, it had survived the hurricane force winds and is still thriving several years later. It was the deep root system which extended far out beyond the trunk that made the difference.

The soul that has emerged from addiction is such a tree. Although some branches may be broken, the root system, anchored in gratitude to the Savior, will allow it to withstand the storm. Douglas Malloch's poem is relevant:

---

[12] Ibid.
[13] Ibid.
[14] Ibid.
[15] Ibid.

The tree that never had to fight
For sun and sky and air and light
But stood out in the open plain
And always got its share of rain,
Never became a forest king
But lived and died a scrubby thing.

The man who never had to toil
To gain and farm his patch of soil,
Who never had to win his share
Of sun and sky and light and air,
Never became a manly man
But lived and died as he began.

Good timber does not grow with ease:
The stronger wind, the stronger trees;
The further sky, the greater length;
The more the storm, the more the strength.
By sun and cold, by rain and snow,
In trees and men good timbers grow.

Where thickest lies the forest growth,
We find the patriarchs of both.
And they hold counsel with the stars
Whose broken branches show the scars
Of many winds and much of strife.
This is the common law of life.[16]

In speaking of how gratitude strengthens and protects us, my wife, Jana, shared some pertinent points on the subject at Brigham Young University's Women's Conference in 2006. She said, "Gratitude to our Father in Heaven and to our Savior, Jesus Christ is the

---

[16] Douglas Malloch as quoted in Sterling W. Sill, *Making the Most of Yourself*, Bookcraft, Salt Lake City, 1971, 23.

root system that keeps us firmly anchored. Gratitude keeps us reaching upward and outward during the calm and peaceful moments, and it is also gratitude that gives us strength to survive and endure the winds of adversity."[17] The formerly addicted and progressively sanctified soul is thus able to first survive, then endure, and finally thrive in the face of formerly irresistible temptation.

It is when we are *alone,* separated from our support systems that temptation strikes. Returning to our initial metaphor about the lion, it is noted that lions don't attack a herd of adult water buffalo. Rather, they separate the old, sick, or young and take them individually. So the adversary isolates first, then like the roaring lion, devours.[18] My wife's comments on how gratitude prevents this isolation are insightful:

> Gratitude is acknowledgement. *To feel gratitude is to know you are not alone.* To know that we are not alone in our trials and challenges and to realize that we are not alone in our triumphs and our successes. Gratitude is to know that someone else has rendered us assistance. When that gratitude is directed to our Father and to His Son, our Savior, Jesus Christ, we feel their divine love and invite a spirit of humility into our lives. Acknowledging God is humility. Gratitude and humility bring perspective to both our trials and our triumphs…As we gratefully acknowledge Him we maintain a spirit of humility and insulate ourselves from pride. *Gratitude and humility thus become a sanctifying cycle where each reinforces the other and helps us reach spiritual constancy.*[19] (emphasis added)

As we leave the sensuality of the world and become focused on the spiritual, our perspective widens and we can see more clearly how

---

17   Jana Hilton, "Gratitude Begets Humility, and Humility Begets Joy" BYU Women's Conference, May 4, 2006.

18   1 Peter 5:8

19   Jana Hilton, "Gratitude Begets Humility, and Humility Begets Joy" BYU Women's Conference, May 4, 2006.

to help others on their way. Gratitude helps us in this quest, and self-sacrifice points us outwardly so we expand instead of selfishly shrinking. When considering how to overcome a resistant addiction for a loved one, or ourselves we may wonder, as did the apostles of old, "Why could not we cast him out?"[20] He may well answer us as He did them, "This kind goeth not out but by prayer and fasting."[21] Fasting is a subservience of the physical to the spiritual. As we de-emphasize appetite, we accentuate our access to the Divine, and selfishness recedes even further. My wife's grandfather exemplified this steadfast humility and unselfishness perhaps as much as is possible under extraordinary conditions, by *remembering* to feel gratitude. The following is given in her words:

> In 1941 my grandparents, Forrest and Esther Packard, made a difficult decision; one that would affect their lives in ways they could not have foreseen. Forrest signed a nine-month contract with a construction company to work on Wake Island, located between Hawaii and Japan. They felt this job would help relieve their financial stress. Esther was expecting their sixteenth child, who would become my mother. The ship stopped in Hawaii while en route to Wake. Forrest attended the temple there and requested a blessing from the temple president. He had deep concerns about leaving his family behind with a possible world war looming. In his blessing President Belliston said, "Brother Packard, I bless you that you will return to your loved ones unharmed and in happiness after much trial and hardship. Your family will be in good condition and their numbers increased. You will be blessed on land and sea. Eventually you will return and find your family chain unbroken." This blessing would be a great strength to Forrest throughout the four and a half year ordeal, which would follow.

---

[20] Matthew 17:19
[21] Matthew 17:21

Seven months later, toward the end of his contract on
Wake, Pearl Harbor was attacked. The following day Wake
Island was also attacked. After sixteen days of valiant defense
by the small band of marines, aided by the civilian workers,
Wake Island surrendered. Forrest spent most of the follow-
ing four years in a prison camp in Shanghai, China.

In spite of extreme hardship and much suffering, grandfather Forrest always *remembered*. Fellow prisoner Charles
Nokes said, "Hunger was something we lived with every
minute of the day. We spent what little time we had thinking and talking about food. The predominant thing on everybody's mind was food, and, believe me, in that kind of
situation, the only thing you think of is food." [22]   Even
though the food was terrible the prisoners would often fight
over small differences in portions. POW Jim Allen once saw
the cooks throw burnt rice, described as charcoal, out on the
ground. A group of hungry POWs frantically scooped the
burnt rice out of the muddy soil.

In this setting, Forrest continued to express gratitude and
humility to his Heavenly Father. Oscar Ray, another Latter
Day Saint prisoner, said, *"We all loved Forrest. He was such a
tremendous example to all of us. On the first Sunday of each
month, [he] would fast. He kept track of the days of the month so
that he could fast on the first Sunday of each month. He would
take his allotted portion of food and give it to another prisoner
who was sick, malnourished, or extremely depressed to lift his spirits."* He also stated that other prisoners who were members of the
Church would try to convince Forrest the Lord would understand
his need for food because they were all starving. Brother Ray said,
*"Forrest did not waver. He lived his religion even while starv-
ing."* [23] The priesthood blessing that Forrest Packard received

[22]   Jana Hilton, "Gratitude Begets Humility, and Humility Begets Joy" BYU Women's
       Conference, May 4, 2006, portions concerning Forrest Packard's ordeal are from
       They Never Wavered by Ellen Dee Leavitt, (2005) 7, 85, 101.
[23]   Ibid.

in the Hawaii temple was fulfilled. He was blessed to return
home, with a spirit of humility and gratitude that would remain with him throughout his life. I thank my grandfather
for *remembering.*[24]

Considering Grandfather Packard's example fills us with
wonder and gratitude. It helps us reach beyond our physical
senses as we contemplate his Abrahamic offering. May we learn
to be "steadfast and immovable,"[25] never wavering, that the Lord
may "seal [us] his."[26]

---

[24] Ibid.
[25] Mosiah 5:15
[26] Ibid.

CHAPTER 19

SCRIPTURAL METAPHORS

And He will feed those who trust Him;
And make their hearts as gold.

Roger Hoffman

In the *Doctrine and Covenants* the Lord tells us, "And the spirit and body are the soul of man."[1] We have spoken of the duality of addiction as a true "soul" sin in that it damages the brain; the very instrument the spirit manifests itself through the body into the physical world. We have thus addressed primarily the healing of the brain by learning to reverse thought process associated with damaged pleasure centers. Let us consider the spiritual healing of the essence of the soul.

To climb up a steep cliff, a technical climber needs two hands. Similarly, to overcome a "soul" sin such as pornography two hands are required, one physical (technical aspects of brain recovery in addiction) and the other spiritual, to heal from sin by coming unto Christ. Both are needed to free the person from this evil.

When the Savior began His ministry, He stood in the synagogue in Nazareth and read the words of Isaiah, thereby defining the purpose of His ministry. It is instructive to read these words in the context of later metaphors He would teach: "The Spirit of the Lord is upon me, because he hath anointed me to preach the gospel to the poor; he hath sent me to heal the broken-hearted, to preach deliverance to the captives, and recovering of sight to the blind, to set at liberty them that are bruised."[2] In the context of our subject, consider

---

[1]   *Doctrine and Covenants* 88:15
[2]   Luke 4:18

the purposes of His mission, culminating in the Atonement. In what more direct way is His purpose accomplished than in preaching the gospel to the poor [in spirit]?[3] Consider how His mission is fulfilled as we "preach deliverance to the captives"[4] who are addicted, and see them "set at liberty"[5] as they are healed of their spiritual "bruise."[6] He "heal[s] the brokenhearted,"[7] both the addicted and their innocent loved ones, as they emerge from addiction. He sees His mission fulfilled in the "recovering of sight to the blind"[8] as eyes turn from evil images upward toward heaven. Based on this description of his mission, let us consider four scriptural metaphors which are particularly relevant and pertinent: light and darkness, sight and blindness, freedom and bondage, and health and sickness. We will first consider light and darkness.

LIGHT IN OUR DWELLINGS

One of the plagues of Egypt was thick darkness. It was a darkness "which may be felt."[9] It had other interesting properties: "They saw not one another, neither rose any from his place."[10] This evil of pornography surely can be felt, and it causes isolation so families don't see each other. The plague was so dark it paralyzed the people so they couldn't be productive, as they did not rise. Likewise, the sin of pornography paralyzes people so they too do not rise to their potential. The next verse, however, contrasts beautifully: "But all the children of Israel had light in their dwellings."[11] As we live worthily and keep our covenants, we become the "sons of Moses and of Aaron and the seed of Abraham, and the church and kingdom, and the elect of God."[12] We therefore will have "light in our dwellings," even in the

---

3   Ibid.
4   Ibid.
5   Ibid.
6   Ibid.
7   Ibid.
8   Ibid.
9   Exodus 10:21
10 Exodus 10:23
11 Ibid.
12 *Doctrine and Covenants* 84:34

midst of spiritual Egypt where many have darkness coming into their homes literally through the airwaves.

Light can apply to us individually as well. The Savior said, "The light of the body is the eye: if therefore thine eye be single, thy whole body shall be full of light. But if thine eye be evil, thy whole body shall be full of darkness. If therefore the light that is in thee be darkness, how great is that darkness!"[13] Pornography enters through the eye and fills the whole body with darkness. The key to freedom is also given: keeping our eye "single."[14] As we "[bring] into captivity every thought to the obedience of Christ,"[15] we keep our eye single in purpose to Him and away from evil.

Lehi speaks of a "great mist of darkness"[16] in his dream which caused many to "lose their way," to wander off and become lost. They also "fell away into forbidden paths and were lost."[17] Others were "lost from his view, wandering in strange roads."[18] Many are lost in midnight binges on the Internet, clicking frantically, lusting after that which will never satisfy. These are the forbidden paths that lead to personal misery. How can flipping through cable channels or browsing the Internet alone at night aimlessly be better described than "wandering in strange roads?"[19]

Now I See

The next metaphor concerns sight and blindness and is related to light and darkness: "And the mists of darkness are the temptations of the devil, which blindeth the eyes, and hardeneth the hearts of the children of men . . . that they perish, and are lost."[20] Temptations lure into sin and addiction and destroy the ability of the sinner to see reality. He believes the lie that there is a life in sin, not understand-

---

[13] Matthew 6:22-23
[14] *Doctrine and Covenants* 4:5
[15] 2 Corinthians 10:5
[16] 1 Nephi 8:23
[17] Ibid, verse 28
[18] Ibid, verse 32
[19] Ibid.
[20] 1 Nephi 12:17

ing that "there is no peace, saith the Lord, unto the wicked."[21] Paul described this lack of understanding: "In whom the god of this world hath *blinded the minds* of them which believe not, lest the light of the glorious gospel of Christ, who is the image of God, should shine unto them."[22] (emphasis added)

The return to sanity from the insanity of addiction allows the repentant to "understand what I did not understand."[23] Daniel said, "Many shall be purified, and made white, and tried, but the wicked shall do wickedly, and *none of the wicked shall understand; but the wise shall understand*."[24] (emphasis added) The Lord has told us that He has given us the Gospel "that ye may understand."[25]

Those trapped in pornography addiction lose the ability to feel and to love, thus experiencing "blindness of their heart,"[26] that they become "past feeling."[27] This sin causes them to worship the physical, the five senses, so faith ceases to have meaning to them. This blindness of both the heart and mind allows some to wander other strange roads into Internet sites of those antagonistic to the Church. It is no coincidence that pornography and apostasy are related. As pornography causes sensation to elevate in importance, the sixth sense of spiritual perception goes silent. The natural, sensation based, or sensual man places no worth on things of the Spirit. One person who felt he had lost faith said God and religion had become irrelevant. I thought of Paul's words: "But the natural man receiveth not the things of the Spirit of God, for they are foolishness unto him, neither can he know them, for they are spiritually discerned."[28]

Repentance opens blinded spiritual eyes, hearts, and minds. The two blind men pitifully called out to the Savior "from the way side" as he "passed by," and "cried out, saying, Have mercy on us, O Lord,

---

21 Isaiah 48:22
22 2 Corinthians 4:4
23 Alan Payton, *Cry, the Beloved Country*, Scribner, 1987 (original 1948) 214.
24 Daniel 12:10
25 *Doctrine and Covenants* 50:10
26 Ephesians 4:18
27 Ibid, verse 19.
28 1 Corinthians 2:14

thou Son of David." [29] Many addicted, spiritually blinded souls sit in the wayside, feeling ostracized and alone. But those who persist in seeking him, as the two blind men did, will find that just as he "stood still"[30] for the blind men, he will also visit them "in their Gethsemane, Savior and Friend."[31] Although he could undoubtedly see that they were blind and knew what they wanted, he asked them, "What will ye that I shall do unto you?"[32] Those spiritually blinded by addiction must also ask him for healing and peace as they did: "Lord, that our eyes may be opened."[33] He then "had compassion on them and touched their eyes: and immediately their eyes received sight, and they followed him."[34] He will also touch the spiritual eyes of the afflicted that they may see and may continue to see as they follow him in the future by maintaining purity. Just as the other young man was healed and given physical sight by the Savior, so many have been healed from spiritual blindness and have also exclaimed, "One thing I know, that whereas I was blind, now I see."[35]

THEY WERE LOOSED

The third metaphor is freedom and bondage. As was discussed earlier, when the Savior read Isaiah 61:1-2 in the synagogue, he was proclaiming his ministry and his purpose. In this initiatory sermon, he stated that he had come "to proclaim liberty to the captives and the opening of the prison to them that are bound."[36] Certainly those trapped in the prison of addiction, their loved ones, and those they have damaged are a significant focus of His ministry and healing. This is in contrast to the purpose of the adversary, who "opened not the house of his prisoners."[37] We have considered the flaxen and

---

[29] Matthew 20:31
[30] Matthew 20:32
[31] "Lord, I Would Follow Thee," *Hymns*, Deseret Book Company, 1985, 220.
[32] Matthew 20:32
[33] Matthew 20:33
[34] Matthew 20:34
[35] John 9:25
[36] Isaiah 61:1-2
[37] Isaiah 14:17

strong cords and how they relate to binding the soul, both brain and spirit. Paul said, "Know ye not, that to whom ye yield yourselves servants to obey, his servants ye are to whom ye obey: whether of sin unto death, or of obedience unto righteousness?"[38] Addiction is a cruel master, forcing its servants to destroy what should be beautiful and holy. Perhaps this sexual control is one of the main components of the binding power of the adversary: "And he beheld Satan, and he had a great chain in his hand, and it veiled the whole face of the earth with darkness; and he looked up and laughed, and his angels rejoiced."[39] Here the metaphors merge again, this time darkness veiling the earth because of this great chain. Indeed, "hundreds of bishops and stake presidents list pornography as their No. 1 concern for Church members."[40] This spiritual and biochemical chain of the adversary binds many, and they carry heavy burdens as a result.

Virtually all who have healed from pornography addiction, who are now strong in recovery, describe gratitude for the spiritual strength they have gained *emerging from addiction*. This transition from darkness to light is a common theme in the scriptures. Some of the most beautiful imagery in the scriptures (again merging metaphors) regarding freeing oneself from bondage and darkness is in Alma chapter 5. These verses describe Alma and the four sons of Mosiah: "They were in the midst of darkness…they were encircled about by the bands of death, and the chains of hell…were they destroyed?…Nay, they were not…he changed their hearts…he awakened them out of a deep sleep, and they awoke unto God…they were loosed, and their souls did expand…their souls were illuminated by the light of the everlasting word…they did sing redeeming love…they are saved."[41]

I have changed the order of some of these phrases to transition from darkness and bondage to light and freedom. One emerging from the bondage, blindness, and darkness of addiction and sin will

[38] Romans 6:16
[39] Moses 7:26
[40] "Protecting Homes from Pornography," *Church News*, March 10, 2007
[41] Alma 5:7-9

recognize the soothing, healing words, such as changed, awakened, illuminated, loosed, expand, sing, and saved.

I Am The Lord That Healeth Thee

The last metaphor is that of health and sickness. In the *Doctrine and Covenants* the Lord warns, "And there shall be men standing in that generation, that shall not pass until they shall see an overflowing scourge; for a desolating sickness shall cover the land."[42] We commonly think of sexually transmitted diseases such as AIDS as being possible candidates for these scourges, and this may be a partial fulfillment, but what about the scourge of the brain-sickness of pornography addiction, which infects electronically and ruins minds before they can process what they are feeling? This desolating affliction brings destruction upon the people as we discussed earlier.

When the Lord brought the Children of Israel out of Egypt, He told them if they would keep His commandments, "I will put none of these diseases upon thee, which I have brought upon the Egyptians: for I am the Lord that healeth thee."[43] When we keep our covenants we are protected from this modern neurochemical compulsion and sin, this disease of the soul. It may be that some of the diseases of the Egyptians were venereal in nature and at least related to health and dietary practices embedded in their culture. The Levitical code provided both physical and spiritual protection to the obedient.

Healing, particularly when surgery is involved, can be painful. When I was an intern in surgery just out of medical school I worked with an older general surgeon as part of my initial training. I learned to hold a scalpel and tie knots, but more importantly I began to learn surgical judgment. One day early in my training, this experienced surgeon told me to come back and drain an abscess on a patient at the bedside. An abscess is a collection of infected material, basically a large boil. At the end of rounds I had numerous tasks to come back and perform, in addition to surgery. That afternoon he asked if I had

---

[42]   *Doctrine and Covenants* 45:31
[43]   Exodus 15:26

drained the abscess, and I realized I had not gotten around to it yet. He firmly told me that left untreated, the infection could spread, get into the blood, and cause a more generalized infection and sepsis. I learned some valuable lessons that day. I learned that an abscess must be opened; it will not heal and will only worsen with time. I determined to act immediately in the future, and over the years the lesson has served me well. I would later treat abscesses deep in the brain and would use the same principles of urgency when confronted with these more serious lesions I had learned as an intern.

Pornography is a spiritual abscess in the brain and spirit. Unless drained through spiritual surgery, it will cause a spiritual coma leading to the second death. Although painful, the "scalpel" of the Lord will heal the repentant, as His word is "sharper than a two edged sword."[44] This spiritual scalpel will cut out the infection; full healing will take effort, time, and "antibiotics," in the form of scriptural immersion, prayer, spiritual guidance from a loving bishop, and support in recovery from appropriate sources.

Those who emerge from the gauntlet of serious illness learn unsolicited but valuable lessons about themselves. If they will see with an eye of faith they may emerge tutored and strengthened. Adversity can purify and cleanse. This can also be true of those fully emerging from spiritual malady. They will be able to reach out to others with an empathy and support unique to those endowed with the knowledge only one soiled, scarred, and subsequently saved can have. Having experienced healing, and now "strong in the Lord,"[45] they can reach out and help others climb out of the mire and move into the light.

---

44   Hebrews 4:12
45   Ephesians 6:10

CHAPTER 20

MY BURDEN IS LIGHT

Wherefore lift up the hands which hang down, and the feeble knees.

Hebrews 12:12

To the afflicted, addicted soul the Lord sends this message: "I am the Lord that healeth thee."[1] In the end we must go to Him in prayer, as President Hinckley said, in the privacy of our closet and plead with the Lord.[2] He will hear our prayer and send help from loving sources, some from this side of the veil and some from the other. All of us will have times when we need to feel his personal love and healing. We may well remember the words of Elder Bruce C. Hafen:

> The lost sheep are not just the people who don't come to church…The lost sheep is a mother who goes down into the valley of the dark shadows to bring forth children. The lost sheep is a young person, far away from home and faced with loneliness and temptation. The lost sheep is a person who has just lost a critically needed job; a business person in financial distress; a new missionary in a foreign culture; a man just called to be bishop; a married couple who are misunderstanding each other; a grandmother whose children are forgetting her. I am the lost sheep. You are the lost sheep. "All we like sheep have gone astray."[3]

---

[1]   Exodus 15:26
[2]   Gordon B. Hinckley, "A Tragic Evil Among Us," *Ensign*, November 2004, 59.
[3]   Bruce C. Hafen, *The Broken Heart*, Deseret Book, 1989, 60.

We all experience periods of trial. Some trials are self-imposed, and others seem to find us unsolicited. At times, we are all "the wounded and the weary"[4] and those whom "in the quiet heart is hidden sorrow that the eye can't see."[5] At times we are the healing hands; at other times we feel other hands gently healing us. It is because we have all been the lost sheep that we know where to look for others; it is in the depths of the soul that pain is felt but not always seen.

HEAVY BURDENS

"Come unto me, all ye that labour and are heavy laden, and I will give you rest,"[6] He pleads. Few carry more heavy burdens that those struggling with sexual addictions and sins. He is anxious to take these burdens away and carry the pain for us: "Take my yoke upon you, for I am meek and lowly in heart: and ye shall find rest to your souls. For my yoke is easy, and my burden is light."[7]

Contrast His burden with the weight of sin and addiction. Those who have freed themselves from addiction through the power of the Lord describe feeling light. They have experienced atoning forgiveness, and like the sons of Mosiah, feel their "souls expand,"[8] as they are healed both brain and spirit.

In his masterpiece *The Lord Of the Rings*, J.R.R. Tolkien tells of Frodo, a hobbit who must destroy the evil One Ring by returning to the dark land of Mordor and casting the ring into the Crack of Doom. Frodo carries the Ring throughout the dangerous journey with his faithful friend Sam supporting him. The Ring has some interesting parallels with addiction. Frodo hates carrying the Ring, but finds he doesn't want to part with it. In fact, he becomes angry and frantic when anyone threatens to take the Ring away. Naturally kind and thoughtful, he becomes selfish and cruel when this happens. When he puts the Ring on, he becomes invisible while wearing it and is alone (the isolation of addiction). The Dark Lord, Sauron,

4   "Lord, I Would Follow Thee," *Hymns*, Deseret Book, 1985, #220.
5   Ibid.
6   Matthew 11:28
7   Ibid.
8   Alma 5:9

can sense his weakness when he wears the Ring and gains power over him. Sauron made the Ring to captivate: "One Ring *to rule them all,* One Ring to *find them.* One Ring to *bring them all,* and *in the darkness bind them. In the Land of Mordor where the shadows lie.*"⁹ (emphasis added)

Pornography is like the captivating Ring, trying to find and bring all it can to the mental and spiritual land of Mordor where the shadows lie, the shadows of addiction. Note the similarities—the lust for the Ring, its power to isolate and make invisible (hide). Frodo also feels the Ring getting heavy as he nears Mordor and describes it as a great burden. Indeed, at the end of the quest when they are ascending Mount Doom itself, Frodo is so weak he can hardly move, and Sam must carry him: The words describing the scene are pertinent and compelling:

> *The night seemed endless and timeless, minute after minute falling dead and adding up to no passing hour, bringing no change…* "Now for it! Now for the last gasp!" said Sam as he struggled to his feet. He bent over Frodo, rousing him gently. Frodo groaned; but with a *great effort of will he staggered up; and then he fell upon his knees again.* He *raised his eyes with difficulty* to the *dark slope of Mount Doom towering above him,* and then *pitifully he began to crawl forward on his hands.*
>
> Sam looked at him and wept in his heart, but no tears came to his dry and stinging eyes. "I said I'd carry him, if it broke my back," he muttered, "and I will!"
>
> "Come, Mr. Frodo!" he cried, *"I can't carry it for you but I can carry you and it as well.* So up you get! Come on, Mr. Frodo, dear! Sam will give you a ride. Just tell him where to go, and he'll go."¹⁰ (emphasis added)

---

⁹ J.R.R. Tolkien, *The Fellowship of the Ring,* The Easton Press, 1984 (originally Houghton Mifflin Company, 1954, 60.

¹⁰ J.R.R. Tolkien, *The Return of the King,* The Easton Press, 1984 (originally Houghton Mifflin Company, 1955, 217-218.

Even at the end, he cannot voluntarily thrown the Ring away by himself. The tormented Gollum attempts to steal it back, and it is destroyed with Gollum in that struggle. Just before he enters the Land of Mordor, the Elf Queen, Galadrial, gives him a gift to help him as he faces his great task:

"And you, Ringbearer, I come to you last who are not last in my thoughts. For you I have prepared this." She held up a small crystal phial: it glittered as she moved it, and rays of white light sprang from her hand. "In this phial," she said, "is caught the light of Earendil's star, set amidst the waters of my fountain. *It will shine still brighter when night is about you. May it be a light to you in dark places, when all other lights go out.*"[11] (emphasis added)

Anyone who has faced this burden himself or struggled like Sam to help and carry a loved one will recognize the similarities. Those addicted will feel they are in an "endless and timeless night." With "great effort of will" they fight the compulsion, only to fall "upon their knees" again. They "raise their eyes with difficulty" to the "dark slopes" of their personal "Mount Doom" of addiction, and "pitifully crawl forward" on their hands at times. They can't do it alone, and sometimes the "Sams" in their lives will have to carry them, although the "Sams" cannot carry the actual addiction for them. And most importantly, those bound in addiction, like Frodo, have a light to shine in "dark places, when all other lights go out." That light is the Savior, Jesus Christ.

HE IS MIGHTY TO SAVE

Elder Jeffery R. Holland said, "Are you battling a demon of addiction...the pernicious contemporary plague of pornography?...Whatever other steps you may need to take to resolve these concerns, come *first* to the gospel of Jesus Christ."[12] All the coun-

---

[11] J.R.R.Tokien, *The Fellowship of the Ring*, The Easton Press, 1984 (originally Houghton Mifflin Company, 1954, 393, compare with 2 Peter 1:19.
[12] Jeffery R. Holland, "Broken Things to Mend," *Ensign*, May 2006, 69-71.

seling or cognitive therapy in the world will not break a pornography addiction without the Savior. He understands all pain and temptation because He descended below all. He understands addiction because He felt the *pain of the addicted*, although never experiencing addiction himself: "And he will *take upon him their infirmities...that he may know according to the flesh* how to *succor* his people according to *their infirmities.*"[13] (emphasis added) He carries the burden because He *knows*: "By his knowledge shall my righteous servant justify many, for he shall bear their iniquities."[14] His unconditional love for us caused Him to feel "the travail of his soul"[15] in bearing the travail of all our soul sins, not to mention our "griefs and sorrows."[16] In gaining this knowledge of us he was "satisfied"[17] that He could "justify many,"[18] namely, each of us, by his personal and collective knowledge of our sins and pains. Undoubtedly the crushing pain of addiction, tormenting He who was never addicted Himself, contributed to his agony in the Garden of Gethsemane and on the cross: "My soul is exceedingly sorrowful, even unto death: tarry ye here, and watch with me."[19] The soul sins, with the pain of the tormented and all their innocent victims were seen, understood, comprehended. The pain of isolation was felt, reminiscent of the lines from Ella Wheeler Wilcox's poem:

> *All those who journey, soon or late,*
> *Must pass within the garden's gate;*
> *Must kneel alone in darkness there,*
> *and battle with some fierce despair.*[20]

---

[13] Alma 7:12
[14] Isaiah 53:11
[15] Ibid.
[16] Ibid, verse 4.
[17] Ibid, verse 11.
[18] Ibid.
[19] Matthew 26:38
[20] Ella Wheeler Wilcox, "Gethsemane," in *The Poems of Ella Wheeler Wilcox*, Nimmo, Hay and Mitchell, 1910.

Even He did not want to be alone, to be isolated: "Tarry ye here, and watch with me."[21] Yet at the end it was necessary for Him to experience the pain of separation from the Father we all experience when we sin: "My God, my God, why hast thou forsaken me?"[22] In the Garden he experienced the acute pain those seared by soul sins feel: "My *soul* is exceedingly sorrowful, even unto *death*."[23] Speaking of his repentance process, Alma describes a similar level of pain: "After wading through much tribulation, *repenting nigh unto death*."[24] Those who have fully emerged from addiction will recognize the word *tribulation*. They will have, like Caleb, successfully looked at their personal Mount Doom, and said, "Give me this mountain,"[25] recognizing this as their personal cross to bear, their unique sacrifice to lay on the altar in their quest for perfection. And surely some of these purified souls, who have "waded through much tribulation,"[26] like Alma, will be among those described by John:

> After this I beheld, and, lo, a great multitude, which no man could number, of all nations, and kindreds, and people, and tongues, stood before the throne, and before the Lamb, clothed with white robes, and palms in their hands; And cried with a loud voice, saying, Salvation to our God which sitteth upon the throne, and unto the Lamb.
>
> And one of the elders answered, saying unto me, What are these which are arrayed in white robes? and whence came they? And I said unto him, Sir, thou knowest. And he said to me, *These are they which came out of great tribulation*, and have *washed their robes*, and *made them white* in the *blood of the Lamb*. Therefore are they before the throne of God, and serve him day and night in his temple: and he that sitteth on the throne shall dwell among them. They shall hunger no

---

21 Matthew 26:38
22 Matthew 27:46
23 Matthew 26:38
24 Mosiah 27:28
25 Joshua 14:12
26 Mosiah 27:28

more, neither thirst any more; neither shall the sun light on them, nor any heat.

For the Lamb which is in the midst of the throne shall feed them, and shall lead them unto living fountains of waters: and God shall wipe away all tears from their eyes.[27] (emphasis added)

While serving as a mission president in Manila, Philippines, my father recorded in his journal: "I have realized that we have many types of trials. Some we bring upon ourselves because of transgression and are called 'stumbling blocks' and 'pitfalls,' and others the Lord places upon us to test, try, and prove us."[28]

Alma's trials may have largely been stumbling blocks by my father's definition, yet Alma described them as his personal tribulation. It is likely that Alma will be among John's multitude, the multitude who came out of great tribulation. It is noted that they had to *wash* and *make* white. Surely some of these are those people who struggled through and overcame sin and addiction in an extremely wicked world and then became sanctified. John the Beloved's parting admonition regarding the will and desire of these exalted ones is enlightening: "Blessed are they that do his commandments, that they may have right to the tree of life, and may enter in through the gates into the city...And whosoever *will* let him take the water of life freely."[29] (emphasis added) May we say in our hearts, and with our thoughts and lives, as He said, "Not my will, but thine be done."[30]

In the end mortality is a test. We will each have our own exam, however, individually experienced as we walk the challenging road of life. The lie of addiction says, "You can't change," yet the Savior's arm is "stretched out still."[31] If you can only desire to return, or hope to heal, He will come with forgiveness and peace. As Joseph said to the repentant and returning W. W. Phelps, "It is your privilege to be de-

[27] Revelation 7: 9, 10, 13-17
[28] Personal journal, Donald L Hilton, 1992.
[29] Revelation 22:14, 17
[30] Luke 22:42
[31] Moses 7:30

livered from the powers of the adversary."[32] Many who have felt the
hopelessness of addiction for themselves or their loved ones have felt
much like Peter on the ship "in the midst of the sea."[33] They are
"tossed with waves"[34] of despair and blown about with winds that are
"contrary."[35] It is the "fourth watch of the night,"[36] and the blackness
and depth of the forbidding water fills them with despair. It is *especially* at times like these that the Lord Jesus Christ comes walking on
the water, takes our hand and invites us to walk with Him, saying
"Be of good cheer; it is I; be not afraid."[37] And we, like Peter, take
our initial tentative steps, and then begin to walk toward Him as He
bids us to "Come."[38] But when we see the "wind boisterous,"[39] we,
like Peter, are afraid. We may begin to sink back into addiction or
into despair over a beloved husband, son, wife or daughter.

"And immediately, Jesus stretched forth his hand, and caught
him, and said unto him, (I picture gently and lovingly) "O thou of little faith, wherefore didst thou doubt?"[40] Only then, when He had
saved his sinking, but beloved, Peter, did the wind cease.

I testify and promise all who have felt pain and despair for themselves or loved ones that "He is mighty to save."[41] He will come to
you in the midst of your blackest night, when waves toss and winds
blow and hope seems impossible. It is *especially* then, when we are
sinking, that we must remember to cry, as Peter did, "Lord, save
me."[42] He who touched the blind eyes and caused them to see is real
and loving, and He will immediately "[stretch] forth his hand."[43] The
touch of His hand will grasp and save. *He can also touch the damaged
brain and soul, and cause it to feel and to think and to love again.* He

---

[32]   *History of the Church*, Volume VI, LDS Church, 1949, 163.
[33]   Matthew 14:24
[34]   Ibid.
[35]   Ibid.
[36]   Matthew 14:25
[37]   Matthew 14:27
[38]   Matthew 14:29
[39]   Matthew 14:30
[40]   Matthew 14:31
[41]   Alma 34:18
[42]   Matthew 14:30
[43]   Matthew 14:31

who healed the leper can heal the damaged marriage and help the be-trayed loved one to hope and to heal as well. There are many who wandered in "strange roads,"[44] who are now on the "strait and narrow path,"[45] and can say, "He restoreth my soul."[46] There are many who wandered in the "mists of darkness"[47] of addiction who now say, "One thing I know, that whereas I was blind, now I see."[48] That we may see with eyes purified from lust, anger, judgment, and fear, and know that in a better place "God will wipe away all tears from our eyes,"[49] is my prayer in the name of Him who saves us all.

---

[44] 1 Nephi 3:32
[45] 1 Nephi 31:18
[46] Psalms 23:3
[47] 1 Nephi 12:17
[48] John 9:25
[49] Revelation 7:17

APPENDIX A

WHAT WORKS FOR ME: THOUGHTS FROM A MAN IN RECOVERY

A recovery story of one who is now an experienced facilitator. His wisdom and insight will hopefully bring understanding to those who seek peace.

My addiction to lust, pornography, and masturbation started when I was about twelve years old. I didn't really think much of it at the time, but being raised in the LDS church, I knew that what I was doing was wrong. I didn't think I was hurting anyone, so I continued to use the addiction as an escape from depression and loneliness (though I didn't know that was what I was doing at the time) and to cover whatever I didn't feel like dealing with. Around age sixteen, I became more rebellious and started drinking alcohol with my friends as well. I graduated and left home to go to college 600 miles away. Free at last! I got involved with the wrong crowd and partied with my new found friends. My sexual addictions were always there in their various forms but I kept them very private. I isolated from friends at church and eventually stopped going to church completely. I was often around large groups of people but I always felt completely alone. Plain old normal TV (not cable, not satellite, not videos) was my main source of inappropriate material along with people I would see throughout the day. I was nearing rock bottom as I would regularly use lust and alcohol to numb my pains and escape from life.

At age twenty-two, I had some experiences that led to a change of heart. I really started to care about what I was doing and how it was hurting me and my future wife and family I wanted to have some day. I found out later that this change of heart had come to me as a result of my parents' prayers, fasting, asking people in their ward to pray and fast, and continuously putting my name in the temple. When this change of heart happened, I was able to walk away from alcohol, partying, everything except the sexual addictions. At this point, I actually wanted to walk away from those too, but over the years it had turned into a strong addiction that was much more powerful than alcohol or anything else I had experienced up to that point. As I would soon find out, I was completely unable to overcome it on my own.

For the next ten years, I tried to overcome my sexual addictions and failed miserably. I would mentally beat myself up every day for being such a failure. I went on a mission around age twenty-five. I did get a two-year reprieve from acting out my addictions physically during my mission, but lust was still with me throughout that period. After my mission, when the Internet had matured enough for me to get into it more fully, is when what people would consider "real pornography" entered my life. This new found material locked me into the addiction even tighter. I could find no way out of it.

At this point, I was a full tithe payer, temple recommend holder/attender, and active member of my ward with leadership positions. It seemed that I was doing everything in my power to do everything else in my life perfectly to make up for the sins of my hidden life. At times, my pride would convince me that I was such a great person that I had to have this addiction just to keep me humble. Thoughts like that almost got me to stop fighting against it and just accept it as a necessary evil that, by keeping me humble, did more good than harm. I found out later that I was completely wrong about that! I also thought that once I got married, the problem would go away because then this "appetite" would finally be satisfied. I found that to be completely wrong also by talking to other people who were married and still had the problem. I found out later that just as one in addiction is never satisfied with one piece of pornography for their whole life, one's wife could not satisfy lust for very long either. I found that love was completely different than lust and that I could only find happiness if I removed lust from my life completely. I discovered that love is personal and different for each person that I love. I also found that lust is generic and can be transferred from person to person. That is what is done as a person views several images of pornography one after the other, transferring lust from one to another to another.

Around age thirty-two, one of the many bishops who had tried to help me overcome this addiction told me about a 12 Step program for sexual addiction. I didn't even know what a 12 Step program was, but my bishop told me that another member of my congregation had found success there. At this point, I was willing to try anything. I went to my first 12 Step meeting and was very nervous. It turned out that the people there were just like me and had been in predicaments similar to mine but were now changing for the better. I identified with what they were saying, and I got hope in that first meeting that this might actually work. I was no longer alone. I kept going back to the 12 Step meetings, started "working the steps," and began to see real changes in my behavior and in my level of peace and joy. It was a rocky road in the beginning for a while, but with a lot of meetings and working the steps, I became free from these addictions and then started to work on overcoming the effects that all of those years of addiction had on me.

I didn't become free from temptation, but I no longer felt compelled to give in to temptation and I was finally free to choose to turn away from these addictions and was finally free to choose other, better things in life. I am finally happy and free. I still have to exert effort to maintain this freedom, but it's nothing like what my life of addiction was like. Instead of fighting the addiction directly, I now work to provide an environment where the Spirit and Christ can come in and gain victory over the addiction. I also work to rid myself of the pride, resentment, judgement, and unresolved sins in my past and present that were causing the misery that I tried to cover up with my addiction.

After a while, I started going to LDS-sponsored 12 Step pornography addiction recovery meetings as a facilitator. A facilitator is just someone with a certain length of sobriety who has experience working each of the 12 Steps and who is there to share their own experience along the path to recovery.

I want to share a few things that I have learned on my journey through recovery – things that I have learned from my own experiences as well as from the experiences of several people that I have met in these meetings along the way.

THE PURPOSE OF THIS ARTICLE

The fundamental principles of the 12 Step program were not new to me. I found that, for me, the core of 12 Step programs matched something that I was already familiar with - the Gospel of Jesus Christ – faith in Jesus Christ, repentance, baptism, and the gift of the Holy Ghost. I had known about the Gospel of Jesus Christ for most of my life, so what was so different about these 12 Step programs? Why should I bother learning about similar things I had been learning at church all those years? It was obvious that simply possessing knowledge of these things in my mind had not freed me of these addictions up to that point in my life, so why would learning about these same principles again make a difference this time around? I think I found the answer to this question, and I want to share what I have found with you.

The main difference I could see was in the meetings themselves. The inherent safety and anonymity of these meetings permitted a level of humility and faith in Christ sufficient to allow the repentance process to work for me. The meetings are safe simply because everyone there suffers the effects of the same addictions that I do. Therefore, I can have confidence that they will not gossip, backbite, judge, or condemn in the same way people might in other settings. Attendance in these meetings changed me from the inside out – slowly but surely – in very important ways that I will describe below. It wasn't as much the content of the meetings as it was the safe environment that allowed my heart to open up and my faith to increase to the point that I could finally be healed and be set free from the chains that had bound me for twenty years - one small step at a time. There are other important aspects of the 12 Step programs besides meetings themselves that have positive effects, but I found that without going to the meetings, it just didn't work for me (and others I know).

Therefore, the purpose of this article is to help people who are currently trapped in addictions to understand a little about how this program works in an attempt to help them continue firmly on the path of recovery that is now before them.

THE MEETINGS –
CHANGING FROM THE INSIDE OUT

"And the church did meet together oft, to fast and to pray, and to speak one with another concerning the welfare of their souls."

Moroni 6:5

I didn't speak with people in my church meetings about my addiction. It just wasn't a safe (or appropriate) place to share such things. Because of this, half of me has been at church all these years while the other half has not really been there. Therefore, the addicted part of me has truly been inactive in the church since the addiction began. I have been split in two – the "church" or "public" me and the "addicted" or "private" me. The 12 Step meetings are like a desperately needed Sunday School class specifically for that addicted part of me. There is priesthood authority in these meetings in the form of LDS Family services missionaries. Taking an active part in the meetings is called "step zero" by some. For me, the rest of the program doesn't work without going to these meetings regularly – kind of like being inactive in the church never worked very well for me either, surprisingly enough.

INCREASED HUMILITY

These meetings increase my humility (decrease my pride). For me, this means that they increase my capacity to be aware of the true nature of both my strengths and weaknesses. This is the first missing piece to the puzzle and is also what the first of the 12 Steps is about. This self-awareness increased as I attended the meetings. This was very important to me because without self-awareness and impeccable honesty, I couldn't begin to see clearly what things I needed to do in order to start overcoming these addictions. I also learned that without such humility and self-awareness, I was a horrible judge of my own progress. Months would go by with me thinking nothing was happening. Luckily I kept going back because later I would look back and see that a solid foundation was being put in place while I was unaware. I kept going back regardless of what my blind eyes told me about my progress.

INCREASED FAITH IN CHRIST

Faith in Christ is the second missing piece to the puzzle and is also at the heart of Step 2. I found an interesting quote in the Bible dictionary under faith. It describes two ways to increase faith:

> *"Faith is kindled by hearing the testimony of those who have faith . . . (Rom. 10:14-17) strong faith is developed by obedience to the gospel of Jesus Christ; in other words, faith comes by righteousness."* Bible Dictionary, "Faith"

The 12 Step meetings increase my faith in a few ways. First, I start to believe that Christ wants to help me and actually has the power to help me. This faith isn't a learned thing. I can't get it through reading a book or having someone tell me about it. It came to me through hearing and bearing testimony about the reality of our individual situations while sitting in these meetings. It also comes from my own righteousness as I gradually move away from my addictions and replace sin with righteousness. I have not found any other way to increase the kind of faith in Christ necessary to be freed from these addictions and the underlying problems that the addictions are covering up.

The second way my faith in Christ increases deals with believing that Christ loves and respects me – warts and all. As I see people in the group respect each other even though we all know the truth about each other's problems, I think to myself, "If these guys can love and respect me, maybe Christ is also capable of that kind of love and respect for me too." The testimony of the other members in the group increases my faith in Christ's capacity to love. I ended up loving and respecting myself more also, which I found to be very important too.

INCREASED CONNECTION WITH OTHERS KNIT HEARTS

I had been isolated for most of my life when it came to this part of my addiction. Just showing up to the meetings was not enough. I needed to "connect" with the people there. I needed to come out of isolation where satan could have his way with me and form bonds with others that could allow me to share burdens with them when I was weak during meetings or through phone calls. Just as I cannot do very well in the gospel when I isolate myself and stop going to church, I cannot do very well isolated with regard to this addiction on my own - just like a hot coal from a fire taken away from the main pile of coals soon becomes cold and goes out. I could, even in the safety and brotherhood of these amazing groups, find reasons not to connect with others - judgement, pride, putting myself above or beneath the group, etc. can all keep me going through the motions of going to group meetings but still isolated and dying on the inside. As I faced my fears and talked to and called these men, I found myself beginning to progress at a much faster rate with a much more solid foundation than I did before I really started connecting with others.

With these key pieces of the puzzle finally falling into place (humility, faith in Christ, and my heart knit together with others in the groups), I can finally move to the next steps of repentance (Steps 3 through 9), and then endure to the end (Steps 10 through 12).

ONE DAY AT A TIME – CHANGING FROM THE OUTSIDE IN

Going to meetings put me into an environment where Christ could finally heal me from the inside out. I started to turn to Christ more and more for comfort and support, but this, by itself, I found was not enough. I found that I also had to work on myself from the outside in too. In other words, I had to change behaviors and habits to the best of my ability. I had to do all I could do and let God and Christ do the rest. Below you will find some of the daily things I learned from others and on my own that helped me to make progress from the outside in.

LUST AND SELF-AWARENESS

"He that looketh on a woman to lust after her...
shall not have the Spirit, but shall deny the faith and shall fear."

D&C 63:16

I found that these addictions start with lustful thoughts that I was completely unaware I was entertaining – hours, days, weeks, or even months before any physical manifestations of addiction. As I started going to the meetings and working the steps to start working on myself from the inside out, I then started becoming more aware of how much I was lusting after people each day. As I become more and more aware of it (I never knew how much I was looking and lusting before I came into the program), I try to let go of it at the earliest stage possible – when it's easier to let go of it. It's kind of like the easiness of pulling out a new weed compared with the difficulty of pulling out a weed that has been growing all summer long. My capacity to turn away from the temptation to lust is directly proportional to the strength of the faith and self awareness that I build in these meetings.

WORKING THE STEPS

I learned that it was essential to work the 12 Steps, or lasting progress would continue to escape me. To me, the Steps are just the Gospel of Jesus Christ broken down into manageable pieces. The Steps are progressive in nature and they build upon each other. I have found that it is essential to work the Steps thoroughly and in order from 0 to 12.

There are many books out there that cover the steps so I won't do much here other than give an extremely brief overview. Step 0 is attending and being a part of the meetings - helping and connecting (becoming friends) with those in the meeting. I mainly worked on Steps 1 and 2 (humility and faith) by going to the meetings and making phone calls - building a tightly knit fabric of connections between myself and others in those meetings. I think of Step 3 as repentance - surrendering my will to God's will in all things, not just the surface addiction. Step 3 relies on the foundation of humility and faith continually built by working Steps 1 and 2. Steps 4-9 deal with clearing out the junk from my past. This junk gets me feeling unhappy and depressed and therefore tempts me to cover it all up with my addiction. It also stands between God and me. Getting rid of it helps me to not have as much of a need for the addiction to cover up those negative effects of the past. It also enables me to have a more pure relationship with Christ. The character defects found in Steps 4-9 for me were worked on in Step 10 rather than in the steps in which they were identified. Steps 10 through 12 deal with preventing more junk from building up, positively seeking out God's will for me, and sharing what I have found with others -enduring to the end. Enduring to the end while experiencing motivating changes and progress that happen even faster once the addiction is set aside. I have become more patient, kind, and approachable just to give a few examples of how I've been changing once the progress-stopping addiction was out of the way. I still have a long way to go but the joy and freedom I see each day now amaze me and motivate me to continue working hard on my character weaknesses after the addiction is set aside. If I choose to stop working on these things, the addiction awaits me. If I continue doing the things that helped me to let Christ in to gain victory over the addiction, then I will continue to remain free from the addiction one day at a time.

BOUNDARIES

Another thing that has helped me in this process is to set boundaries. When I have sprained my ankle in the past, I usually have needed to put a brace on it to prevent re-injury while my ankle healed. This is how I view boundaries. I put them in place to allow myself to heal while they help to prevent re-injury. Some examples of boundaries would be not watching TV alone, not surfing the Internet alone, not having the Internet at all, not going places that are triggering, etc.

I must define my own boundaries. Any time I fall, I identify which boundary I broke leading up to that fall and move that boundary back to a more safe location, for example, changing a "no Internet while alone" to "disconnect the Internet completely and just use it at the library." Learning from each fall instead of beating myself up is very helpful. Boundaries are like crutches. The real healing and progress takes place within the protection of those boundaries. As healing occurs and my faith is strengthened, some boundaries can be adjusted to match my faith and strength, if absolutely necessary.

The adjusting of boundaries takes a great deal of rigorous self-honesty. I found that some boundaries are good to keep forever though, like not watching inappropriate media.

It's strange because in the beginning, I had trouble keeping my boundaries. It was as if I hadn't ever learned to protect myself. I would do anything to keep my children from harm, but I wasn't doing that with myself. It's something I had to learn to do and part of that seems to have something to do with loving myself. As I worked the program, I gradually started to love myself and then was more able to protect myself from harm that existed beyond these boundaries and I became willing to keep these boundaries - to keep myself from harm. I became one of my own "loved ones" and only then did I truly protect myself at all costs. I never realized how much I didn't like myself before coming into the program. But now, I can say that I like myself and am starting to truly love myself as a person and that love fixes a lot of things.

SELF RESPECT AND LOVE

For this topic, I offer an analogy that played out in my heart that had a profound effect on me.

Before I got into true recovery, I met Christ at the door and told Him that He didn't need to come in - I made the mess, I would clean it up and some day my house would be clean enough for Him to come in without judging me and thinking I was stupid, slothful, and filthy. I sent Him away empty handed.

Once in recovery, I opened the door to Him, and quickly handed out a gift-wrapped bag of garbage for him to take with Him. I offered Him some surface temptations for Him to take. I made sure they were ok so He wouldn't hate me and think I was a slob.

Next, I finally realized I couldn't clean up my house by myself. It was a filthy house and I was ashamed of it. Satan whispered "quick, hide" whenever Christ came. I was done hiding and finally, with so much fear, let Him in. I showed Him around nervously just waiting for Him to start telling me how dumb I was to have let my house get so dirty and for not knowing how to clean it up. I wept inside, bracing myself for His wrath. Instead, He quietly knelt down and started cleaning, inviting me to help where I could.

After a while of this, He was over helping me clean again, and He heard cries coming from the basement - a place I had not taken Him yet. It had barbed wire and insulation stacked as high as I could get it to keep it hidden. He said nothing - waiting for me to invite Him down there. Once He left, I went downstairs and found myself as two people sitting on the floor exhausted from one of me beating the other for years. Neither of them knew how to stop it. They both looked at each other and cried. They had had enough and in their hearts they invited Christ into the room. He walked in and quietly took the place of the one of me being beaten.

My heart changed that day and will never be the same. His Atonement is quietly making its way into every aspect of my life in every waking moment - not just to resurrect me at the end of my life, but to receive the temptations I give to him, to make right the offenses I give not only to others but to myself. The only way I can pay Him is to willingly open the next room, willingly open my heart to Him one step at a time.

Participation in the recovery groups has brought me to this place because when I see a group of men nodding and understanding me, loving and respecting me, warts and all, I see Christ sitting before me - knowing me and what I'm going through and not condemning me but helping me clean.

I can't get that anywhere else in the world but in meetings. I can't read it in a book. I can't be told it. I must live it by placing myself in those meetings that expose me to the most Christlike experience I've felt.

SELF CARE

Taking care of my spiritual, physical, social, and emotional needs has also been a huge part of recovery and enduring to the end for me. I must study the scriptures and pray and do other things that nourish and strengthen my spirit to be able to more effectively turn away from temptation.

Interestingly enough, I must also take care of my body by getting enough sleep and healthy food at regular mealtimes. I must also stay connected with others and stop isolating. These needs are very important for me to fulfill the right way so I don't end up trying to fullfill them in the wrong ways. Spencer W. Kimball once spoke about the result of unmet needs:

> *"Jesus saw sin as wrong but also was able to see sin as springing from deep and unmet needs on the part of the sinner. This permitted him to condemn the sin without condemning the individual."*
> Spencer W. Kimball, "Jesus: The Perfect Leader," Ensign, Aug 1979, 5

When I don't take care of myself in these ways, temptations end up being more difficult to turn away from. In fact, not taking care of myself in these ways is usually the main cause of me being triggered." If I skip breakfast, lust plagues me more that morning than if I had eaten a good breakfast. I don't know why, but knowing why isn't as important as just taking care of my needs because I know that works for me.

Phone Calls

It is also helpful to get a few phone numbers of people in the group to call throughout the week when I need a boost and to build unity. This also does two other things. It increases my humility by admitting that I need help since the act of calling someone is an act of humility. It also defeats isolation. Isolation halts my progress. I need to get with and connect with people instead of just being alone. This doesn't just mean calling people in the group. It can also mean being with good friends who have a good influence on me.

Goals

My whole life, I had been setting goals that had to do with the addiction, like "I will remain sober for fourteen days," or even worse, "I'll never do that again." Since I had no control over the addiction (according to Step 1), I was making goals that dealt with outcomes that I had no control over. Not too surprisingly, this would usually end up in depressing failure after depressing failure.

I didn't realize it at the time, but I now see that when I came into the program, I started changing the types of goals that I made for myself. I started making goals about completing certain steps or getting to a certain number of meetings per week, etc. These were different than the old goals I used to make because I actually have control over the outcome of these goals. I can work on the steps five minutes per day or complete Step 4 by the end of next month or attend at least two meetings each week. I had control over these things; and therefore, I had a say in whether or not I achieved these goals. What a concept!

Because of this change in the types of goals I was making, I started seeing success in meeting these goals and started seeing a correlation between my efforts and my successes – something I rarely saw when working on goals that dealt with my uncontrollable addiction. The old addiction-related goals didn't work. The new recovery-related goals worked.

REPROGRAMMING

Not only did I need to reprogram how I thought about women and other triggers, but I had to reprogram my deeper thoughts about being worthless, needing to be perfect to be loved, etc. I found that reading a list of statements daily helped me to do this. Over time, I found out what lies I was believing from satan and reversed them. For example, one lie he told me was that "I have to be perfect to be loved or helped by God". I reversed that to say "God will help and love me when I'm imperfect". There are many more statements I read each day. Something about saying those things over and over gets me to believe in them more each day. I get the negative versions whispered to me every waking moment so I deserve to have someone (myself) tell me the truth instead.

HABITS

Recently, I changed the location of the trashcan in my cubicle at work from my right side to my left side. It had been on the right side for several years. After switching it to the other side, I spent a lot of my time turning to the right to throw away trash, realizing in frustration that the trashcan was no longer there and then turning to my left to finally throw the trash away. With time and patience, I started catching myself earlier on and only started thinking about turning to the right, and finally, I now just turn to the left by habit.

As I change addiction-related habits that I have developed over the years, I have to be very patient with myself. I slowly change habits in the same way I was changing my trashcan to the other side. Beating myself up out of impatience and frustration never helped at all. It only made things worse. I had developed habits of looking at people in cars as they pass on the freeway or looking around at people in public in order to feed lust. I acted on these habits without even being aware I was doing them most of the time.

It took time, awareness, and a lot of patience with myself to slowly change these habits, but they did change as I kept working on them.

DREAMS

One other area that was troublesome to me was inappropriate dreams. I had heard that I am not responsible for my dreams and sometimes I would look forward to them just to relieve the pressure of my lust. I never felt good about that though. I found that inappropriate dreams went away completely as I stopped stuffing myself with lust all day long. After I learned to let go of lust and stop letting it into me throughout the day, I could go for years without any sexual dreams at all, nor did I want them or need them for relief. The pressure went away once lust went away.

Now, I use dreams as an indicator of how well I am letting go of lust. If I have a dream, I immediately begin to search my memory of the past day or two and figure out what lust I didn't let go of, and I let go of it again and again until it stops coming back to my mind. I find something I had been holding onto every single time, and the dreams go away once I have let go of that thing. In this way, I have been able to be aware of when I'm not letting go of lust. This awareness is essential for maintaining freedom from these addictions. This awareness is so easy to lose over time without some sort of indicator like dreams.

SURRENDER BEFORE SLEEP

Speaking of dreams, I have learned to take a few minutes before bedtime and think back on the day to see if any triggering memories from the day pop up. I have learned that if anything pops up, I didn't really let go of it during the day, and so I have to let go of the thought or visual again and again until it stops coming back to my mind.

When I do this, I have a more pure sobriety and am much more lust free, and the lustful dreams don't happen. Again, I don't know how this works, but it does. I talked to someone who was at an earlier stage of recovery who had tried this, and he said that unless he was in a really good place spiritually, thinking back on the day would bring up things that they were unable to let go of and it ended up making things worse. Through that experience, I have learned that I must be in a good spiritual place and must be able and willing to surrender my lust before I can use this technique successfully.

THE "LUST BALLOON"

When I entered the program, I acted out almost daily. As I progressed, I would end up acting out weekly, then every two weeks, then every month, etc. It seems to me as though I have some sort of capacity to hold lust within me. I'll call it a lust balloon. Once I have filled this balloon to capacity with lust, it explodes (figuratively speaking), and I feel compelled to resort to my addiction through acting out physically.

There seem to be three things I can do with a lustful thought: 1…Let it go completely (surrender) and voluntarily, 2…White knuckle it down into my subconscious, or 3…Dwell on it and feed it until it overpowers me. When I let go of all lust completely (which capacity gradually increases as I work the Steps and connect with others in regular recovery meetings), the lust balloon never fills up, and I am never compelled to resort to my addiction. If I let go of 95 percent and stuff the other 5 percent into my subconscious, then the lust balloon may take two weeks to fill up, and then I am at the point of being compelled to resort to my addiction. If I dwell on it in my conscious mind, then the balloon fills up quickly, and I end up acting out later that day.

Letting go of lust for me takes a prayer telling God that I am willingly giving Him this temptation (not "take it from me" as I grip it tightly), praying for the person I'm lusting after, and when those don't make it go away, calling another member of the group to explain to them (without graphic detail) what I'm struggling with and surrendering it to God while on the phone. I don't know why that works, but it does. It does. At first, when I gave my struggles (and this works with any temptation, resentment, etc. too) to Christ, I only imagined the thought or temptation going out of me, but one day I decided to visualize it going to Christ and Him struggling with it for me. Boy did that change my experience! It deepened my appreciation of what He really has done for me and it also helped me to realize that I don't know Him well enough! The man I was giving my temptations to was a stranger to me and it gave me a deep desire to know Him more fully.

Of course, my ability to let go of lust completely depends largely upon my attending meetings and thereby increasing my faith in Christ and my humility (self awareness). I won't let go of lust or any other sin or drug if I don't have more faith in Christ than I have in that drug. And I can't let go of something that I don't even know I'm holding onto.

TRAVELING AND UNSTRUCTURED TIME

For some reason, when my surroundings or schedules change, usually by traveling somewhere or during a holiday season, triggers get stronger. Some boundaries that are usually in place, like Internet filters or TV channel filters, may not be in place in my new surroundings. Idle time is deadly. It has been said that Christ chose His disciples when they were at work and Satan chooses his disciples when they are idle.

There may also be family-related triggers around holidays. Making some arrangements to call a member of the group each day while traveling or during a holiday helps a lot. This is especially the case for many people if they are traveling home to their parents. It seems that many of the issues they had growing up come back to trouble them, and they look to numb those issues out through the addiction.

Unstructured time also seems to be a trigger. It's important to have a purpose and a schedule during times when there's nothing on my schedule. This could be on weekends or during breaks from school or work.

PRAY FOR HER

One other method that I learned from others and that I have used is to pray for the person I am lusting after. Pray for them to have a good day, to get married in the temple, to overcome the challenges they face, etc. This changes the selfish lust into giving blessings and turns the "object" I'm lusting after back into a child of God who has thoughts, feelings, dreams, and who cries and is joyful just like I am.

CONNECTIONS

Before recovery, almost all of my connections with women were lustful and dysfunctional. When I got into recovery, I started disconnecting in those lustful ways from women - largely through surrendering lust as described above and through avoiding people and places. A few years later, I started to feel a sadness about being isolated away from half of the people around me because of my fears and triggers. A counselor I was seeing at the time suggested that I try connecting in a healthy way by saying "hi" and getting to know people just as I would a man or someone I wasn't triggered by. It is important that I point out that I could not do this earlier in my recovery or these attempted connections would have gone back to being lust based. Amazingly, when I said "hi" the lust disappeared and the anxiety left me as well. To those to whom I couldn't say "hi" or that it wouldn't be appropriate to say "hi", I would think about going up to them in my mind and tell them "I just objectified you and I'm sorry for that, I hope you have a good day" without them saying anything back (in my mind) and that helped me as well. Again, I could not do this before a few years into physical sobriety from the addiction, but now I feel that through positive healthy simple connections, I can have freedom from the anxiety and temptations that up to that point I just had to wait around for and then let go of when they came along. It's amazing but it does take a lot of time and complete honesty. Again, this progression took years and had to be taken in the right order and at the right time, but with each step, I found more freedom and happiness.

Years of addiction had really messed me up and it takes a while for God (with my help) to untangle that mess. I don't know if I'll ever run out of things for God to untangle, but that's ok, because at each stage, from the first moment I stepped into a recovery group, I have had more and more freedom, hope, happiness, and motivation to keep going.

"Take it from Me"

Many times I would find myself praying for God to take this addiction from me. In my mind I would quietly and subconsciously add, "so that I don't have to give it up of my own free will." He won't take it from me against my will. He'll wait until I get strong enough to give it to him of my own free will, kind of like putting it on an altar and walking away from it and then letting him burn it away.

Good Music

I have found good music to be very helpful in fulfilling some of my spiritual needs. Good music means music that helps me to feel the Spirit instead of music that pounds my spirit numb. I used to use music to numb myself in the same way I can use pornography or substances to numb myself. Good music has become a way to re-sensitize myself and help me to be more sensitive to the Spirit's gentle promptings.

ADDICTION SWITCHING

Speaking of using music to numb myself, I have found that I can switch between addictions quite easily. Some people switch between abusing drugs and using pornography. Some switch to video games. Books, hard music, caffeine, and junk food are also very common things to switch to for comfort, numbing, or escape from the pains of reality. Other more emotional addictions I can switch to are resentment, fear, co-dependency, aspiring to high callings, etc.

I have found that as I turn to these various addictions instead of turning to Christ for comfort, it's as though I am putting other Gods - the Gods of addiction - before Him. Oh, and that doesn't work very well for me. Resorting to any of these addictions halts or slows my progression.

IT GOT WORSE BEFORE IT GOT BETTER

When I stopped acting out and lusting, things got worse! What? I thought things would get better when I stopped acting out. Why are things getting worse? I learned that I had been using these addictions to escape and numb out the negative feelings I experienced. For example, if I were feeling depressed or unloved or worthless, I'd resort to my addiction to cover those feelings instead of looking to the Atonement and Christ and His sacrifice for me to derive my sense of self worth.

So, when I stopped acting out, these unresolved feelings of anger, resentment, fear, depression, etc. that had built up throughout my life came bursting out. Many times this convinced me to run back to the addiction instead of waiting for God to help me feel better. The analogy below touches on this concept also.

ONE DAY AT A TIME

This general concept deals with breaking things into manageable pieces as well as living in the now instead of the past or future. I don't sabotage myself with thoughts of how I'm going to stay sober for the rest of my life – just for the rest of this minute, hour, or day. I don't beat myself up because of the past. I learn from it and apply those lessons to this minute or this hour. Living life one day at a time, one hour at a time, or one minute at a time helps me to not become overwhelmed and it just works.

SELF-SABOTAGE

During the time between getting into the program and getting some serious sobriety, there was a time of self-sabotage. I really just wanted to resort to my addiction, and so I'd find ways to do it by crossing boundaries, neglecting my needs (like food, sleep, or scripture study) to make myself weaker, surfing for seemingly innocent things that I know might accidentally lead me to something bad, but at least it wouldn't be my fault that I accidentally found something bad, right? Insanity.

These were attempts for me to resort to my addiction without feeling quite as guilty. These things pass, once the part of me that wants to quit gets stronger than the part of me that wants to resort to my addiction, so just be patient and keep coming to the meetings and working the steps. It will get better.

THE BANDAGE

I learn by analogy, and so I will share an analogy that has helped me to understand these addictions better. A certain man got wounded, and he didn't know how to take care of the wound. He did not clean it out, apply ointment, or put a bandage over the wound to protect it. After a while, the wound got infected. It was painful and wasn't very pleasant to look at, and so he put a bandage over it. That kept things from bumping into it and kept it from being so unpleasant to look at. This worked for a short time. After a while, the bandage started to leak and the pain got worse, so the man put another bandage on the one that was already there. It worked last time, so it might just work again. After all, it would be too painful to pull off the bandage and clean it out. This continued until the pain and mess became unmanageable. The only option was to pull off each bandage and then clean out the wound, apply ointment, and then put a bandage over the now cleaned wound so that it could heal properly.

In this analogy, the wound represents the unresolved issues from my past – the things that I got rid of in steps 4 through 9. The bandages placed over the infected wounds are my addictive behaviors and my pride. These serve to numb out the pain and keep me from addressing the real problems within me. Addiction (or sin that is too much for me to overcome on my own) and pride are just painkillers to cover the pain of an infected spiritual wound.

SHARING EXPERIENCE, STRENGTH, AND HOPE

By following a simple rule, I get the most out of my sharing whether that sharing happens in a meeting as a participant or as a facilitator or if I'm on a phone call or as a sponsor. The rule is this: I share my own personal experience – what did "I" do this week or during my lifetime of recovery and what was the result of "my" actions? That's all. There are many things that this does. It keeps the "philosophies of men" out of the meeting or phone call. If I'm just sharing what I did and what happened as a result, that's pure truth and the Spirit can confirm the truthfulness of it. If I start preaching, I might end up injecting my own ideas into what's going on and they may be wrong and the Spirit can't confirm that.

As a member of the group, I don't have the authority or stewardship to suggest to someone else what he or she should do. Preaching to the group and telling them what they should do or how they should work the steps or what "we" should do is not my job. My job as a member of the group is to talk about what "I" did this week and what happened to me as a result of my actions – sharing my experience, strength, and hope with others. Having worked all 12 steps is one prerequisite for becoming a facilitator perhaps for just this reason. If I haven't worked Step 10, for example, how am I supposed to share my experience with it? If I haven't worked a step but must share about it, I would then have to resort to preaching about it instead of sharing my non-existent experience about it.

I really don't know what is best for other members of the group and so telling them what they should do may even get in the way of their own progress. I leave the saving of others up to God. He actually knows what He's doing in their lives. I don't.

The same principle of sharing experience and not suggesting or guiding applies to facilitating a meeting or taking a phone call from someone else in the group. If someone calls me and they're having a problem, instead of suggesting things for them to do, I just tell them of experiences I had that are similar and what I did that worked for me. If I'm facilitating a meeting, I just share my experience that I had with the step being studied and what worked for me, and that's it.

I also shared two or three other specific pieces of information, which kept me focused on what works. I shared my length of sobriety (which was difficult to do when I only had a day or less every week), which step I am currently working on, and in some meetings, I would report the number of phone calls to other members in the group I had made that week.

Being "Healed of this Addiction"

Many times, I (and others I have listened to) say that they want to be "healed of this addiction." Many times, what they mean by that is that they want to never be tempted again. In my experience, that's not how this works. I was not "healed" from ever being tempted by these addictions again. The healing I have seen in myself happens at a much deeper level than the addiction, and so the need for the addiction as a painkiller becomes diminished.

At the same time, my faith in Christ increases so that I end up wanting Him and His peace more than I want the false relief of the addiction. Before, I couldn't choose to resort to my addiction or not. Now I can choose to resort to my addiction or not. I can choose!

I don't want my agency to be "healed" or taken away from me, I want my defects to be healed and faith to be increased so that I can finally choose to walk away from these addictions in peace. This has happened to me, and it is a wonderful place to be. Of course, since I still have agency, I must maintain the humility and faith necessary to remain free by choosing to walk away from addiction and sin.

PRAY FOR EACH OTHER

Praying for other members of the group gets me out of my selfishness and also adds strength to the other members and also builds unity. I can pray for them to have a good day, to have more faith, to get to the meetings, to work the program, etc.

MARRIAGE DOESN'T CURE THIS

I once thought that lust was just a normal appetite, and therefore, once I got married, the addiction would be satisfied and go away. I learned, mainly through the experience of others I have met in the 12 Step groups, that this is a false assumption. Most I know end up returning to these addictions within a few weeks or months of getting married.

The reason for this seems to be that lust is never satisfied, and it gets bored with the same thing. That's why a twelve-year old boy doesn't get one pornographic picture and keep it, never looking at anything else for the rest of his life. He must always have something different. His wife becomes his next piece of pornography, and then he must move on to something else once the lust is no longer satisfied by her.

Lust is unnatural and must be replaced by love. Love is connected to just one person at a time, forever, and it is completely satisfied with that person. Lust can be transferred from one person to the next. Love is giving and lust is taking. Repeatedly conditioning myself with lust decreased my ability to love, but in sobriety and recovery I am reversing that process.

CODEPENDENCY

Codependency is a universal underlying addiction that I found out about around a year after giving up the addiction (as do many others I have talked to). Just as removing the main surface addiction reveals resentments and fears, removing some of those things then reveals codependent behaviors, whether speaking of marriage (or facilitating or sponsoring).

So, what is codependency? In my experience, it is simply when I am dependent upon someone else for my happiness. They in turn can be dependent upon me for their happiness, turning it into a vicious cycle. Perhaps a few examples will clear up this abstract idea. The wife of a person addicted to pornography could feel sadness when her spouse falters in his addiction. Thus her happiness is tied to his acting out or not acting out. When she is sad or angry because he has faltered, he can also become sad. When I need someone else to behave a certain way in order for me to be happy, I then feel a need to control his or her behavior, so that I can be happy.

So a wife may feel the need to control what her husband does or experiences so that he won't falter so that she won't be sad. A husband, knowing that his wife depends on him being perfect with regard to his addiction, might decide to control her environment by not being truthful with her regarding him faltering in his addiction. I have found that control or unrighteous dominion is one result of codependency.

In one case, I personally was dependent upon my wife being happy for me to be happy. She was dependent upon the kids being obedient for her to be happy. Therefore, I had to control the kids to make them obedient so that my wife would be happy so that I would be happy. Once I figured out what I was doing, I stopped controlling the kids, but quickly resorted to telling my wife what to do to control the kids. So my codependency was now four levels deep: I controlled my wife to control the kids to keep her happy so I could be happy. Codependency can get really messy and I have found that the spirit is not with me when I engage in the powerful addiction of codependency.

In the context of facilitating a 12 Step group, my happiness may be dependent upon how well people in the group are doing or how big the group is getting or how much people in the group praise what I'm doing or how smart they think I am. If this is the case, I may feel that I have to preach or give the members of the group a sales pitch to save them from walking away from the group meetings because of ignorance or a lack of faith in the program or in Christ. This is a particularly deadly practice because I have seen the spirit leave me as a facilitator as I resorted to this addiction of codependency. Without the spirit, nothing else matters. It is very easy for me as a facilitator to become the savior or salesman for the group when I'm struggling with codependency issues.

One of the main focuses of the family support groups (that go along with the 12 Step groups for those with sexual addiction) is overcoming codependency. Many times it's easy for family members to become addicted to monitoring and trying to control the one with the sexual addiction's behavior because they feel their own happiness is dependent upon them. When codependent, the family member can become miserable each time the one with the addiction falters. So the family member, not wanting to be miserable, will try to control or help them to not falter. From what I have learned from people who attend these family support groups, they learn to rely on God for their happiness instead of relying on the perfection of an imperfect human, and they become happier and less controlling because they don't need to any more because their happiness comes from their dependency upon God and Jesus Christ.

The only way I have found to overcome codependency is to work the 12 Steps and try to be aware of when I'm controlling and surrender my will to not do that. As my faith in Christ increases, my dependence upon other people decreases, and that's the only way out that I know of. Just like any other addiction, codependency seems to permeate every relationship I have in one way or another, and I have found that escaping this addiction little by little is very rewarding and liberating.

BUMP ON A LOG

I found that once I was able to completely give up lust, I became a bump on a log when it came to appropriate intimacy. This is because I had been approaching intimacy in Satan's way my whole life, through compulsion. I would feed lust until I was compelled into intimacy.

I found that I had to give and serve of my own free will and choice instead of having lust compel me toward intimacy (sometimes against my own will). I have learned that it takes a long time to distinguish between lust and love. I had to be patient and work the steps and the program, and things gradually came together. I still have a long way to go.

PRIDE

I have found that pride is similar to codependency in its sneakiness. One good way for me to detect pride in myself is how good of a follower I am. In the context of being a facilitator, for example, I can ask myself if I am following the guidelines (and my leaders) or not. If I am following them, am I following them with all my heart, wanting them to work, and thereby I am being a good follower? If I do my own things that I think are better, then I am seeking praise for doing those things because my idea was better than the program's. This is the same thing Satan did with God's plan. If Satan is anything like me when I'm doing this, he didn't want to follow the plan because he could get glory for coming up with a better way of doing things.

In the context of my main addictions, pride can blind me to my weakness, and like the addiction itself, can numb me to the point that I don't think I need God's help. The only way I have found to keep from falling to pride is through contact with group members through phone calls or at meetings. I am, through that contact, constantly reminded of my weaknesses and strengths and am kept on track.

SELF CONFIDENCE

I found over time that I started to have more self confidence, not just with being able to choose what's right with regard to the addiction, but in standing up for myself. It's strange, but it seems that since I was so riddled with guilt and shame all these years I felt like I deserved anything that anyone did to me that was mean or abusive. I felt I had earned it. I was beating myself up so much that I welcomed it when others did the same - hey I deserved it, right. It was like it was my punishment for doing so much wrong. Once I stopped beating myself up so much, I started being offended when others would beat me up and I would stand up for myself. It was scary at first and I had feelings of hypocracy and unworthiness, but each time I did it, it got easier. Another thing I realized was that there was a wrong way to stand up for myself (which was to be mean back to the person) and a right way (simply stating how I felt when the person did what they did and if needed, distance myself from them without resentment or hatred).

IMPECCABLE HONESTY

If I can't be honest, I can't heal or progress. If I can't share exactly where I am, not just with the group, but more importantly with myself, how can I see what really needs to happen for me to progress? I lie (or rationalize, minimize, omit details, intellectualize, etc.) to myself and others because of shame. Ironically, being honest against the fear of shame in the safety of the group helps my shame disappear. I can share where I'm at (without graphic details) and what I'm struggling with or having success with and people start nodding their heads in understanding instead of running from the room in horror! No shame there. I can then learn to stop shaming myself and can then become impeccably honest. Then Christ can heal me. If I go to the doctor and say "I'm ok - it's not that bad" the doctor will ask me why I'm there and will send me on my way. The same seems to be true with my Heavenly Father - until I'm willing and able to be completely honest with myself and others, I can't truly be honest with Him and He won't reward my dishonesty by helping me. He seems to wait until I'm ready to come to Him (and myself and others) with the truth, then He starts working miracles.

THE RESULT

Though my journey toward recovery is difficult, I am happy now and have enjoyed a few years of freedom from the compulsion of these addictions. Someone who is stuck in the middle of these addictions asked me if this is all worth it. If giving up the addiction is really worth all of this trouble. They also asked me how much better it was to be free of it than to give into it. On the surface, the answers to these questions may seem obvious, but to the person trapped in this nightmare, there is real doubt that escaping it is truly worth it.

His questions made me think. Has this been worth it? How do I know? The first thing I told him was that being able to stand up straight before God and know that I'm doing what He wants me to do instead of cowering behind some rock fearing that God doesn't love me or care about me is a thousand times better and is completely worth it. And that's just the beginning. If that was the only thing I got out of it, that would definitely be completely worth it. However, escaping addiction with Christ's help has opened up a whole new world of progress to me that I had never even thought about. I have become more patient and loving, less abrasive and sarcastic, etc. These things didn't come automatically as I left the addiction, but leaving the addiction allowed me to start working on them and actually make true progress. I now see why Satan wants me to sin. It stops me from becoming more Christ-like. It stops my eternal progression. I have so much more progress to make, but at least now I am able to make it.

I also told him that one reason that the addiction might look better than recovery is the same reason that a starving man just loves to eat garbage. A starving man who hasn't eaten in weeks just loves to get his hands on garbage. It's the best thing in the world! However, if a man is not starving, garbage suddenly doesn't look so appetizing. A man who is eating good food and eating regularly won't have the starvation necessary to compel him to eat garbage. When in the addiction, I was believing in a false dichotomy; that I had only two options: 1...Depression and misery, or 2...Acting out the addiction. When I thought I had only those two choices, I picked number 2. I have found now that there's a third choice: Recovery and joy through Christ.

When I resorted to these addictions, my soul was starving to the point of death, and so the addiction looked like an acceptable escape from my starvation. The problem is that the addiction is worse than garbage because it actually takes more energy out of my starving soul than it pretends to put in. Life is good now, and I choose, one day at a time, one hour at a time, one minute at a time, to stay sober and live life to its fullest. Thanks for letting me share.

APPENDIX B

SUPPORT FOR WOMEN WHO STRUGGLE WITH SEXUAL ADDICTION

Written by LDS women who are in recovery from sexual addiction.

This information is intended to help ecclesiastical leaders, parents and women understand and recognize the patterns of behavior in sexual addiction. It consists of some questions that can help determine if a woman has a sexual addiction, suggested questions and responses when interviewing and reaching out to those struggling with this challenging problem.

For many women, sexual addictive tendencies can start at a very young age. However, many years may pass before the actual sexual addiction is manifested. Some women started in their addiction very innocently, not comprehending that what they were doing was wrong. Sometimes sexual addiction may begin out of curiosity as they have innocently begun to self stimulate, not understanding what they were experiencing. They only knew that what they were doing was creating a feeling that was powerfully enjoyable. Many others were exposed to pornography at early stages of their lives, or were sexually, verbally or physically abused as a child. Others may have had emotionally traumatic experiences that propelled them into their addiction. When a child becomes emotionally wounded through abuse, many seek escape from the emotional pain they are feeling through sexual acting out. Sadly, some women were raped as children and/or as teenagers and others may have been pressured or forced into sexual experiences by peers and/or boyfriends. They were vulnerable to these demands because they were seeking love and acceptance. In any case, it is essential to comprehend that something has "triggered" them and lured and seduced them into sexual addiction.

Sexual addictions in women are increasingly becoming more common. Television, movies, magazines and music videos promote decadent sexuality as good, desirable and acceptable but never reveal the negative consequences of these behaviors. Many are constantly influenced and exposed to the following sexually damaging behaviors:

- "Acting out" through inappropriate sexual encounters with men or young men is common in both younger and older sexually addicted women. This can include, but is not limited to: sexually suggestive or explicit conversations either in person, on the phone, texting or on the Internet; petting; heavy passionate kissing; sexual acting out while remaining clothed; and giving or receiving oral sex.

- Behaviors may or may not include sexual intercourse. A very common symptom among sexually addicted females is fantasizing or daydreaming about "acting out" in different ways. This problem is enhanced and cultivated through romance novels and movies. These "so called" romance books and movies can become powerfully addictive. Women are very vulnerable to become addicted to sexual fantasy.

- Often the addiction begins with thoughts, which eventually lead to actions. Some women are addicted to pornography in the same manner that men are addicted, which may also involve masturbation (self-stimulation). The pornography industry has been targeting women for several decades. They have completed research and developed pornography sites just for the purpose of seducing and capturing women.

Some questions that may be helpful for individual women in determining if they are sexually addicted:

- Do you seek situations (dances, parties, concerts, etc.) that awaken sexual feelings?

- Do you fantasize sexual encounters you read about in a book or see on a screen?
- Do you sometimes fantasize about men and their attraction towards you?
- Do you dress or put yourself in situations for the purposes of sexually attracting men?
- Do you watch sexually explicit scenes in movies?
- Do you have sexually suggestive or explicit conversations in chatrooms, on the phone, or through instant messaging?
- Do you engage in sexual behavior on the phone or on web cam?
- Do you watch the sexual behavior of others on web cam?
- Do you send or receive pornographic pictures of your self or of your friends?
- Do you regularly seek out and view pornography?
- Do you regularly turn to masturbation for comfort or stress relief?
- Have you ever thought you needed help for your sexual thinking or behavior?
- Do you resort to sexual activities to escape, to relieve anxiety, because you can't cope, or to feel loved?
- Do you feel guilt, remorse or depression afterward?
- Has your pursuit of sexual activities become more compulsive?
- If you are married, does this compulsion interfere with intimacy in your marriage?
- Do you resort to sexual images or sexual memories in order to have intimacy with a spouse?
- Does an irresistible sexual impulse arise when another person flirts with you or sex is offered?
- Do you keep going from one "relationship" or lover to another?
- Are you involved in several sexually suggestive or emotionally intimate relationships at the same time, either online or in person?
- Do you feel the "right relationship" would help you stop lusting, masturbating, or being promiscuous?

- Do you have a destructive need - a desperate sexual or emotional need - for someone?
- Does the pursuit of sexual activities make you careless for yourself or the welfare of your family or others? Do you lose time from work for it and risk being fired?
- Has your effectiveness or concentration decreased as your sexual behavior has become more compulsive?
- Are sexual urges interfering with your daily activities?
- Do you turn to a lower environment when pursuing sex? Anyone, anywhere?
- Do you want to get away from the sexual partner as soon as possible after the encounter?
- Although your spouse is sexually compatible, do you still masturbate or have sex with others?
- Have you ever thought that you should stop "giving in" to your sexual behaviors?
- Do you feel sexual urges are controlling your life?
- Have you ever tried to stop or limit doing what you felt was wrong in your sexual behavior?

Some questions that may be helpful for ecclesiastical leaders and parents in determining if a woman or girl is sexually addicted:

- Are you currently or have you ever regularly participated in self-stimulation (masturbation) to achieve a desired sexual response?
- Are you reading sexually explicit romance books or are you watching sexually explicit videos or movies?
- Are you involved in sexual conversations on the phone or Internet or sexual texting with others?
- Are you seeking out sexual encounters with others?
- How long have you been struggling with these type of behaviors?
- Are you ready and willing to seek help to overcome these struggles?

Suggestions for leaders and parents in supporting a woman or young woman who may be exhibiting symptoms of a sexual addiction:

DO

- Assure her that she is loved. Heavenly Father still loves her and she needs to be reassured that He does. Parents need to express their love and encouragement for her as well.
- Prayerfully ask the appropriate questions. It is important to understand the types of sexual behaviors that she is involved with her addiction without going into explicit details.
- Witness to them that through the Atonement of Jesus Christ she can receive the forgiveness and the strength and support needed to overcome this powerful and destructive addiction. Encourage her to find help through the LDS Family Services 12 Step Recovery Program. (This may not be available in all areas, and in that case, other 12 Step programs can be helpful too.)
- Help them find professional counseling if they feel they desire it. Oftentimes a licensed therapist experienced in addiction recovery can offer help in ways an ecclesiastical leader and parent can't.
- Ecclesiastical leaders are encouraged to regularly meet with women who are seeking to overcome addiction. Having someone to counsel with on a regular basis will help to spiritually strengthen her recovery. Never give up on their recovery. It takes time and commitment on the part of those in addiction to make progress. These women need to regularly attend support group meetings for however long it takes to find healing and recovery. Relapses are not uncommon, but can become learning experiences for those struggling with addiction and eventually help them find full recovery.

DON'T

- Don't make her think she is a unique or rare case. She is not alone and needs to know there are many others struggling with this same addiction. The shame she feels can be very debilitating.

- Don't be afraid about what you may hear. She needs to feel safe and to be able to trust that she can confide in you. If you act nervous about what she may say, she may be reluctant to talk to you again. You do not have to know specific details, but she does need to feel validated and have the opportunity to confess and begin repentance.
- Don't push or force her into recovery. Recovery is always a choice and it needs to be her choice.
- Don't excuse masturbation as nothing. It is HUGE! It is a brain drug addiction that completely interferes with recovery. It is just as serious as pornography or other issues involving young men or men. It needs to be addressed with as much seriousness as any other sexual sin.
- Don't mistakenly think that if she has never had sex, she is not struggling with sexual addiction. Many women/young women caught in sexual addiction have never been intimate with a man/young man. Many may have been sexually addicted for years before acting on their addiction with someone else.

Sexual addiction is becoming a plague in the modern world. Pornography is everywhere, although many people are not aware of its influence and do not recognize where it exists. Some different types of pornography include:

Obvious ones such as:

- Pornographic Internet sites
- Pornographic magazines, movies, and videos
- Sex scenes in movies and television
- Sending inappropriate pictures to friends' phones ("sexting")
- Listening to music with sexually explicit lyrics

Not so obvious ones such as:

- Romance novels and other sexually stimulating books (i.e. Harlequin, Kensington, Avon, Twilight Series, Romance E-Books, etc.)
- Fantasizing and sexualizing yourself through using role-playing computer games or other virtual reality sites on the Internet

- Most teens' and women's magazines
- Immodest and provocative clothing
- "Sex talk"/"dirty talking" with friends or significant others, either on the phone, via chat/instant messaging, or in person Crude sexual jokes
- Non-pornographic Internet sights that facilitate emotional connections (i.e. Myspace, Facebook, etc.)
- Advertisements where the models are not fully clothed
- Many PG-13 and even PG movies contain sexually stimu- lating conversations and scenes

A key element in avoiding this type of addiction is education. We must teach our children and our young women and young men about the dangers of pornography and sexual "acting out". We must not be afraid to teach them how addictive these behaviors can become. The more they know, the more empowered they are to avoid it. Parents and spouses need to comprehend that sexual addiction can afflict anyone. Sexual addiction is not gender or age specific. Even those who are raised in loving, stable, religious families can become trapped in this addiction. Both young and adult church members who are regularly attending may be afflicted with this powerful addiction.

Many women, who have struggled with sexual addiction and have found recovery, witness that their best help has been the support of an understanding and encouraging ecclesiastical leader, good friends in a 12 Step support group and a loving and supportive family. When ecclesiastical leaders are willing to confidently ask appropriate ques- tions, many women begin to realize they have an addiction and be- come empowered to seek help. Addiction is not something that can be overcome by will or determination – the very definition of addic- tion denotes that those caught in this trap cannot stop on their own. They need help. Recovery is possible! Most women know that what they are doing is wrong and they need someone to lovingly confront them about their behavior. They also need to believe that Heavenly Father still loves them and that repentance and forgiveness are avail- able to them through the Atonement of Jesus Christ.

STORY 1:
FINDING HEALING
FROM EMOTIONAL SCARS

I am a female in recovery from sexual addiction. From the time I was born, my life was filled with many challenges and struggles. An unstable home environment, physical and sexual abuse, and my mother's struggle with two failed marriages all contributed to severe emotional scars that impacted my ability to feel safe and loved.

I was born to a loving mother and a very abusive father. He would manipulate my mother by threatening that if she didn't do what he wanted he would injure me. He beat my mother severely enough that my mother went to the emergency room. This abuse continued until my mother was brave enough to leave the marriage. She was granted a divorce, but unfortunately for me the State decided that I had to continue visiting my father until I was eleven years of age. My brother and I both experienced continual physical and emotional abuse while visiting in my father's home.

As a single parent, my mother decided to return to school to improve her education. Starting at age three, I was left home with various sitters and family members. My sitter would show me attention and started sexually molesting me. This caused a physical reaction in me that I have fought for years to overcome. I felt many conflicting emotions because as a hurt and lonely little girl it felt good to feel some sort of physical love even though it was molestation. I was finally able to tell someone about the molestation and it was reported to the police and the sitter was taken away. However, the damaging impact of emotional and sexual abuse had inflicted great harm upon me, which as a small child I wasn't capable of processing.

In time, my mother married again. My new stepfather was wonderful – at least at first. He always seemed to want to touch me or play with me. Because of the previous struggles in my young life, I was a very angry and rage-filled child. My stepfather would give me a back rub to help calm me down. Unfortunately, he used the massages to begin molesting me. When I tried to talk to my mom about it she didn't believe me. Due to the impact of the sexual abuse and the lack of support I was getting, I began reacting with anger towards my parents. I would scream, hit and kick my mother and stepfather. Out of desperation and frustration, I would run away. I began a pattern of lying and stealing to get what I wanted. Because of the abuse by my father and stepfather, I came to the conclusion that if you try to love someone you will end up being hurt by them. As a result, I became filled with anger and manipulative of others. I learned to trust no one. My mother tried to help me by placing me in many facilities for out of control children. None of these places really helped, I just felt even more abandoned and out of control.

My mother finally divorced my stepfather and in time married again. My third stepfather was everything I had been missing in a father. He disciplined me and made our house a home. Because of his influence I started to try to control my anger and my out-of-control behavior. I began to understand some of the confusing feelings that had contributed to my anger and rage. I know that I owe much of my life and happiness to his lessons and his love. He is the one who finally convinced me that I had taken enough abuse from my biological father and he convinced the courts that I didn't have to see him anymore. That started helping me to trust men again, although it wasn't very easy.

Sadly, no human being can take away all emotional pain and I began to turn to books for some measure of comfort. It started out with fantasy books. They would take me to faraway places that didn't have horrible fathers who abuse you. I could leave the challenging life I had endured behind. I stumbled upon my first pornographic book when I was about twelve. It came in the form of a romance novel. By then my mom was so used to me always having my nose in a book that she didn't think anything of it. I began to feel strong sexual reactions that were fueled from my early molestations. The sexual feelings that this created in me made me want to escape even more.

From then on I would do anything to get a book with sex in it. I bought used book and I began stealing books. I found a neighbor who also had an addiction to sexual romance books and I was able to get them from her. I loved imagining myself feeling loved again. My child abuse had polluted my understanding of being loved and so the romance books supported my confused understanding of what love was. I became deceived that love had nothing to do with an emotional and loving relationship. It was just about sex. I kept trying to stop reading the books but I couldn't. I recall throwing a book across the room trying to get away from the words and feelings in the book but they haunted me and wouldn't leave me.

The damaging process had begun through the sexual romance books and slowly with each passing boyfriend I began acting upon my sexual fantasies and going just a little bit farther with each one, until I had lost my virginity by age sixteen. I deluded myself into feeling that the only way I would fill the dark, gaping emotional hole inside me was to make myself into an object to be loved. I was not being loved as a real person. To obtain this confused image of love, I became a chameleon. I tried to be what I thought people wanted me to be. I grew increasingly empty with each passing relationship. I didn't care that my grades were failing or that my relationship with my mother and new stepfather were crumbling. All I wanted was my sexual "fix" so that I would be able to survive life.

In this incredibly vulnerable state, my family moved to another town where I lost any support for making better choices, and I felt so alone. The worst word in the dictionary to me is the word "ALONE". It terrified me. So I did the only thing I knew how to do, which was to find a boyfriend and get out of the pain of everything through finding my comfort in a sexual relationship. I found someone. Even though I hated him, I needed him to act out my sexual addiction. When addiction is your master there is no logic or good choices involved, only the demands of the compulsive behaviors and powerful cravings. Finally, after running away for a night and lying about it, my parents sent me to a recovery center.

The center was a haven for my poor battered soul. In this environment I was faced with the reality of what my life had become and I received the opportunity to start applying the 12 Steps. They referred to a higher power to help you to get free from your addictive behaviors. I tried a lot of different higher powers but none of them seemed to work until I chose my Lord and Savior, Jesus Christ. I remember exactly where I was when I realized that sweet, sweet concept. I was lying in a girl's bedroom after the lights went out, and I realized I could not do this by myself anymore. I finally prayed to my Heavenly Father even though I had rejected him all the previous years in my life. I felt like I was placed underneath a waterfall of the Spirit, and I received a testimony of Jesus Christ and that He loves me. This witness and powerful love carried me until I graduated from the program at the recovery center.

Three months after I graduated, I relapsed back into my addiction worse than I had ever relapsed before. I reverted back to sexually addictive relationships, dating online, and one-night stands. I realized I was out of control! This time I knew what I needed to do to find peace. I went cold turkey from my addictive patterns, but I was afraid to go back to church and face the disappointment of my Savior. My mom bribed one of my friends to take me to church on Sunday. The lesson was on the law of chastity and keeping yourself clean for your future husband. My perception of what my life had become was completely shattered. I felt like it was a message from my Heavenly Father to get my act together and prepare myself for the time when I would meet my husband. I decided to meet with my bishop regularly and I practically ignored all men. I discovered my testimony of Christ's atonement again and became ready to take the sacrament. With the help of my bishop I felt that I was better prepared for marriage when I eventually found and married my husband in the temple.

After I was married, I became angry, co-dependent and emotionally dysfunctional again. Our relationship began to crumble from the moment we returned from our honeymoon. For a time I lost the relationship with my Heavenly Father again. I expected my husband to fill the gaping, emotional hole in me that had been there for so long. I had unrealistic expectations of what to expect from my husband. We tried going to counseling and talking with our bishop but nothing seemed to fix our relationship. The biggest step in the saving of our marriage was when my husband and I got pregnant, only to lose our baby a few weeks into the pregnancy. At this point I hit rock bottom, and could no longer depend on myself for anything. I became sick after the miscarriage and was bed-ridden. I had to depend on my husband for everything. I was reminded once again of my powerlessness and how I desperately needed to rely upon my Heavenly Father. As I began to rely upon the Savior, He began to heal me from the emotional pain I was feeling from the loss of our baby.

After the loss of our child, a missionary in the LDS 12 Step Addiction Recovery Program spoke in my mother's ward. He said that there were support group meetings to help both men and women who struggle with sexual addictions. My mother, being the wonderful woman that she is, volunteered me to attend the support group meeting for women in sexual addiction. I began attending the meetings and was invited to become a facilitator in the LDS 12 Step PASG Addiction Recovery Program.

I think the first beginning months of participating in this program were more for me than for anyone else. I recovered from the pain of the loss of my unborn child, as well as from everything that had ever happened to me – the abuse, the neglect, and all the hurt I had caused myself by participating in sexual addiction. By continuing to apply the 12 Steps I deepened my resolve to get to know and trust my Savior every day. This spiritual understanding takes time to fully apply. My marriage improved by leaps and bounds and four months later I discovered that I was pregnant again. Imagine the fear I felt as I begged my Heavenly Father to not take another child from me. Then humility came over me as I finished that particular prayer with: "If it be Thy will that I lose another child to learn more about my recovery I will accept Thy plan for me."

That's when I realized how dedicated I am to the recovery program that we have. My whole life has been centered upon this God hole that was gaping open in my heart. No matter what I threw at the hole, it could not be filled. The 12 Steps have helped me learn to find the healing I finally needed and that healing could only come through the Savior.

I would like to describe my life to you now that I am in full recovery. I have a beautiful baby girl who is so precious to me. My husband and I are again best friends, like we were when we were dating, only our relationship is better because we rely upon our Savior who is with us in our home. I am assertive about my feelings and I have learned to not let them build up because of the fear of being misunderstood and rejected. As a facilitator, I currently serve my fellow sisters seeking recovery from addiction with joy. Each week I watch them go through the same journey that I have experienced with 12 Step recovery. I am motivated to serve my family and I have wonderful relationships with my parents and siblings.

Most importantly I know that my Savior is truly my Redeemer. I know that there is not another method on this earth that will bring the peace, love and joy that we need other than the Atonement of the Lord, Jesus Christ. I know that He "remembers my sins no more" and because of that I feel, like Alma, that my joy is greater than my sorrow. I know that true peace is possible because I have felt it in my own life and I encourage each of you to find out for yourself that He lives. For those of you reading my story please know that Jesus Christ and Heavenly Father love you and are there for you. There is hope for full freedom from your addiction.

STORY 2:
FROM A WOMAN JUST
BEGINNING TO SEEK
RECOVERY FROM
SEXUAL ADDICTION

Sexual addiction is difficult for many to comprehend or understand. It is the darkest, most hopeless and loneliest experience in life. During the times I indulged in my addiction, I felt like I was stuck in a sealed well – completely dark, cramped – with walls so high I couldn't see the top. All I could hear was my own echo as I called for help but was only met with silence; nothing but piercing silence… silence from my friends, from my family and from the Lord. I felt silence everywhere. I felt completely alone.

By nature we are social beings. Even if we are shy, everyone needs to know they are loved and cared for and that they hold a place on this earth and would be missed if they were gone. I began to doubt that anyone cared. I felt that no one loved me, and that I had no purpose and value in this life. Even if I tried my hardest, there would always be better, more righteous people than me. I felt that if I wasn't going to make it to the Celestial kingdom anyway, then why try at all? Why even BE here on this earth where people would waste their time and energy on me? I felt my spirit and my soul literally rot from the inside out.

So, I trudged through life, day after day, keeping a pasted smile on my face so no one would know the real pain that ruled every aspect of my life. Eventually, though, the darkness began to lift. Writing played a huge roll in lifting the despair I was feeling. I would just sit with pen and paper, and write for hours and hours, tears staining the pages. Then I would close my journal, and the pain would stay in the book. All my ugliness would pour through my fingers into the book and I could capture it there, and I would feel better.

Music was (and still is) another outlet for me. I relate to music so much. I can find music for any mood and relate to it. I have found though that I tend to mirror the music I listen to. If I am listening to "I hate myself and my life stinks" music, then that is how I'm going to feel. But, if I listen to more uplifting and meaningful music, then my heart is much lighter.

Another key element in my healing is meeting with my bishop. Satan works day and night to keep me down but I have found that he is left at the doorstep to the Church building when I see my bishop. My bishop's office is my sanctuary and I long for those meetings each week. I long for his council and the constant reminder *that my Father in Heaven does love me* - and eventually, I began to believe it.

I came to realize that the silence I thought I was feeling wasn't coming from my family, my friends and my Heavenly Father. *The silence was coming from within me.* It was all me, and I had the power to overcome it. All I had to do was believe. I had to reach out just a little, even though it was terrifying, and believe that someone would grab on and pull me out of that cold dark well. And I did. I decided to believe, because it was either believe, or be miserable the rest of my life. Once I reached out, I found so much love and warmth on the other side. Everyone whom I thought would not be there for me, or would judge – didn't. They embraced me.

I was absolutely terrified to go to a 12 Step recovery meeting. I was terrified that people would look at me and just KNOW, and I would know they knew. I was so fearful that I would see people that I would know. I realize now, that Satan was working mightily to keep me in that fearful state of mind. I am very fortunate to have a recovery friend who is in my ward. Over a few months our Bishop slowly got us together and we started communicating so neither of us felt alone. Through much prayer and discussion with my husband, I was able to muster up the courage to go to my first meeting, and I thank my Heavenly Father for carrying me there. When I first arrived at the meeting there was only one sister there. She welcomed me so warmly that I felt relatively comfortable. However, as I sat there and more women filtered in, I felt my fear returning. I shrunk in my seat and didn't make eye contact with anyone all the while holding my recovery book close to my chest not wanting anyone to see it. I found myself wondering what I was doing there, and how it would help me. At that time, I felt no one, and nothing could help me. However, as the meeting started and the facilitator began speaking, I felt the spirit enter the room and spoke firmly to me that I was in the right place. The tears immediately started streaming, and they really didn't stop until I went to bed that night. With each woman that shared, I felt not waves of shame, but waves of validation. Validation that I wasn't alone; that I wasn't just a sick and perverted person. Never in my life prior to that had I received ANY empathetic validation, and here I was suddenly faced with a room full of beautiful daughters of God that were faced with the same challenges and on the same journey as me.

At that time, I literally purged so much pain and anguish from me just through tears. I sobbed the entire meeting and it was so cleansing. I committed to myself that night that I would attend meetings as often as possible and I haven't missed one yet. I walk away from them with renewed hope each week that I am not alone in my journey. I have met many wonderful people at group that have lifted me many times since I started, and I only hope that I have, or will, return the service. I am most grateful to my Heavenly Father who has shown nothing but love and encouragement for me since I began this journey four months ago. I would not be where I am if it were not for his loving guidance and forgiveness. I pray constantly that women will be blessed with courage to see their Bishops and seek out our meetings. I feel so fortunate to be apart of such drastic life changing events in these women's' lives.

I struggle with my addiction on a daily basis. This world can be so dark and sometimes it just seems like it would be SO much easier to give up. But, as long as I keep focused on what is on the other side of my life, if I live it to its fullest, live it as a humble daughter of my Heavenly Father who loves me – then I feel purpose and I know the reward for doing what is right, and fighting this disease is far more rewarding than the instant pleasure I get from indulgence. My sexual addiction is only a symptom of a greater tragedy; not realizing my worth. If I can combat that, then I have won.

STORY 3:
HEALING THE
EMPTINESS INSIDE

I am in recovery from sexual addiction. I am happy to share my story and hope it will help another woman who is struggling with this devastating addiction. I don't know exactly when my addiction started, although I suspect it stems from how I wanted and needed more love and attention from my father when I was a young girl. My parents were good people and did the best they could with their large family. I learned many good LDS virtues and principles at home. Still, I felt that there was not enough love for everyone, and my siblings and I all innately and viciously fought for that scarce resource.

As a teen-ager, I desperately wanted a boyfriend to fill the ever-growing emptiness inside me. I found my first love at age 14 and was ready to get married and live in bliss. Unfortunately at this same time I read my first pornographic book and began acting out sexually. The relationship ended, but my vices were already in place – I was drinking, shoplifting, skipping school, and acting out sexually, although I wasn't involved in sexual intercourse. In a desperate attempt to get attention, I half-heartedly attempted suicide at one point.

I developed a split personality, as many who have a sexual addiction do – my parents in fact wondered if I had schizophrenia, as I seemed perfectly rational and normal around them, but when at school or with friends, was a completely different person. I looked for any chance to drink, drug, or be with boys – and yet somehow I managed to keep these behaviors hidden from my parents most of the time.

I was very willful and stubborn, and managed to convince my parents to enroll me in college and move me to an apartment with college-age roommates at age 16. By now I had lost my virginity and was promiscuous, drinking and drugging any chance I could get. Addiction is progressive, and I was spiraling into more and heavier drug use. I felt that my primary addictions at this time were alcohol and drugs, and after four months of heavy binging, I hit a low point and reached out to my bishop. He worked lovingly and patiently with me. I quit "cold-turkey" and somehow managed to stay mostly clean from the sex, alcohol and drugs.

I tried to get my life back on track, and a few years later met my husband. After a whirlwind romantic courtship of two weeks, we were engaged. We were both from LDS families, but were not active. Fortunately any residual drug use either of us had indulged in stopped when we met: we enjoyed each other's company so much that having a chemical reaction between us was a distraction. We did on occasion drink alcohol, but not frequently. We were married and enjoyed several years of happiness together. A year after our wedding, we became active in the church again and were sealed in the temple; a year after that, our first son was born.

While it seemed that my checkered past was really in the past, my previous addiction was merely waiting to reappear. I unconsciously began seeking sexual encounters again, sending out sexual signals. Because I was active in the church, I knew better than to use alcohol or drugs, but sex was an acceptable activity within marriage – although I often fantasized being with other men in order to achieve a stronger sexual high, and would occasionally masturbate, watch pornography, or read sexually stimulating stories when my husband wasn't available. Eventually I met someone who responded to my sexual energy and had my first extramarital affair. Although I never had full sexual intercourse, the relationship was sexual – but somehow I had convinced myself that if I never had intercourse, it wasn't quite so bad.

I managed to break off the relationship and worked with my bishop and my husband to repent and repair our marriage. It worked — for a while. After several years of being clean from any obvious addictive behavior, I began looking for relationships on the Internet – again, seeking attention by putting out sexual energy. I began with online friendships, which soon escalated into pornographic chats, acting out sexually on web cam, telephone conversations, and some real life encounters. At the height of my sickness, I had online relationships with several men around the world and was having sexually explicit conversations with most of them daily. Again, I tried to rationalize that if I didn't have intercourse, I wasn't breaking my temple covenants – but still, I knew that what I was doing was wrong, and somehow managed to hide it from my family and coworkers.

Addiction is progressive, and as I moved from the virtual world towards in-person encounters, my behavior became too erratic and nonsensical to ignore. My husband was inspired and able to catch me in the addiction. At this point, he was again devastated and unable to heal or forgive. I promised him with all my heart and all my conviction that it would never, never happen again – I swore that I would die before I let it happen again!

We limped along for several years, and you can imagine my despair when I felt that sexual energy pushing forth out of me again. When I realized that I was going to enter the cycle again, I contemplated throwing myself off a bridge to fulfill the promise I had made. By now we had three children, though, and I knew that suicide was not a legacy I could leave them. Instead, I tried to stave off the impulses and cravings as best I could, but when I inevitably began seeking again, my husband knew it as well as I did. I finally was honest and admitted that I would never be able to stop this behavior. He left me emotionally and physically for his own protection.

Fortunately this time I wasn't as far along in the cycle, and so was not "beyond feeling." I was able to take my despair and anguish over myself and the devastation I had caused my family to God. I felt the love of our Savior sweep me up and encompass me. I was able to realize that continuing behaviors even when your family and your work are being destroyed by them is symptomatic of an addiction. For the first time I realized that I didn't just have isolated incidents of bad choices; I had an addiction, and I couldn't control it or stop it on my own power.

I began to learn all that I could about sexual addiction and started attending the LDS 12-Step Addiction Recovery Program. I have now been in recovery for six months and am halfway through the 12 steps. It has changed my life for good in enormous ways – I now have hope of recovering and living a pure and virtuous life. I think the most important thing to know about my story is that I was active in the church throughout my life and throughout the 20+ years of my addiction. One of my cycles started while I was a teacher in the Relief Society; another started when I was in the Relief Society presidency. Sexual addiction, like most addictions, begins with feelings and emotions, and is fed by thought patterns, which lead to rituals and behaviors. This all happens first in the privacy of the mind and heart, and eventually in the privacy of home or work. In the early stages of my addiction, it would have been impossible for someone other than myself to diagnose or recognize what was happening. Only in the final stages of acting out is the addiction easily evident, when the addiction is fully rooted and bearing fruit. Of course, even in those final stages, there is always hope for recovery, but I would like to see women recover from sex addiction by recognizing the addiction in themselves and seeking recovery before their lives become unmanageable and they cause such terrible destruction to their spouses and children. I hope my story can help other women yearning for recovery to know that they are not alone in this addiction, and they are not beyond the reach of the saving grace of Jesus Christ. He loves us all so much and He is just waiting to redeem us.

STORY 4:
MY FIRST
12 STEP MEETING

As I attended my first meeting, I just wanted to hide and I didn't want anyone to talk to me. But I was kindly greeted by a sister mis-sionary and the facilitator. I sat in the circle and waited uncomfortably for the meeting to begin. We started the meeting with only five women. A prayer was offered. In that prayer a simple plea was made that I will never forget, "Please Heavenly Father, help other woman find us." When I heard this I knew I was in the right place.

A few rules about privacy and respect were reviewed. The process of the meeting was explained. Then we opened our Addiction Recovery books and began to read out loud; Step 3 TRUST IN GOD. After that the facilitator then started the Sharing Time by giving her own testimony of the gospel, the Addiction Recovery Program and how it has helped her in her life. She then invited each woman to take the opportunity to share. They shared their sweet thoughts, fears, and tears about their struggles. This opened my eyes and helped me realize that I am not alone in this struggle.

When it came around to my turn to share I had planned to say no. But before I knew it I was talking and this is some of what I shared:

"I had a dream a few weeks ago. I was alone and it was dark and quiet and I was very frightened. I called out and no one answered. I came to know that I was dead. As I stood there I realized that I had died without repenting of my sins. I was in a place that my husband, father, mother, sisters, and brothers could not come. The sorrow and the pain I felt was very real. I was in despair and there was no escape. I had procrastinated the day of my repentance.

As this realization came to me I woke up. But I was not overjoyed that it had been only a dream; the dream was my reality. I wept and prayed to God to help me, as I had done so many times before. I felt hopeless and thought that I have tried so many times

before to rid myself of this addiction. How can I do this again?
Comfort did not come.

A few days later my husband got a call. The bishop wanted to
meet with us. I dreaded going into that office. I resolved to pre-
tend like nothing was wrong. As I sat across from the bishop next
to my sweet husband, the bishop asked, "How are you doing? We
miss you at church. Is there anything I can do for you?" We an-
swered these questions as best we could. But I knew that I was not
being honest.

Then I remembered that awful dream. The bishop looked at
me and I knew in that instant that I was going to confess my sins.
I was overcome with sorrow at what I had led myself into. I could
not speak for several minutes and tears streamed down my face.
My husband picked up my hand and held it and squeezed it. I
told the bishop of my sins. The shame was very intense. I don't re-
member much of what was said after my confession. But these few
things I do know. One, I felt an immediate relief and knew that
I had taken the first step to preventing that dream from becom-
ing my reality. Two, my husband still loved and supported me.
Three, the bishop still loved and supported me. And most impor-
tantly, Jesus and my Heavenly Father still loved and supported
me.

God gave me the strength over the next few days and I felt
like a rock and that nothing could touch me. I could NOT be
tempted. I was prompted to look up the nearest meeting for sex-
ual addiction. And here I am. "

This meeting was a lighthouse on a very stormy sea. I learned that
"I" was not part of the equation. It was only WE. Only with God
and Jesus Christ could I return to the knowledge the Gospel provided and live righteously. It has not been easy and it will not be easy
for a very long time. I know this, so I cannot cease to pray. I have
not been perfect in this journey. But it has been the most bittersweet
experience of my life thus far. I have learned so much and my testimony has grown. I feel the love of God in my life.

Please, please, please go to a meeting. It will be a great help to you.
The spirit of God is strong and it is a holy thing. You will be able to
overcome your fears there. Eventually you will no longer care about

who may see you or what they may say. Your only care will be what God says. My prayers are with you in this very scary time. Don't give up. You ARE a beloved daughter of God.

I have a testimony of the grace of God and the plan of salvation. I know that Jesus Christ is my Redeemer and that it is the will of the Father that we partake of the Atonement. He loves you. Be brave, and the fire of the covenant will take flame in you. I now car-pool to our meetings with a sister I met at the meetings! We are able to strengthen each other in recovery with God on our side. I have very recently returned to the temple with my husband. I had tried to do the 12 Step program on my own. But the addiction recovery meetings made a huge difference. It taught me that I could not have done it on my own. I now love myself.

STORY 5:
SEEKING UNDERSTANDING
ABOUT MY PAST

I can't say I honestly know how or when my addiction started. I really can't remember much of my childhood either. From what I can remember, I had a good childhood. I have very loving parents who would never let anything happen to me. At times, the fact that I have a sexual addiction seems surreal because I've had such a good childhood.

From what I've figured out, it all started when I was about five. My older sister was diagnosed with a chronic illness and immediately all attention was on her. My mom had recently given birth to my younger sibling. My two siblings were now the main focus of both my parents. I was, in a sense, cast aside. I was old enough to not need them for every little thing like my baby brother, and I did not have a health problem that required constant attention like my sister. I just felt so neglected. I don't remember a whole lot about my life after that. The few parts in my life that I do remember bring feelings of shame. I only remember the hurt I gave my parents. I started acting out in different ways to get their attention. I'd steal, lie, cheat, throw tantrums, cry, fight with my siblings, and do whatever it took for them to notice me. I remember once, after stealing something and then having a huge fight with my parents, that I didn't feel bad for what I did. I knew it was wrong but I didn't feel bad. I think at this point they started worrying about me. I was about ten at the time. I now realize that I was seeking attention and love and sought to get it any way that I could.

At home, I always acted out and I felt like I was a horrible child. At school, I was the exact opposite. I always did well in my classes although socially I was struggling. I never had many friends even though I got along with people just fine. I was very shy and would often go off by myself during recess. I never got any attention unless I had something someone wanted. I ended up getting bullied a few times. It was always the same girl. I don't remember what she said,

I just remember that I felt so bad about myself after it was over. This bullying went on for about a year and then she changed schools. I never told anyone about it. This is how I was, never talked about anything that went on and never discussed my feelings with anyone. I just kept it all inside.

Junior high hit and I feel that's where things really started for me, although I don't know for sure. I started reading lots of books - whatever I could get my hands on. Not all of them were appropriate. I remember the first time I read one book in particular and got a feeling that I liked from it. I loved that feeling and would read those sections in the book over and over. They made me feel so good so I sought out more books of that nature. I had no idea what that feeling was or why I liked it but I knew I wanted more. I kept this up for years until I hit high school. I started searching out things online that would give me the same feelings the books gave me. It wasn't necessarily bad stuff but it wasn't good either. I started getting thoughts in my head and I'd obsess over them. I was making up fantasies constantly and that's all I could think about when I tried to focus on anything else. Finally, it hit a point when my thoughts just weren't enough and something happened that I didn't understand but it was the best thing I had ever felt. I tried over and over for this same reaction and I got it every time. I had no idea what I was doing or that it was wrong. I always felt that it wasn't right but since I was never taught anything about pornography or sex, except that it was bad, I just pushed my guilty feelings aside thinking everything was okay. This went on for a couple years and then my life started to crumble.

After my junior year, a boy my age had moved in over the summer and we became friends quickly. I would hang out with him constantly and we talked about everything. I thought things were great but then one day, out of nowhere, he got really mad at me. I don't remember why but he just started yelling at me, telling me what kind of garbage he viewed me as. I thought he was just in a bad mood so I brushed it aside. It didn't end. When we were alone, he'd get mad easily and remind me of what he thought of me. When we were with friends he would tease me about little things, but from what he had told me in private I knew he wasn't joking. One time he got very upset about something and ended up slapping me in the face. I started to tear up and then he yelled at me for crying and said that I had no reason to cry. Another time when we were out with other friends he punched me in the arm. It left a bruise. I never dated him and we were always just friends but that never stopped him. He spread a few rumors around about how badly I treated him and that I wasn't someone to be trusted. He ended up distancing himself from me, but because of my need for attention and my fantasies about boys, I clung on to him. For some reason, halfway through the year I gave up. I wasn't getting any kind of attention and so I had no more drive to be around him.

By this point in my life, I had given up on doing anything. I fell into a deep depression and no one seemed to notice or care. My grades went from being a 3.95 GPA my sophomore year to barely being a 1.9 my senior year. Around this same time, my one constant and closest friend transferred schools and all my other friends abandoned me. I tried hard to be a part of a group but gave up after no one noticed I was there. I started missing classes on a regular basis and rarely turned in homework. I didn't seem to have anything going for me and I felt so alone. I turned more and more to those thoughts and actions that made me feel good and occasionally, when things got overwhelming, I would burn myself as a distraction from my emotional pain. I always thought I felt happy after burning myself or fantasizing but I'd wait a few minutes and feel horrible again. It never went away. I had a hole in me and it was growing.

I barely graduated from high school. I see it now as a miracle from Heavenly Father because statistically, I shouldn't have graduated. After high school, I didn't feel the drive to do anything. I wanted to just pack up and move away from it all. I wanted to start fresh but I knew that wasn't a choice. I didn't have a job or go to school so I would sleep most of the day and then wallow in my self-pity when I was awake. My older sister convinced me to take an institute class with her so I did. I originally had signed up for one class but on the first day, I didn't want to be there so I found another class. It was on the first half of the Book of Mormon. I really enjoyed the class and for the first time in years, I looked forward to going somewhere and doing something.

One day as I was sitting in the lesson, my teacher started asking us questions. He'd ask, "How would you explain this situation to a five year old?" Or "How would you explain to a five year old the importance of this principle?" And then he asked the question that changed my life, "How would you teach the law of chastity to a five year old so that they would understand?" No one knew the answer and so he gave a very simple answer. I honestly don't remember what he said but once he finished, I knew I had to talk to my bishop. I still had no idea how to label what I was doing, I just knew it was bad and that I needed to see my bishop as soon as possible. I made an appointment that next Sunday and then I searched out the name of what I was doing so I wouldn't have to describe it to him.

The Sunday I met with him was one of the hardest things I've ever done in my life but it was such a relief once I was able to open my mouth and speak. It felt like I had just given him two 50-pound bags that I'd been carrying around for years. I continued to meet with him for a year and things got better but I still had a hole inside. I did slip into old patterns a few times and would beat myself up because I just couldn't stop. He finally convinced me to see a therapist and the first day I saw the therapist, she told me I had a sexual addiction, plain and simple. This shocked me. It was something I couldn't grasp but I was willing to try. I told my bishop about it and he agreed. I felt heartbroken. What kind of girl was I to have a boys' problem? I honestly thought something was wrong with me and so I desperately sought out any other woman with my problem so I didn't feel like such a freak of nature. During this time, I had a boyfriend and I'd complain constantly about how I felt so alone. He was struggling with addiction as well and would try to comfort me, saying he understood. It didn't work and I'd get dangerously close to going back to my addiction. Luckily for me, the whole time I dated this guy we never got into serious trouble. He was very respectful but occasionally he'd let himself get a little carried away, although he'd always stop before anything happened.

I continued to meet with my bishop regularly until he was released. At this time, I had broken up with my boyfriend and I finally found another woman with an addiction like me. We talked regularly but I was still struggling with staying sober. I had also struggled with some serious health issues. Because of these health issues and the desire to stop my addiction, I turned to other things to ease the stress I was under. One night, after crying all day because I was tired of being sick, I took a handful of pills and ended up in the ER. I was just fine but very depressed.

Almost three months after my new bishop was called, I relapsed hard. I did something I had never done before. I involved another person in my addiction. It was my ex-boyfriend. We picked up where we left off and went as far as you can go without actually having sex, which I am still grateful that we didn't to this day. I was so devastated and ready to give up but at this point, I realized that I couldn't do this on my own.

The first time I met with my new bishop, I explained my background a little. The more I explained, the more terrified he looked. Finally, I told him what happened. He tried to be as sweet and caring as he could but I could see the fear in his eyes. I was struggling with something that he had never heard about or experienced before. My struggle was something new to him and that was terrifying to me. Luckily, I had not done anything with this boy that would require a disciplinary counsel but my bishop wanted to meet with me regularly. I agreed and I also suggested to him that I needed to attend a support group. After calling LDS Family Services, we were able to track down a women's only group. I was both excited and nervous to go.

The first time I went it was a sister missionary, one other woman, and me. I was devastated but I needed this so badly that I kept coming. After about a month, we were told we were getting a facilitator. Within a couple of weeks a sister missionary and our beloved facilitator were assigned to our meeting. The first time the facilitator shared, I felt a sense of hope. She was someone who had gone through the very same pits of hell that I was going through, and she was now successfully married in the temple and had been sober for several years. I clung on to the hope she gave me. I needed it like oxygen.

Our group stayed about this size for quite a while. Every once in a while, we'd get someone new but then never see them again. Even though our group was small, there was such tremendous strength. It helped that hole inside me shrink so small, that I'd forget it was there. I started working the steps, struggling with the fact that I had an addiction. It's something I didn't fully believe. I became depressed and severely relapsed and hit rock bottom. I felt I had hurt my Heavenly Father worse than I had hurt myself. I felt so horrible about what I did that I threw myself into the 12 Steps. I started praying harder than ever and reading my scriptures more and more. I felt God's love for me and my efforts to change and it lifted me to a new height.

My life started getting better after that. I found a new hope I hadn't felt before. I felt empowered and wanted to shout it from the rooftops. I wanted everyone to know how great I felt and how the 12 Step program had helped me. I discovered things in my life that I had never known and eventually came to understand what had made me vulnerable to addition. As soon as I figured this out, my hole closed. I felt 100% complete, something I had never ever felt. It gave me such a deep gratitude for my Savior and all He has done for me. Our group has grown since my first time there. Slowly, one or two brave women at a time have shown up. I am pained to see another woman suffer as I did but I am so happy to see them come and find hope and joy and peace.

Thanks to working my steps, I now have a sense of peace. It is such a wonderful feeling. Life still isn't easy, I have occasionally relapsed and there are still times when I wonder if it's all worth it. Then I go to group and I see and hear those women around me talk about their struggles and their triumphs and I realize that I can do this. I am also able to talk about my feelings honestly without worry of being judged, and because of this I am able to have stronger relationships with everyone around me. I have learned to rely on the Savior for everything and I am so grateful to Him and the many blessings He has given me especially in times of need. I am improving myself slowly and I have learned to love who I am. I have come to accept that I have a serious addiction, but through the help of the Lord I can overcome it.

APPENDIX C

HUSBAND – WIFE RECOVERY STORY

*A couple shares their journey out of darkness
and despair to hope, healing, and love.*

HUSBAND: When I was deep into my addiction it was as if I were two different people. I thought that I was functioning fairly well in my job and church callings or at least I could appear to be. But I could leave church or the temple and go straight to the addiction.

WIFE: During that time, I was anxious and felt concerned that there was something wrong inside my husband but dared not infiltrate his personal space. I was scared to find out what the problems were. Even if I thought that something evil was influencing him, I was a practiced avoider. I hoped that if I did what I was supposed to do, such as being a good Mom, doing my work and going to church, that God would protect me. If I did my chores better, so to speak, God would protect me better.

HUSBAND: It was amazing but it seemed that spiritual experiences would invariably provoke or bring on dreadful addictive behavior. There were two different, conflicting and competitive individuals dwelling in me. There was the "righteous me" which was real and sincere and there was the "addict me," also very real.

As I taught others about the Atonement my hopeless belief was: "Well that is wonderful for them but not for me. I have lost that chance. It is beyond me." I was fully convinced that I was not savable by the Atonement and was unredeemable. I came to the conclusion that perhaps I could help other people find the saving power of the Atonement but it was beyond me. I was just too bad.

WIFE: I would pray for everyone except myself. At the end of my prayers I would think, "God, if you have any extra blessings, could you give me some? You know all about my troubles so please fix them. It's too hard for me." I could not bring myself to face the effects of Satan's influence in my life and my family. Evil was too frightening. I opted to avoid and ignore the warning signs of my failing marriage and focus instead on the more pressing chores of raising our young and demanding family. I pretended that somehow someone would magically rescue me and make my fears and problems disappear. My thinking was so flawed.

HUSBAND: Yes, I wanted God to fix me and take away my addiction. How easy it would be, it seemed, if I could just say, "I'm really sorry." Then He would say, "That's okay. Tomorrow you won't be troubled by this anymore." But I came to understand that what I wanted was more akin to the Deceiver's plan when he said that he would save all men (by force) and none would be lost.

WIFE: I fell for that plan too and became a terrible controller. I thought if I could manipulate you and the children to do what I thought you were supposed to do, we would all be safe and acceptable to God, our neighbors and friends. I proceeded to assume the rights of everyone in the family, thinking I knew what was best for you. Consequently, you all became resentful as well as dependant on me. We all suffered under my oppression. I think my core issue was that I was afraid of life. I was scared and lived in fear all the time.

HUSBAND: I was very fearful of admitting mistakes. As a child, revealing mistakes only brought on the wrath of my dad. Why should I tell the truth if I would be yelled at, belittled or kicked around? Instead I would lie or try to "wait it out" hoping to not be discovered and avoid the inevitable punishment. As a young boy I really didn't do terrible things, but the punishments always seemed severe to me. I could never please my Dad.

Belittling is such a destructive controlling power. Our Father in Heaven doesn't belittle or try to make us feel insignificant and worthless but Satan does.

WIFE: Then because of our weakened self-concept we become vulnerable to his traps and addictive lures. The Controller gains a foothold because we have forgotten who we are.

HUSBAND: When I became engrossed in pornography there was no one I trusted to hear me out and understand my concerns. I became a practiced avoider and continued the same pattern of escape and avoidance that I had learned as a child. I worked real hard to look good to my parents and friends but harbored too many secrets to have any self-respect.

WIFE: As a married couple we followed similar patterns without recognizing them because they were deeply entrenched within us. We came to realize much later that we were estranging ourselves from each other by escaping. Our relationship grew colder and more withdrawn. Even though we stated that we loved each other deeply, we didn't act truly interested. We became more self-centered, more selfish, and more aloof.

HUSBAND: I am sure we fed off of each other's escape and controlling patterns which weakened our relationship. Could we see it and understand it at the time? I don't think so.

WIFE: I became consumed with the children and you just disappeared for long periods of time. I would ask you to take the children for special time but you didn't want them to come. You said you preferred to be alone. We all felt so estranged. My controlling ways probably chased you further away.

HUSBAND: When I was frustrated with the way you treated me, I would escape and because you were frustrated with the way I was escaping, you would treat me poorly and neither of us knew how to handle those feelings.

WIFE: When we were engaged, we made an agreement that we would never fight or quarrel. We thought we could ensure success in our marriage if we would never fight. But in so doing, we never addressed any frustrating issues.

HUSBAND: That naïve goal sounded so sweet and hopeful but it wasn't realistic. It was not healthy for us because it meant that we would not discuss things that were important in our marriage. Some have advised couples to take a walk and cool off rather than fight. Although anger should not have ruled our discussions in the marriage, we should have learned to communicate and work through our problems. I took a walk when I was angry or frustrated. I took a walk into my addiction.

WIFE: Retreating to our hiding places was probably easier than admitting and exposing our weaknesses to each other. When I finally went to a counselor he said that I had built a child-like defensive shell around me that was based on fear. He said that it was normal for children who had suffered as I had, to be afraid of the world. He explained, however, that when I grew up I was supposed to be able to work through my fears with the understanding that all people make mistakes. He assured me that I could learn, but that I would need some new tools.

HUSBAND: Didn't that make you mad?

WIFE: No, it didn't make me mad. The concepts were new to me, like a foreign language.

HUSBAND: I didn't consider myself an addict. Addicts were wicked people. I just knew I could not stop doing what I was doing. I would resist for a while, but sooner or later I would fail. There was nothing I could do to quit the cycles. I fooled myself into thinking that if I did everything right I would be able to overcome turning to pornography. The time of overcoming, however, was always in the great distant future. It was never present because I knew that to stop in the present was impossible.

I thought I could reach some point where "my will" would be strong enough to stop. Then when I failed, I considered myself weak. But I came to realize that my "self will" would never be strong enough.

WIFE: It was the same with me. I kept trying to fix myself. It had nothing to do with the Savior. But somehow neither of us understood the love of the Savior. We needed to turn to His great, patient and enduring love.

HUSBAND: Yes, that's right, but I mistakenly felt that I wasn't good enough to go to the Savior. I had determined that once I stopped, I would go to the Savior for help and He would love me. I was quite sure that He would not until I cleaned up my life. If I couldn't do that, I would lose my chance to be loved by Christ. And that is ridiculous!

WIFE: I didn't understand God's plan either. I thought if He loved me He would resolve my concerns and rescue me. When He didn't, I felt more betrayed by Him than by you. Neither of my "knights-in-shining-armor" had saved me. I felt confused and lost. I didn't understand my responsibility to learn from my experiences and to seek help for my problems rather than run away from them. I had to learn to think and choose for myself or remain that hopeless, helpless woman. I needed the healing principles of repentance and forgiveness.

I mistakenly thought that I had to be a good girl because good girls didn't have problems. Good girls wouldn't suffer. And so I thought if I could be good enough, I wouldn't suffer either.

HUSBAND: My way was to emphasize the good and hide the bad.

WIFE: Basically that was what I was doing too. I didn't realize that there was no way I could be good enough to avoid suffering. It is just part of mortality. But I didn't understand that. I just thought I could "fake" it. If I could just fake it well enough, then I would be all right.

Both of us had ways of avoidance, and pretending and really did not enjoy life. We wondered what happiness felt like and knew we didn't have it. We wanted to be a great couple but we each had a cold emptiness inside. We tried to fake it, to raise our children, do our jobs, wear our suits and look good. We had hurts that needed to be fixed but we ignored them.

HUSBAND: Neither of us knew what the term "escaping" really meant. We had learned to escape as children, dealing with our exposure to a corrupt and unpleasant world. We didn't recognize the patterns for what they were. I never said to myself, "Oh, I am going to start escaping now. I am going to go here and do this and hide from life."

I understand now that a person trying to escape from oppressive controls and exposure is an easy prey to addictive behavior. They become susceptible because their pattern of solving problems is to get away, to escape. Escape is not a solution, just a transfer. It is taking the power from one source and giving it to another, rather than assuming personal responsibility. That is why the addiction can get such a strong hold because any frustrating emotion will cause the brain to presume the desired solution and send you down the addictive path. Somehow that pattern has to be broken. It is called becoming a "new creature."

WIFE: I now know that learning from my own experiences and mistakes, with God's help, frees me from bondage. My counselor taught me that making mistakes was part of my mortal experience and that learning from them could actually help me make better decisions. I had to allow you to make mistakes too. We could talk about our mistakes and learn together. That was a huge step for me.

HUSBAND: My concept of God was distorted by my childhood experiences. It seemed that there was no compassion or room for mistakes. If I made a mistake as a child then I was whipped and belittled by my father. When I did something worth approval it was only considered what I was supposed to do so why make a big deal of it. I erroneously judged Father in Heaven to be the same way.

When I was exposed to sexually deviant behavior at scout camp, I came home and went into the basement and cried for three hours. My father became impatient but didn't ask why I was crying. He ridiculed me and ordered me to stop. I was left feeling ashamed and worthless. I was afraid and felt I had to hide my shame from God. After that time I didn't cry, couldn't cry, for 37 years.

WIFE: One of the most important turning points for me was recognizing that you had been injured and that your injury hadn't healed. My focus began to shift from your addiction to your feelings. I was surprised to realize that you were suffering from more difficult issues than pornography.

HUSBAND: My pornography addiction was the outward manifestation or symptom of deeper struggles and pains unrequited. These unmet needs had accumulated over time and were heaped up inside my soul without any avenue of release.

WIFE: Once I realized that pornography was just a symptom or outgrowth of bigger problems, my perspective changed. As the layers of grief and loneliness peeled off you I discovered a witty, clever and interesting man. I felt like I was being introduced to you for the first time and wondered why I hadn't noticed you there before. I grieved at the time I had lost, of hearing all the interesting and delightful things you might have said and enjoying life with you. Why hadn't I listened to you or valued what you had to say all those years?

HUSBAND: Yeah, we really did fall in love again. Well, not again, but for the first time, actually. We never did love each other like this before. My sister mentioned that we were acting like newly weds.

Well, let's get back to the story.

WIFE: This is the hard part.

HUSBAND: We had learned that our son had a pornography addiction. After the birth of their second child you had traveled to their home to help and realized that I needed to be there as well so I came.

WIFE: One of our son's questions was why you had not been there for him while he was growing up. It was then that you told me in privacy that you also had a pornography addiction. The next morning we called and made an appointment with our Bishop for that evening and left.

HUSBAND: I certainly was ill equipped to help him with his problems.

WIFE: Me too. As we drove home you began telling me a few superficial things about your addiction. Confined to our van for seven long hours, I asked questions. I realized that you were unable to tell me without my gentle probing. As the heart wrenching truth just kept coming and coming, I felt like a huge glass dome was shattering around me. Shards of glass seemed to be flying everywhere, penetrating my poor soul. My heart, my face, my head, everything hurt so badly. It all came crashing in on me.

HUSBAND: I don't think anyone with a strong addiction of any type is going to reveal it on their own. Maybe some do. But I suspect that most in addiction have to be found out. I had to be discovered and un-covered. The protective mechanisms I had were too strong to risk say-ing, "I've got a problem and I need help to fix it." The thought of losing everything was too great and I was convinced that I would lose it all. I had become expert in hiding from the world. The thought of exposing or baring my soul was frightening. Whether it is drugs or alcohol or pornography, the addictive behavior is where those in addiction go to hide from life. It was a natural and comfortable thing for me to continue pretending to be someone else.

WIFE: The flood of information overwhelmed me. I wanted desper-ately to jump out of that speeding van just to escape the horror and not hear anymore. But I couldn't escape. I was stuck in that van for hours and I couldn't leave because we had to get home to our Bishop.

I had not realized at that time that I also had become expert at escap-ing from problems and that my protective shell had to break. It had to come down. Because of it, I never really trusted or loved anyone, even the Savior.

HUSBAND: I remember being surprised that I was rather calm and felt some confidence even though I was exposing my most dreaded secrets. Maybe I was numb or in a state of shock.

WIFE: I think we were both in a state of shock. But I remember feel-ing the calmness of the Spirit too. We were a miserable pair.

HUSBAND: Yes, God is so quick to send His spirit anytime we turn our head even just a little bit in His direction.

WIFE: I felt our marriage was an empty shell. We had nothing. But I told you I still loved you and would stay with you if you would show me that you wanted our marriage to last.

HUSBAND: That was a shock to me. Satan had told me that if I ever confessed, you would leave me. Do you remember how I answered your question?

WIFE: You quietly responded that you did want our marriage to last but I wasn't sure that I could believe you. I had little hope for us. I felt that all our covenants meant nothing. It was all a farce. How could I trust in covenants when they seemed empty and aborted? It seemed that all my defensive structures had come down upon me with the fractured dome.

HUSBAND: The devastating thing was that when I was in my hiding place, my pornography addiction, I had no hope either. There was no light and there was no chance of recovery because the addictive power was far greater than my will to overcome it. And so I lost all hope which perhaps was Satan's greatest power over me. It was not until I could say, "This is who I am, this is what I've done, and this is where I've been" that I began to feel hope even though the fear remained that I would lose everything.

WIFE: I had a lot of pent up feelings too that I would never have expressed because I was a "good girl." Once my hiding place was demolished my angry and hurt feelings just came bursting out of me. I needed someone I could talk to. We had agreed to keep this secret between our Bishop and us.

HUSBAND: I guess we were still hiding.

WIFE: Maybe so but I felt such shame and contamination. You had chosen pornography instead of me. I didn't face those emotions very well. I was miserable and confused.

HUSBAND: Once I confessed to you and then to the Bishop, I actually sensed relief. I could finally begin to get help. I gave away my black suit because it was such a symbol of the false pretense and the lies I had been living. I really wanted to quit the addiction for myself. I realized that I could not do it for my Bishop, for you or for my children. I had to do this to save my own soul. I had to say, "I quit this battle of wills. I will take whatever is going to happen and surrender all I have and am to the Lord."

As I went to counseling, I learned to let out my struggles, uncover my pain and express my feelings. Sometimes I would yell and cuss and the counselor just listened. I had not been able to show emotion for many years, but for the first time since childhood I learned to cry again. Then the miracle began!

WIFE: Now he cries all the time and it is good for him to feel and express emotion. And it is so good for us to hear each other's hearts. We finally care about what the other thinks and feels. We listen and share ideas.

HUSBAND: When I went to a counselor, she helped me realize that I was beginning to heal. In time, I learned to turn to the Savior for help. I had to go slowly to gain back my faith and trust little by little. I realized that the Savior's whole motivation for helping me was based on love. And now my motivation is based on love too. I have learned to love both the Savior and you and I know you both love me too.

HUSBAND: After my first relapse, you told me I had to leave. I had lost my job and moved into a cramped, dark basement apartment which I shared with two other men. I was lonely and miserable but determined.

My prayers were now connecting to the heavens. I would cry to the Father and plead for His mercy and the grace of Christ. There was nothing else that I could do. It's very sad that I had to hit the bottom before I would consent to be lifted up. This is when I told the Lord, "Do to me anything you want. I will suffer anything, just save my soul."

WIFE: During the first year after you confessed, we worked secretively just you, me, our counselors and the Bishop. We didn't tell other people about your addiction. We finally included our two children who were still living at home and then we started telling our other children. There was so much grief.

HUSBAND: Yes, there was and because they took your side I was pushed out of the family. And perhaps that was the right thing to do.

WIFE: No it wasn't the right thing to do. I was bitter. I felt like I was the abandoned one. I was the victim and you were the bad guy. I felt you behaved so poorly against our marriage covenants.

HUSBAND: Yes, I felt that I had betrayed my children and you and so *I was* the bad guy.

WIFE: I felt so much anger and shame. I had to have help from the patience and grace of our Father in Heaven. He gave me little bits of information and I progressed very slowly through this miserable time. I was not good at dealing with this problem. I was mean and cruel and I wouldn't even let you sit with us in church. I made you sit somewhere else.

HUSBAND: Yes, and I figured that I deserved it. I felt privileged to be in the same building.

WIFE: As your Dad and siblings learned about your addiction, they were wonderful to me but none of us knew how to reach out to you.

HUSBAND: Yes, they pretty well ignored me. Most people ignore those who have trouble, particularly something that is so poorly understood as a pornography addiction.

WIFE: Nobody knew how to address our core problems. It was just the pornography that got all the attention. That was so bad.

HUSBAND: That is such a dilemma. Discovering that your spouse has a pornography addiction is so shocking. Addiction, however, has little to do with the "choice of drug" people take. The "drug of choice" – alcohol, illicit drugs, over-eating, over-working, pornography or any obsessive pattern – is only the "choice of escape" from the real problems. Giving in to that choice doesn't address the problem you are trying to escape from and over-emphasizing the choice of escape clouds the real issues.

WIFE: The more I fixated on your addiction, the further I strayed from understanding our problems. I was so busy feeling hurt and betrayed and blaming and accusing you that I never recognized the pain and the heartache you were suffering. And so I did things like not allowing you to sit on the same bench with us at church. I treated you like you were filthy. I had no understanding of your feelings.

HUSBAND: I never had any understanding or cared much about your feelings either. Certainly, as one in addiction, my feelings and concerns were for myself. There wasn't much left over after that for anyone else – you, the kids or the Lord.

WIFE: That was one of our core problems in our marriage. We said we loved each other but didn't seem interested, unfortunately, in each other's feelings. We were caught up in our own concerns but didn't share them with each other. We alienated ourselves from each other. I left you out of the family decisions and happenings. I just tried to manage the family alone and only discussed surface issues with you. This was such a cold and sad way to live and makes my heart ache now.

HUSBAND: Yes, but we sure wanted to look good to the members of the ward. I remember we loved having folks tell us what great kids we had or how we were such a wonderful couple because "we still held hands." I tried so badly to be the model priesthood holder in public but had pretty well removed myself from my family in private. I didn't have anything left to give. The addiction took it all. So I became more and more isolated and non-caring. I felt filthy and I thought I deserved what ever you could do to me.

I was denied partaking of the sacrament and couldn't exercise the priesthood. To me being separated from you at church was part of letting the Lord punch down the clay. I had read in Jeremiah chapter 18 when the Lord sent the prophet to the potter's house. The vivid, almost startling, impression or picture that came to me at that time was watching the potter vigorously punch down the "marred vessel" with his fists until only a mound of shapeless clay remained. The potter I saw was not angry or vicious but determined to create a thing of beauty. So he punched down the clay and started over.

I recognized the potter as Jesus Christ. I said to the Lord, "Whatever you want to do to me or whatever happens I will take it." Even if I never could go back to my family again, I covenanted to still take the punching. I wished more than anything that God would make of me a beautiful vessel. My hope at that time had changed, not because I thought I could make it but because I knew that Jesus Christ could make something of me.

WIFE: That reminds me of a dream I had some time later. I was sitting on an old wagon seat beside a weary driver. It seemed I was interviewing him. The countryside was bleak, shapeless and without color. Trudging behind the wagon was a group of injured, bedraggled people. Most were hunched over and bandaged heavily. Some stumbled along on crutches but all were supporting each other as they plodded along behind the wagon. I sensed they had fought some great battle.

All of a sudden a flashy, colorful character arrived to join the group. He was bare-chested with huge muscles, all greased and tanned. He burst on this dreary scene as if to say, "Your hero has arrived!" Then he looked around in shock and distain as he truly noticed the battered crowd. Appalled at their wasted condition, he wanted nothing more to do with them or their cause if it meant his gorgeous body might be marred. In disgust, he dashed away, leaving the humble followers and their master.

I asked the driver who these war-worn people were. He said they were his army. I scoffed and said, "Some army." But the master answered, "These will never leave me." I thought of that flashy, wimpy warrior and knew that he had not been willing to suffer what these valiant had suffered. I knew then that no matter what this weary army was called to endure, they would remain faithful to their master. As the dream ended, it came to me that the wagon driver was the Lord Jesus Christ. I wanted to be part of His army but was sobered at the cost. There was nothing pretty about being in His army, certainly nothing to brag about. I often reflect on that dream and ask myself which kind of disciple I am acting like, as I am involved in the Lord's battles.

HUSBAND: I remember early in my recovery walking outside and looking at the sky. It was beautiful! I looked at the trees and actually saw distinct and separate leaves instead of the blur of green I had grown accustomed to. I remember a wonderful feeling that I don't ever remember feeling before in my life.

In my newfound exuberance, I told my counselor "I feel great! I feel wonderful! I feel new and I want to share that with people. I want to share with people and be happy and I want to show love." I didn't understand why my family was still so miserable. He told me that I was the one that had pulled the trigger that had shot a bullet into my wife's chest. He said I had now laid down the gun and felt better, but that she still had the bullet in her chest. And it was still there festering. So as much as I wanted to be filled with joy and happiness and thrilled with the grace of Christ because I had been able to lay down this burden and get rid of it, everyone around me was still hurting. I still had to live with that.

WIFE: I was still in stages of shell shock. It seemed like you were working on your addiction and getting help. I was hopeful but then you just
seemed to give up the struggle. I didn't understand it at the time but you
had relapsed and were hiding secrets from me again and didn't seem to
care. That was when I said you had to go. Our concerned Bishop asked
me if I was sure this was right and I replied, "He has to go, he cannot
stay." I called and cried to our oldest son that night and it was an awful
time. He told me I had done the right thing. I cried all that night because it hurt my heart so much to make you leave.

HUSBAND: Boy, do I remember that phone call. My determination still
stood, however. I would do, I would suffer whatever the Lord thought
to inflict upon me. This was for me, not for you.

WIFE: After this it seemed like your heart changed so much. You became gentle and humble and caring. You would call me sometimes and
would tell me about what you were going through and what you were
learning. And so I began the process of learning to trust you again. You
talked about repentance and spoke of the Atonement. I knew the word
but had not really understood what it meant. I thought that repentance
was only for "bad" people. Once as a young woman I recalled hearing
the word atonement in a sacrament meeting. I thought, "I do not know
what that word means." And then the Spirit bore witness to me that
someday I would.

HUSBAND: It was during that lonesome time in that dark and cold basement that I was finally humbled enough to try the one thing that I had
never tried before. I decided to try the grace of Jesus Christ. I prayed
constantly and read some really great books. I continued to visit with the
counselor. Once after spouting off about other people's faults he said,
"Quit being a Pharisee." That really hit me. I began to realize my "whited
sepulchure" was so full of corruption that it made no sense to criticize
anyone else. The Atonement began to take effect. I felt the grace of a loving God for me and had little concern for condemning others. After all,
if Jesus Christ would forgive me, "though my sins be as scarlet," what place
did I have in worrying about the "mote in my brothers eye?"

WIFE: I started watching you. You seemed happy but I was still feeling
quite angry inside. As the victim, the shame, the anger, the unfairness kept

me suffering. You had experienced sacred time with the Lord and when you came around me, you had a peace inside you. There came a point in those few months we were separated, where the spirit witnessed to me, "Your husband is going to move on and if he has to he will find another woman who is willing to go with him. If you want to be that woman, it's up to you. But he is going to find a happy life with or without you."

I was still felling miserable but this message from the Spirit startled me and brought me to a frightening and humbling awareness that I had a choice to make. I could remain bitter and accusing or choose to be your wife and companion and follow you into this new life that seemed to bring happiness. I came to understand that I also had much to repent of and needed to find the Savior myself. You taught me how to do that and explained to me the meaning of the Atonement. It sounded sweet to me. I saw its affect in your life. I wanted the peace and calm that you had found.

HUSBAND: That's the amazing thing about the Atonement and repentance that we sometimes don't understand. *Repentance is the greatest gift that God has given us.* The ability to change and have all this garbage taken away from us is so wonderful!

WIFE: I decided to follow you on your trek into this new kind of life you were living. I wanted to see what you were doing that was making you happy. I wanted to trust you but it was slow in coming. I would go back and forth because it was so scary to put my trust in you. You taught me about the Savior and you shared books about the Atonement that helped me gain a deeper understanding.

I finally realized that we were both crawling on our hands and knees back to the Lord. Bit by bit I felt that you were becoming a safe place for me. I invited you back into our home. We have been together on that path toward the Savior for over 10 years now.

HUSBAND: I remember one night after leaving the church building and walking down the hill to our home I could see the Temple beautifully lit up in the night sky. I was praying out loud, as I do now all the time, I told my Father that someday I wanted to be back in that temple. And He said to me, "I have prepared an escape for you."

I was told that I had to start doing everything differently than I had done before. I could not eat the same food, not watch any TV, not listen to the same radio stations and not drive the same way down the road. I had to be a totally different person. If He was going to make me a "new creature" I had to change the way I did everything.

It may seem silly to change all those little things, but I learned I had to change completely every minor detail of my life. And in each and every thing I changed I would say, "Father, I am changing because I need the grace of Christ in my life." And it didn't matter what it was, nothing was too minor to me. I wanted to become a new creature in Christ. I had to leave everything of my old self behind do things differently. The consequence was that I began to think and act differently too.

WIFE: We learned at an addiction seminar, that even small changes begin to alter behavioral patterns in the brain. We learned about recognizing all the trigger points that pulled us into our avoidance and addictive patterns. The seminar really helped us. My attitude shifted to this being "our recovery." Since then, working together, we have had more hope.

HUSBAND: After being sober for a long time, you may think that it is okay to add back some of the triggers (or small habits) that you had before and you will be all right. But if you do, you may not see it happen that day, but it will happen and you will have a relapse. Sure as sure. It will always come back. The brain will shift back into the pattern you had before.

WIFE: It seems to me that both of us had lost our sense of personal value until we humbly came to the Lord and relied completely upon Him. When I finally realized that this was my recovery as well as yours and in fact very separate from yours, it was my journey to come to Christ all by myself. It really didn't matter what you did, it was my job to find Him myself. Then Christ brought us together beautifully. That is His gift to us.

HUSBAND: He does not mass save. He saves one soul at a time.

WIFE: When I found out that He loved me all by myself, I came to know of the great love He had to give us all and I felt peace.

HUSBAND: It was remarkable to me that when I was fully exposed and everyone knew about my addiction, Jesus still loved me. That was a shock to me. That was something I did not imagine could be possible. He never did yell at me. He always spoke quietly and sweetly and confidently and kindly. And He never did accuse or belittle me. Satan accused me a lot in a very loud, condescending and belittling manner. The Savior never speaks that way. I learned to tell the difference between the Savior's voice and the accuser's railings by how they spoke to me.

WIFE: In the scriptures it talks about despising the shame of the world. I cried to the Lord, and was despising this miserable world I was in and living through. I learned He despised it too and realized He hated the whole misery more than I did and still loved me through it all. I realized finally that we had both been wounded and that He loved us knowing of our wounds. He wanted to help us through them. He didn't despise us. He despised the shame of the world. But He loved us.

One of the most important things I came to understand is that we are to learn from our experiences and our mistakes. We learn to say; "Lord could there be a better way that I could do this?" "Could you help me find out what it is?" That was the best thing that ever happened to me. I realized that was one of the purposes of repentance and that the Lord loves me and He is going to help me change and do better if what I am doing now is not working. And then He helps me progressively feel the spirit about what works and what doesn't. It is repentance. It is an ongoing process. It's the greatest thing that could happen to a person.

Thanks to our Savior who has given us this gift through His sacrifice for us. This is the best news to me of our time. I can learn from mistakes, I can change and that with God's help and His Son and the Holy Ghost I am a better woman. It's not just bad people that make mistakes. We are children in a mortal experience and we are learning by our mistakes. That does not make us bad.

HUSBAND: The prophets tell us to remember who we are and that we are children of God. When we discover who we are, loved of our Father in Heaven, purchased by our Lord and Savior, we realize that we have great potential. We do not need to succumb to the control of the destroyer. This confidence in our position with God helps us to not be affected by the deceiver's belittling and name-calling.

WIFE: Just because we do not have an addiction to pornography or some other overpowering sin, we must never think we have nothing to repent of. If we are so blind as to ignore our own many sins, we cut the very lifeline to our own personal salvation and happiness and our Lord's saving grace, which we so desperately need.

HUSBAND: Often when others find out what addiction I have in my life, they want me to name three or four steps to solve the problem so they can help someone they love find hope and recovery. I can't do that. The only thing I can say is that it takes the Savior to fix it. He is the only one that can resolve it. The only way recovery comes is by a total surrender to Him. Complete, total surrender to His way, to His grace, to His benevolence.

Only through Christ can anything be accomplished and particularly when it is something as drastically difficult and consuming and addictive as pornography or any other addictive patterns in our lives. Only Christ can fix it. Our wills are not strong enough. Our Bishops are not enough, our wives are not enough, and our children are not enough. They can only love, accept and pray. The Redeemer can take our grief, pain and sorrow and somehow – somehow make those powerful in our lives. Only then can change happen, can redemption come. It isn't over in a flash, and it isn't over in a year, and it isn't over in fifty years. It's a cleansing and learning process I will continue forever with Jesus Christ, my Savior.

As did Nephi, I declare with grateful adoration, "…I glory in my Jesus, for he hath redeemed my soul from hell."

WIFE: The privilege of repenting and becoming new creatures is our greatest gift through our Lord Jesus Christ, no matter how long it takes. As we gain understanding of each other, our fears, our heartaches and negative behavioral styles seem to fade away.

HUSBAND: We also learn the magnificent nature of God our Father and begin to understand His plan for our personal development and growth. We begin to appreciate Jesus Christ as The Way, The Truth, The Light and our Beloved Savior.

WIFE: The Savior releases us from bondage and we become free to choose for ourselves. We can then choose a better way. So how bad is that?

HUSBAND: It is wonderful, isn't it?

LETTER TO A BISHOP FROM A RECOVERING WARD MEMBER

*A young man, now in recovery, shares his thoughts
with those who may be facing the road to recovery themselves.*

Dear Bishop,

Thank you for following the Spirit of the Lord in helping me to begin a lifelong path to recovery from this debilitating addiction. I hope that now I can share some things that I have learned with others. I must emphasize the fact that this is a lifelong path and that I am only beginning down it. This is one of the most important things that you and others have helped me to learn.

First, I would like to give my heartfelt thoughts to those who feel they are or may be addicted. You are free to share this with anyone whom you feel it would help. Here is what I would say to others:

Friend,

You and I are in very similar situations. I am a student, I am recently married, and I need the healing that comes from the gospel. I attend a ward much like the one that you are attending right now. I may even be in some of your classes. I want to share my experience with you in hope that it will help to bring healing and peace into your life. I suffered from an addiction on and off for seven years before discovering the path to healing.

If you think that you might have an addiction, you probably do. The good news is that you are not alone. The path of addiction and bondage is a crowded one – some addictions just happen to be more visible and harmful than others. If you have a serious addiction, one that excludes you from temple service, you are not alone either. Many, many people suffer from serious addictions to alcohol, drugs, and pornography.

If you are suffering, please understand that the first step is clear. To help you understand what that first step is, let me first share what it is not. I have tried each of the following and have been unsuccessful:

- Tell yourself, "I can quit, I will NEVER do this again, I don't need this, I don't like this…etc."
- Try to ERASE the past by yourself.
- Tell yourself that the Lord will forgive you if you just pray to him and ask for his forgiveness and then never do it again.
- Hide your addiction and try to wean yourself off it.
- Expect yourself to be healed quickly just because your intentions are good.
- Imagine that it will just go away with time because you are married and your wife will help straighten you out.

Just ask yourself this question: If an arsonist started your house on fire and then hung around to try to show you how to put it out would you listen? You don't want the devil's solutions to the devil's problems.

The gospel gives us the solution and has been the only source of real healing that I have experienced in my path to recovery. The wonderful thing about the gospel is that the steps are the same for everyone. Gospel principles apply equally and in the same sequence for everyone.

I can tell you that the only first step that has brought me peace and put me on the path to recovery is this: Admit to myself, to my wife, and to the Lord that I have a serious problem that needs serious attention. There is no way around this step. Do not try to talk yourself out of this step. Do not let others try to talk you out of this step. Do not pass go.

Do not collect $200. This can be painful but ultimately leads to a peace that will last as you continue down the path to recovery. If you try to skip this step you may:

1. Get caught in your addiction.
2. Lose complete control of your life.
3. Lose any desire that you may have to give up your addiction.

Wives, try everything in your power to be supportive of your husbands. Listen as they share and seek forgiveness. It may be very painful and it may take some time, but understand that your husband is sharing these things with you because he loves you and because he seeks healing and forgiveness. Accompany him to your bishop, and he will help to guide you through the inspiration of the Lord. Seek out a professional counselor if you need to. Do not let go of whatever love you have for your husband. Let that love be the channel through which you attempt to understand and work through these challenges. Please understand that your husband thinks that you are beautiful and that nothing you did caused or contributed to his addiction. Pray that you might not take it as a personal attack on you. At this point of honesty and humility, your husband would love nothing more than to be healed of this addiction and to be forgiven by you and by the Lord.

Let me emphasize once more that this is the ONLY first step. There are no other alternatives. Honesty is the first step to recovery. You will not need to open up to everyone you know, but you will need to open up to your wife, God, and your bishop.

At this point do not even worry about the second step. I have found that when I try to look ahead to the next step, I doubt myself, I get scared, or I talk myself into giving up. Sometimes I wonder what will happen if I "mess up" again. Those are times where I am vulnerable to temptation. If I look forward to one day of success at a time, I have found that to be very manageable. If you are suffering in secrecy, look forward only to completing this first step of honesty.

Once you have committed to this first step I know where you can find the remaining steps that will lead you to recovery. The church has a program called the Addiction Recovery Program. If you need to find your nearest meeting, go to www.providentliving.org. There you will find many resources and locations for your nearest meeting. Go to the distribution center and purchase the book *Addiction Recovery Program*. If you need to know where it is in the Provo distribution center, just go inside, turn immediately to your left, and it should be on the top shelf. When I first committed to take the leap into this program these were my thoughts:

- I don't want to go to something like Alcoholics Anonymous. I'm really not doing that bad.
- I can do this on my own. I'll buy the book and work through it with my wife.
- If I can just develop habits like prayer and scripture study, I can conquer this.
- I don't want to run into someone I know at a group meeting.
- I don't want to commit myself to a lifelong schedule of recurring meetings.

Rather than tell you why these aren't good reasons for not attending the Addiction Recovery Program, I will let you examine each excuse for flaws and play Angels Advocate. Let me just tell you this, I would not be on the road to successful recovery if it were not for this program. I have never seen anyone overcome this challenge without following the steps of the program. (That doesn't mean you won't be the first, but it sure sets a difficult standard.) I have never seen anyone be unsuccessful who comes to the meetings and works through the steps. They have a meeting for wives as well. They can go and understand what you are going through and receive help and support for their personal issues.

When I first started to attend these meetings, I hated them. I felt uncomfortable sharing that I had an addiction and that I needed help. I looked around the room imagining that I was better than everyone else. Now I love going to meetings. I encourage others to go. I hope to see you there if you need the support. If you are one of those who are looking for healing, please ask the Bishop to point me out, and I will gladly share with you my experiences and accompany you to a recovery meeting. We have become friends at these meetings. I cry tears of joy when I hear of the success of my brethren. It is a reminder that you are not alone. It is a way to maintain honesty and show the Lord that you are willing to do what it takes to remove addictions from your life. It is the best thing that ever happened to me.

I want you to know that I love you, whoever you are, and hope from the bottom of my heart that you can take the first step. Honesty is imperative in your healing. Don't look beyond that step. The Lord will take care of you as you take this leap of faith.

Thank you for listening. I hope to see you and your wife at a recovery meeting soon!

> With love and sincerity,
> Your Brother and Friend

Bishop,

Thank you again for your love, support, and friendship through this challenge. I am grateful that we have been able to share with each other and grow stronger through this process. I feel the Atonement beginning to work in my life and the peace that comes from that. My life is filled with hope and with love. I am grateful for the blessings of temple worship and hopeful that others will find this path as well. Let me know what else I can do to help.

AN APPROACH TO COUNSELING ONE SEEKING REPENTANCE AND RECOVERY

A perspective from one strong in recovery from pornography and sexual addiction and who is currently serving as a facilitator in the LDS PASG 12 Step Program.

Dear Bishop,

I'm writing this to you, my common judge in Israel, to offer a perspective that may help you better work with someone like me.

Recently, I came to you after mustering all the courage I could, and I confessed my sin. "I have a problem with pornography," I said. Your response was encouraging and lightened my burdens for sure. You told me to forsake my sins (D&C 82:7), to strengthen my testimony, to serve others, to get back on the strait and narrow—all appropriate counsel. You may have even disciplined me in some way, formally or otherwise. And I thank you for your dedication, time, love, and fellowship. You even indicated that you would follow up with me, and I'm sure you will.

I thank you for walking around your desk, looking me in the eye, taking my hand, and thanking me for having courage. I thank you for trying hard not to say, "Oh my" or looking shocked. I'm in desperate need of both help and hope. You have given me both.

I'd like to offer some insights into my problem. I don't mean to make your job harder. I may have come to you because I got caught or because I was tired of having this problem. I may have done this many times before with you or other bishops. But, simply put, I have never really been able to do much more than dust off a life full of pain and "many strugglings, which have been in vain." I may need more help than you can provide because "I trust there remaineth an effectual struggle to be made" (Mosiah 7:18). I believe, because I've begun to hear the stories of success, that with your guidance and the intervention of others, I might be delivered from bondage and make the mighty change described in the scriptures (Mosiah 7:33, Alma 5:12-14). And I pray that you will help me initiate this by asking me several probing questions and helping me open up about the pattern of sin in my life. I need you to help me realize how caught I really am in this problem.

So here are some suggested questions that will probably make us both uncomfortable but questions that will nonetheless begin to rescue me from a problem that will continue to ravage my life and the lives of numerous others unless and until I get help. I need you to be direct in asking me the following questions (you may be the first person who ever has):

What's your pattern of use? Will you tell me more about what you mean by "a problem with pornography?" What is your pattern of use and frequency of indulgence? What size is this problem? What accompanies your use (masturbation, inappropriate relationships, other forms of "acting out")? (Please ask, "Tell me what you mean by…" when you hear words that sound like I may be minimizing or rationalizing.)

What's your duration of use? How old were you when you first viewed pornography? When was the last time? How often in between have you viewed it? How long have you gone without viewing pornography?

What's your pattern of confession? Have you ever confessed this sin to a bishop before? How many bishops? And how many times? (You will likely uncover a pattern of confession that precedes our relationship and may involve many bishops on many occasions. Please work with me to review what has taken place across the scope of my life, not just since I last met with you or another bishop.)

What efforts have you made to get help with this problem in the past? (You will likely learn that while I have read scriptures, prayed for miracles, read books, and even sought professional help, I'm much better at confessing than forsaking my sins.)

Who else knows about this problem? (You will likely learn that few if any others know, other than someone who may have caught me in the recent past. I have kept this secret well, for the shame that I feel is overwhelming.)

At this point, you now know more than anyone ever has about my problem. You'll probably be quite shocked. You may not know what to do. That's okay. You will sense my fear and shame. You will wonder how someone like me could have a problem like this. You will wonder what help you can provide.

What I need most now is:

Willingness to Change. Ask me to what length I would go to have this problem taken from me. Would I move to the North Pole? Would I crawl across broken glass? These sound extreme, but I have wanted to change, perhaps for years, and yet have no idea how to—all at the same moment. I will likely continue to try the same broken strategies again and again, hoping for a different result (someone's definition of insanity). Telling me to "just stop" probably won't mean much to me, because of myself, I have no idea what to do, and I'm scared that I've lost my opportunity for eternal life—that being a ministering angel or less would be okay. If there is a way for me to escape this pit of despair, I want it. (If at this point I say that I'm not so willing, you can rest assured that I'll be back in your office or see another bishop sometime in the future.)

A Divine Source of Power. Help me begin to see that there is a way to change. Ask me: What is the source of your power? I will likely say, "Me," for I know no other Savior (despite the fact that I haven't been able to save myself yet). Who is smarter—you or Satan? I will likely say, "Me," for I have no other source of hope. Again, you will expect my understanding to match yours that Satan has thousands of years of experience tempting millions of my brothers and sisters, but I am confused and stuck in a self-sufficient, self-deceptive mode of existence.

A Realization that the Atonement is for Me. Help me to know that the Atonement is for me. Do I believe in the Atonement? Yes. Do I believe in it for me? No—I likely have a long pattern of doubt or at least a sense that it's only for people who have done far less than I have or who have lived clean lives for much longer than I ever have. I likely have a distorted view that the Atonement will apply to me only when I can deliver a long period of clean living to the Lord. I hope you and I will have many wonderful future conversations about this topic and that you'll help me understand that the Atonement is for me today, and that it can help me become spiritually fit now and forever.

A Sure Solution. When the cost of the solution looks less than the cost of the problem, I **will** be ready to change. Would I be willing to participate in a process that has helped people recover from problems like this? When I say "yes," introduce me to the LDS Family Services addiction recovery program (at www.lds.org you'll find meeting times and locations for pornography and sex addiction group (PASG) meetings. Give me a copy of the Church's Addiction Recovery Program: A Guide to Addiction Recovery and Healing ($5 through LDS Distribution Services). Read through the "introduction" with me. Tell me that you know I want and need help, that you'll support me through the full process. Help me get to that first meeting—it will likely be the hardest thing I have ever done. You might even consider attending with me or at another time to experience this process yourself. (If appropriate, encourage me to invite my spouse or another support person, such as a parent, to attend the spouse support meeting that occurs at the same location, same day, same time.) Your encouragement and support will give me courage to get there and attend regularly. There I will be surrounded by others who, like me, are breaking away from a pattern of sin and into a life of recovery. (My spouse will be surrounded by others who, like her, are striving for full recovery as well.) At this point, there's no need to over-emphasize the word "addiction." I will learn that this word applies to me soon enough as I begin a process of rigorous honesty, humility, hope, self-discovery, moral cleansing, spiritual maturation, restoration, turning my life over to God, and recovery—a mighty change of heart. You will see the evidence soon enough and feel rewarded for your patient coaching.

Regular Follow Up. I don't expect that you'll have many of the answers to how I go about forsaking my sins and becoming a new man, yet I will appreciate you holding me accountable in this program of change. Ask "Did you make it to the meeting this week? Tell me about it?" You'll be surprised at the progress I begin to make.

Thank you for helping me see more clearly my pattern of sin and giving me voice for my problem. You've helped me begin building a bridge—one to a life of recovery, the restoration of spiritual blessings in my life, true conversion, and a restoration of hope for my loved ones and me. Thanks for helping me "get real" (maybe for the first time in my life). I can and will change through this process—I will lose myself and gain an understanding of the Atonement. I will learn that only through the Atonement can I stay in recovery and be reconciled with my Heavenly Father, for thousands before me have and thousands more will follow.

Sincerely,
An Adult Male in Your Ward

The thoughts expressed in this document are those of the individual who wrote them and do not necessarily represent LDS Family Services or the Church of Jesus Christ of Latter-day-saints.

LETTER FROM ONE IN RECOVERY FROM SAME-SEX ATTRACTION

Dear Friend,

Well, we haven't met and I apologize for the awkwardness of attempting this in a letter; but I wanted to take a few moments to write to you and share with you my experience of what some might call the *homosexual condition*. I applied the gay label to me for years, that is, until after losing so many opportunities and finding that I didn't fit and wasn't happy in the gay lifestyle. I decided to look for some better answers. The idea that I was born gay I found to be a lie. I'm writing to you to give you some insight to how one man found some different answers and a surety of truth.

Years ago, I had hated the idea of being gay and for so many years fought against accepting that word as a definer of my identity. It may be hard for you to imagine why or how hard it was to embrace the idea of myself being a gay man. The media nowadays makes a skewed but pervasive sales job of the "Will and Grace" or alternate lifestyle mentality. It wasn't so back when I was your age. In high school, I wasn't the macho hang-with-the-guys type. I didn't fit in, but I sure couldn't have endured the labeling of faggot or queer. The teasing I did go through for being non-athletic and different was as much as I could handle.

I wasn't raised LDS, and even at that early time therapists of the '70's advised me to go with accepting homosexuality as an identity. But it didn't feel right. Yet when in despair of struggling with my desires, the furtive looking around in the showers at the gym or bathrooms, the pornography (which was hard for a Midwestern boy to get), I felt that something was deeply wrong with me.

Then I found the Gospel. What hope it gave me. I thought joining the church would be the curative answer. I went on a mission and served successfully although I struggled occasionally with masturbation and a return of the troubling thoughts. But my testimony (earned through that service) deepened in spite of these things and I thought that God would take it away as a reward for my faithful service. Most times it lessened to feeling like distant static over a radio, but it didn't go away.

As I came home, I sought counseling and was told by well-intentioned therapists to "think manly thoughts and get married, and it would take care of itself," as I would then have an appropriate outlet for my desires. Now there's a two edged sword. I'm glad that that type of counsel has stopped, but for me there was good and bad in the prevailing thinking of the time.

I found the girl, got married and fathered four beautiful children (the blessing here is that I found I could respond sexually with a woman—the paradox, it didn't cure anything). I stayed active in the church, served as an Elders Quorum President, served as a temple worker, served as a student body officer in college, and taught religion classes as a TA at a Church school. These were marvelous faith promoting experiences, and again as I immersed myself in the Gospel, the constant feelings of same-sex attraction diminished, but they didn't go away.

Somewhere around my early thirties, my periodic dabbling with pornography and masturbation struggles caught up with me. Satan threw me a curve that I was not expecting (though now in hindsight I should've known because that's how he works). Someone hit on me. Oh, I avoided the temptation at the time, we talked, he propositioned me, and I got out of there. But I was devastated with the power of the temptation. I'd said no, yet for days my thoughts screamed out how I'd missed my chance. I became obsessed with it, didn't feel I could tell anyone my dirty little secret, and was overcome by feelings of suicide.

I again went into therapy, read an amazing book *Out of the Shadows* by Patrick Carnes, and found a 12 Step group called Sexaholics Anonymous (SA) for addressing my compulsive lust desires. This SA group and going to meetings with other men who (though they usually didn't have the same attractions that I did) were finding a faith that worked, faith that addressed deep seeded unwanted obsessive drives and behaviors. I had become a voyeur and cruising took up hours and hours weekly out of my life. Looking at my lust problems from the perspective of a disease helped immensely; but it also wasn't a cure all. I continued to pray and go to Church even though it seemed futile. I felt like I was living the life of "Dr. Jekyll and Mr. Hyde." Yet at times I felt the spirit whispering to me to keep trying.

I took a job as a sales trainer that required me to travel away from my wife and kids twenty to twenty-five days a month thinking that the SA meetings in the big cities where my territory took me would provide the insulation or safety net I'd need. Wow, how deluded I was. I got worse.

This was not because the 12 Step program failed. It absolutely works if you work it. But I was kidding myself on what it would take to get and stay sober (not act out). I did not know how deeply I would need to admit my powerlessness and surrender to my Savior. I still thought I could control things.

About this time I was being considered for a calling, and the Bishop called me in for an interview. Yes, I was living a double life. However, I had always promised that if ever I was asked point blank about what was going on with me I'd tell the truth. This bishop was inspired to ask the hard questions (really a temple recommend interview), and as I swallowed my pride and admitted where I was stuck, I had gone far enough over the edge and was excommunicated.

So within a year I lost my job, lost my membership in the Church, lost my sweet wife and kids, all due to the fact that I would not give up these behaviors and get serious about the consequences of what I had created in my life. I despaired. I thought I should just quit and give in and so devoted 2 years trying to convince myself that I just had to get over my own homophobia and accept myself for who and what I am. I 'came out'.

It got worse. The details of what I did and how bad it got isn't important to tell here. After a year or two of more acting out and more loneliness piercing the plastic smile I tried to hide behind, it was more than I could bear. I knew the jig was up. The promise of freedom in the gay lifestyle just didn't materialize for me. It was a meat market out there, and every one night stand or quick sexual encounter left me feeling soulless and empty.

Also, I couldn't cover up the feelings of testimony I'd had or the memories when I had felt the Lord's tender mercy and blessings. I decided to try again…and what was it that finally took? What finally got me over the blockade? For me, it was a combination of many things.

It was first and foremost letting go of my self-sufficiency and pride. I had coveted my own life, my own desires, my own wants. When those things didn't give me what they promised, I finally submitted deeply to the plan of happiness, the plan of redemption, the Lord's way, His help in all of its forms.

I'm now sure the 12 Step program of SA and the now available, Addiction Recovery Programs of the Church are inspired. Just as I'm convinced that finally surrendering my sense of being a victim to same sex attraction—*finally*, accepting responsibility for my actions (even my thoughts) and temptations was a vital key. I found that serving others both at SA as I helped others get sober, and eventually at church (it took years for them to trust me—for me to trust myself really—before I could get re-baptized) was another great key to my getting over myself. I found that being involved with men deeply, emotionally but realistically in a brotherly way, took much of the sexual attraction out of the picture. I became involved in several men's groups.

I found that another measure of me which I had been ashamed of could be modeled on Christ and therefore seen with different eyes. For example, my tender heart or gentleness and my deep reflective attitude about life and trying to figure it out were to be treasured and not put down by the inward mocking voice of what I perceived to be the 'cool' crowd that I'd caved into in my younger years.

Then too, I've found that there is great safety in boundaries. Just as an alcoholic wouldn't stand around in a bar or take the lid off of a bottle of liquor, I couldn't pretend I was immune to the power of lust and look at pornography in any form, cruise bathrooms, channel surf alone late at night or hang out with people who couldn't support me in my desire for recovery. There are places I just don't go. Now, I'm not perfect but instead of having days or months of binges, I'll have a bad moment (if I'm not careful) wherein dabbling bites me. Boundaries regarding the computer are a gift to me. Pres. Benson put it most poignantly. He said: "When obedience ceases to be an irritant and becomes our quest, in that moment, God will endow us with power." Or as Pres. Faust said: "When obedience becomes our goal, it is no longer an irritation; instead of a stumbling block, it becomes a building block".

Finally, I have read many different books on the subject of homosexuality; being careful to give equal time to read both for and against the concept of recovery. Especially in the beginning, this was a great help. As time went on however, I could see that the anti—you can't change camp--didn't hold a candle to the light and truths found in the Gospel. There were some great insights gained as I read such books as: Fred's Story (Victor Brown Jr.), Elizabeth Moberly's Homosexuality A New Christian Ethic, The SA big book, The Road not Taken by Peck, You Don't Have To Be Gay by Jeff Konrad, Joe Dallas' Desires in Conflict and a host of other's.

I know hundreds of men who've made similar journey's out of the deception that 'you are born gay', who now live lives of peace and truth. *It is the toughest thing I've ever done*—trying to bring my will into compliance and lay it at the altar of sacrifice—*but I know from experience it's worth it.*

Now, with nearly two decades of recovery, I live a life of integrity wherein I serve in the temple, have a loving wife of 18 yrs and all in all, have peace in the knowledge that I'm not living for the illusive moment.

For me, temptation is still out there. This quote in the SA big book sums up how I feel:

> So the realization slowly begins to dawn that we may always be subject to temptation and always powerless over our lust. We come to see that it is alright to be tempted and feel absolutely powerless over it as long we can get the power to overcome. We can look forward to the time when the obsession-not tempta-

tions-will be gone. We begin to see there's no power over the craving in advance; we have to work this as it happens each time. Therefore, each temptation, every time we want to give into lust or any other negative emotion, is a gift toward recovery, healing and freedom—an opportunity to change our attitude and find true union with God.

I have a faith that works and a relationship with the Lord which sustains me and helps me feel deeply, passionately and powerfully that I am a man, a noble son of God.

I hope my sharing this with you will be a blessing in your life now and not after paying the price I did. He calls to you. You are worth the effort to find out if what I've shared with you is true.

APPENDIX G

COUNSEL FOR FAMILY MEMBERS WHO HAVE LOVED ONES IN ADDICTION

Written by those who have family members struggling with sexual addiction, with the assistance of Toni Handy, an LDS Family Services missionary.

When we first discovered our loved ones were struggling with a sexual addiction, many of our hopes and dreams were shattered. We experienced emotional trauma and shock. In this situation, trauma may be defined as a circumstance which inflicts great distress and disruption to our relationships, family, and personal aspirations for those in addiction. This shock and emotional pain has severely wounded us through the emotional complications following the initial trauma. The pain we feel leads to our need for recovery and healing.

Everyone who is in a relationship with an addicted loved one, experiences negative emotions which lead to behaviors that are more hurtful than helpful and result in consequences that are not easily or quickly resolved. Often, family members of loved ones in addiction become codependent. Codependency can begin innocently out of a desire to help our loved one out of a difficult problem. "A codependent person is one who has let another person's behavior affect him or her, and who is obsessed with controlling that person's behavior." (Melody Beattie, *Codependent No More*, p. 31.) For example, many codependents believe, "When the addicted person gets better, I will be better, too." Codependents devote all their time, energy, and emotion into coercing our addicted loved one to "get better," because we believe we will not be at peace until our addicted loved one recovers. Of course we are going to feel natural emotions such as grief, anger, hurt, etc. However, codependency results in these natural emotions becoming unnaturally harmful, intrusive, and destructive to ourselves and those around us. In the meantime, codependent people are missing out on the many blessings they could receive if they were able to let go of their dependence on another person to make them happy and let God heal their hearts instead.

In our attempts to deal with our loved one's addiction, we reacted out of fear, shame, discouragement, anger, self-hatred, and judgment, all of which have harmed our loved ones as well as ourselves. Shaming and condemning those in addiction is counterproductive to their seeking healing and recovery. Eventually, our negative feelings consumed us and controlled our thoughts and actions, resulting in severe damage to our souls and relationships with others. Though we would have liked to have blamed everything on our addicted loved one, we come to understand that we cannot, for we are responsible for our own reactions and responses to others.

However, it can be tempting to be unkind, hurtful, negative, or to slip into a martyr or victim role, and we may feel justified in doing so. We can create a self-righteous realm that harms us and those around us, and this is why we need recovery just as much as our addicted loved one. *"Just as we did not cause the sexaholic's acting out, we cannot 'cure' it – the sexual sobriety of the sexaholic is not our responsibility. While our encouragement and cooperation can be helpful to the sexaholic seeking recovery, real peace of mind for us depends upon changing our attitudes and eliminating our self-defeating behaviors... We commit ourselves to our own recovery, taking full responsibility for our actions and reactions... We focus on taking positive action to make our lives more serene and fulfilling, regardless of whether or not the sexaholic chooses sobriety."* (www.sanon.org/keys.htm)

We go through this humbling, heartbreaking process for some time before we finally realize that we are totally incapable (i.e. powerless) to change the mind or heart of another person. However, when we recognize that we are powerless over our loved one's addiction and its negative effects on us, the black cloud of hopelessness and despair begins to lift. We feel relief and freedom from the responsibility of solving this problem. Releasing our desire to control our loved one actually frees our heart and mind to focus on the one soul we can bring to the Lord for guidance and healing—ourselves. By recognizing our powerlessness, we are free to let the Lord take over. Then we will realize that we are not and were never meant to be "saviors" of our addicted family members. There is only one Savior, who is Jesus Christ. We need to allow Him to do the rescuing and the saving, and we need to learn what our role is in this process. Our role will become evident as we continue to apply the 12 Steps for our own sake. When we understand that this challenge is under new management, miracles will begin. When we *turn* our addicted loved one over to the Lord, in *return* Heavenly Father helps us to rediscover feelings of peace, joy, and hope.

How can we begin to recover? There are 12 Steps, originating from Alcoholics Anonymous, which are spiritual principles of truth that lead us into complete repentance and fellowship with God. Also available are materials specifically for the family members of those struggling with addiction in books such as S-Anon. It is only through God's grace, healing, and presence that we can begin to shift our focus from our addicted loved one to our own need to offer ourselves and our lives before the throne of mercy. The Church of Jesus Christ of Latter-day Saints has adapted the 12 Steps for church members to include repentance to proper priesthood authority and to identify the higher power as Jesus Christ himself. When we work through these 12 Steps, we will begin to recover.

Recovery provides peace, serenity and wholeness when we did not believe we could be whole again. We must do our own work to achieve these things by attending local support group meetings, working the 12 Steps, and beginning the process on our own, for we cannot rely on someone else's recovery to find our own serenity. We are the creators of our own misery or our own serenity, and it is only through our personal relationship with the Savior that our self-inflicted wounds can be healed.

In addition, because we all suffer from human failings, each of us needs a repentance process that is thorough and complete to live our lives to the fullest and reach our potential in Christ. When we are wrapped up in the obsession of someone else's behavior, we cannot achieve our highest potential. We are unable to hear the voice of the Spirit and recognize the blessings we are receiving when our main focus is not on our own hearts, but on that of an addicted loved one. While it is true that a person in addiction needs recovery, by the mere fact that we are human, we all need grace, repentance and healing. Indeed, we come to know, we all are in need of the Atonement of Jesus Christ.

STORY 1:
PERSPECTIVES AND LEARNING

It is very hard to put into words my experience in being married to a spouse with a sexual addiction. It has changed my life. This challenge has been one of my most painful experiences but also I have found great spiritual blessings. It has caused me mental anguish, emotional distress, and even physical pain as I have tried to sort through the lies, the selfishness, and the absolute craziness of dealing with a loved one in addiction.

My husband made me aware of his addiction from the beginning of our marriage. We have now been married four years. We have been through marriage counseling, individual counseling, group therapy, and the 12 Step program. We have gone from the point of divorce and back. Still, my marriage and my husband's addictive behaviors are far from where they need to be. Though this addiction has brought many negative experiences into my life, it has also brought me in contact with the most outstanding people and it has given me the most amazing insight about myself and my relationship with Heavenly Father and Jesus Christ. Through the perspectives I have gained, I have been blessed with some of the sweetest experiences of my life.

At first as I tried to deal with my husband's addiction I was confused, terrified and I didn't know what to do. I lived on an emotional roller coaster from moment to moment. I thought if I stayed on top of things and could be his "policeman" the addictive behavior would stop. But after going through one attempt after another, trying to force my will upon my spouse, I became discouraged, fearful, and felt all alone. We went to the bishop and then to the stake president. I thought, if he would just meet with his priesthood leaders more often... if I could have just one more talk with him... if I could get him to read this one book or General Conference talk things would get better. However, these efforts did not, on their own, help him overcome his addiction. After urgings from my stake president, I went to a LDS 12 Step meeting. There I found understanding, support, love, and especially hope! I found hope that if I put my trust in God… not in my husband and not in myself, but in my Savior, Jesus Christ that all would be well. As I went to 12 Step support group meetings, I met amazingly strong and wise women who knew what I was going through and how to help me. I could feel peace in the 12 Step meetings, and the power of that peace kept me going throughout the week.

At the meetings, I gained insight into my own addictions and codependency behaviors that were creating unhealthy relationships with my husband and with other family members as well. I learned that the focus of my life didn't have to be my husband's addiction. Instead I could focus on my choices and my relationship with Heavenly Father and Jesus Christ. I've been going to 12 Step spouse support group meetings for over two years now. Although I can't make it every week I learn something new each time I go and I find renewed strength and hope. I go home with an increased knowledge and testimony of the goodness of the Lord. My spirit is lifted.

Sexual addiction has struck at the core of our young little family and has humbled me time after time. But I can still say that I am thankful for the place it has brought me in my life and for the spiritual awakening it has given me. I know that my husband's choices are *his* own. I have come to know that I have control over *my* actions and *my* own thoughts. I can choose to be happy. I don't have to live *in* my husband's addiction. My reactions toward his addiction do not have to put me into addictive patterns of trying to control those around me.

Most importantly, I know I can't do things on my own. I need Jesus Christ in my life. I know that He loves me and has a plan for me. A perfect, beautiful plan for me, but not just for me, He has a plan for my husband and for our two children. I am so thankful for this knowledge and for the life I have been given. I am thankful for my agency and the choice I have to *choose to hope*. I have hope in my Savior, Jesus Christ who atoned for my sins. My Savior who knows my pains and sufferings. My Savior who loves me. My Savoir who shows me the way back to Him. This addiction is not the end of my world, but the beginning of my *refining process*.

Story 2:
A Young Wife Shares

I met my husband shortly after moving home from another state. Immediately we hit it off, and I was on cloud nine. A few weeks into our dating experience he told me he had battled addiction and depression for the past few years, and had been working with a bishop to overcome this. I was shell-shocked, but found myself loving him so much that I didn't want to let go of him. I have a couple of close family members who have been in severe addiction, so I don't feel I am a stranger to this. I think this prepared me to initially not be afraid of hearing of this wonderful man's biggest flaw. We were married in the temple a few months after that, and I naively thought that the marriage would solve this problem, I could fulfill some need he was looking for, or that it would all just be ok because we were married in the temple. I thought that he could handle this and we wouldn't have to worry anymore.

We have now been married for two years and are expecting our first child soon. For the first year and a half of our marriage I thought he had taken control of his addiction, and it wasn't a problem anymore. We didn't talk about it much- occasionally I would ask him about what he was looking at on the Internet. A few months ago I felt like I needed to ask him directly, and with a sorrow filled face he told me that he was really struggling. My heart broke. Initially I knew he needed to learn how to overcome this himself, and I wanted him to be the one who was taking his recovery into his own hands. We went to see the bishop, and he told us of the 12 Step program. My husband was very hesitant in wanting to go. But he made the call to the missionary of the program and was told the times and dates. He was also told of a spouses recovery program held at the same time. We both naively thought that this program would be to help me learn how to help him overcome the addiction.

At this point I started to think that my role as the wife would forever be turned into the role of the computer monitor, text monitor, policeman, etc... and forever seems like a long time when you have to worry about making decisions for two people. This started out of concern and love, but very quickly turned into my obsession. I constantly thought of what he was looking at, every day, every hour, and at times it consumed every minute of my day. I worried over the future. I am good at putting up fronts for people, but I am sure those I am close to could tell how drained I really was for those first few weeks. It seemed like I was trying to demolish a mountain with a spoon. I didn't know how to "fix" him.

When I walked into the class that first day I was shocked to see the women who were there. They were of varied ages, and I seemed to be one of the youngest. They looked remarkably happy! How could this be when I felt so terrible? I was very intimidated until the class started and we read though the step we were on that day. Immediately I could tell that this 12 Step program was as much for me as it was for my husband. I felt the spirit so strong in that room of women that I knew I had to come back... not to learn about how to help my husband, but to learn how to help me! The facilitator talked about how there is only one Savior, and we are not Him. We cannot and should not try to save our spouse. There is only one who can save and we need to let Him do the saving. This was my first breakthrough. Just the thought that it was not my responsibility to save him brought me more hope than any looking over his shoulder, or texting him constantly throughout the day did.

I am still very "young" in my recovery process, so I go back to draw on the strength of the spirit in those meetings, and to find hope and courage from those women. One of the most comforting feelings I have received from going is realizing that I am not alone in feeling the way I did. I have learned that through a constant process of prayer, study, and applying the Steps I can turn my will over to the Savior and learn to say... "I can't do this. Will you help me to make my will yours? Please guide me! Help me to live with faith, and not with fear." Just saying these words is such a relief. Then when I actually put them into practice, I feel the happiness that I saw in those women on the first day.

I also keep going because I have found answers to deep spiritual questions I have had my entire life. I've always wondered about the power of the Atonement, and how it could help me, but never realized how real that power is. The 12 Steps have become my practical tools to living as I apply them to my eternal process of turning my will over to the Lord. Forever doesn't seem so long anymore. Now I have a different perspective of eternity. Forever doesn't seem like a mountain I have to take down, but a road I get to travel that will lead me back to my Father in Heaven. If I keep working at the steps and keep drawing nearer to Him, no matter what happens to my husband, I will be ok. Remarkably, when I gained this perspective, which can seem to some like I am giving up on my marriage, my marriage actually becomes better! We communicate better, we don't fight as much, and he can draw off of my strength. It's like we are one body, but with individual hands, each with our own role and working at different challenges. I am not perfect at working this process and I still have many hard days where I tell myself to focus on faith and to turn my will over to Him, but everything is manageable now. I am closer to the Savior than ever before, and I feel hope. What a great blessing.

STORY 3:
THE POWER OF
"LETTING GO AND LETTING GOD"

I grew up in a very dysfunctional home, which included family members struggling with sexual addiction. When a child grows up in this type of atmosphere it is typical for them to feel insecure and to take upon themselves the shame and blame and feel as if everything is their fault. I fit that pattern perfectly. I developed deep beliefs that I wasn't worth anything and that I was very unlovable. I completely believed the lie that there was something wrong with me. As a result of my childhood experiences, I have a hard time bonding with others and giving and receiving love. I isolated myself, believing it was the best course of action to hide myself.

I always wanted a happy home and a family that was safe, loving, and secure. When I met my husband, I thought that finally I would be able to have all those things that I didn't have in my home while growing up. What I didn't know was that I was marrying someone with a sexual addiction just like in my family of origin. Because of my past family experiences, I had become a seasoned codependent with all the confusion, attitudes and behaviors that accompany codependency.

During the first 18 years of my marriage, I lived in a state of denial in relation to my husband's addiction. Even when I found pornography in our home, I just thought; "I guess that's the way men are." I had learned how to effectively stuff my feelings by then and tried to cope by becoming emotionally numb most of the time. I also experienced tremendous fear. I tried to "fix" my husband by controlling him, and I also allowed myself to be treated disrespectfully. During our 18 years of marriage my life came tumbling down when I found out my husband was having an affair with someone at work. I was totally devastated and because of the destructive and false beliefs and patterns of my childhood I thought it was my fault.

I had a hard time setting boundaries, due to my feelings of inadequacy as a woman. We had a large family and I became overwhelmed, severely depressed and unable to function in my life. I am grateful to my Heavenly Father and Jesus Christ for helping me through that time, because I didn't know where to get help for myself. At the time, I didn't understand anything about sexual addiction. I did not know and understand that the Holy Ghost could be with me and help me. I began reading scriptures and praying for help and guidance.

I was directed, through the promptings of the spirit, to a professional counselor who taught me how to surrender and give it to God. I thought he was crazy. But I was in so much pain that I decided I would try it. This spiritual and emotional principle saved my life and that of my family. There is so much power in letting go and letting God. This trust in letting God do what I couldn't do helped me to feel peace and I was able to overcome my despair. I gradually became strong. I depended on the Holy Ghost to guide me, to give me comfort and show me how to deal with this severe challenge.

I filed for divorce. This really shook up my husband and he cut off the affair. He was excommunicated and he went through a repentance process and a church disciplinary council. After his willingness to repent, I thought we would be okay and so I went back to the marriage. We were okay for about 8 years. However, during all that time I lived in fear that it would happen again. I also never really forgave my husband and carried deep down resentment in my heart. I tried to control him to make sure it never happened again.

After 8 years he relapsed. As a result of this crisis we were led to the 12 Step program. Both of us had hit rock bottom. That was 10 years ago. We have worked the 12 Step program diligently. It is a major part of our lives. I have learned to let go and let God take care of my husband's addiction. I can't control it. I am glad to know I can't control it because it is too much for me to carry anyway. I have learned that I didn't cause it. I have come to learn and accept that I am enough. I have come to accept that my husband has an illness. I have come to feel complete serenity and peace. I feel this peace when I work the 12 Step program. I have learned that I am loveable. I can now love myself. I can set boundaries and respect myself. I can take care of myself. I have been able to draw close to my Heavenly Father and Jesus Christ. I have come to know them. They are my whole life. I have come to accept the agency of others and realize that whatever my husband does is between Heavenly Father, the Savior and him. I know I will be okay no matter what happens in my life and that Heavenly Father and the Savior will always take care of me and never forsake me. I feel very grateful and happy. We are still married and we go to meetings together. We have served for over 7 years in the 12 Step program as facilitators. We can even laugh now. Recovery is a wonderful blessing! I am deeply grateful for all the lessons we have learned through the 12 Step program and by walking hand in hand with God.

STORY 4:
THE HEALING POWER
OF THE ATONEMENT

Discovering my husband's addiction was the most painful and difficult thing I have ever had to encounter so far in this life. I am a person who is fiercely loyal and my husband's addiction felt like betrayal to me. As he started into the process of recovery I believed that recovery was a possibility for him but that the wounds and damage that he caused me would never go away. I was extremely angry and felt stuck—stuck in my marriage—stuck in my hurt.

I searched the scriptures and other material trying to find out how or if there was a way to find peace someday. I felt no peace. I felt so alone in my suffering. I felt no one had ever felt what I was feeling. Therefore, I concluded that there was no help for me.

My husband asked me to go to the 12 step spouse support recovery meetings. I agreed to go, but I believed that I would just be listening to a bunch of tolerant and passive women who had been so hurt they were unable to find their own happiness. I quickly discovered that the women at these meetings weren't what I had imagined. They were hurt, yes, but those in recovery and healing were strong and full of faith. The material we discussed wasn't what I had imagined either. I found that we read and talked about principles that helped me with my issues with healing and changing, not my husbands.

I am learning through the 12 Step process that there is hope and healing for the spouse of one struggling with addiction. It is through the Atonement of Christ. But even His Atonement cannot heal me unless I let it. I learned that I was the one getting in the way. I would think and worry and cry about how I had been wronged. But all the Lord wanted me to say was, 'I am hurt, this is bigger than me and it is ruining my life, therefore, I give it to you.'

The Savior can make our burdens light. He already has paid the price. He has placed His help upon the table for us and we can choose to walk away from it or pick it up and enjoy it, but He has paid the price either way. I have to remind myself every day that He is in charge, He loves me and He can make sense of what makes no sense. I just have to let Him.

STORY 5:
SPIRITUAL HEALING

My husband planned an anniversary cruise for our 25th wedding anniversary. On our drive home from the cruise he opened up and shared with me his struggles with sexual addictions that had spanned his 40 plus years of life, starting with the sexual abuse he endured as a child. He had started attending the LDS 12 Step Pornography Addiction Support Group (PASG) several months before, and was finally finding hope that he could overcome his addictions. I'm sure that he expected me to clap my hands and join with him in his excitement, but my reaction was quite different than that. Probably because of the horrifying details and specifics of his addictions that he shared with me, combined with my 20 plus years of hurt and anger and resentment towards him, I was devastated. I felt betrayed, used, unbearably hurt, bitter and alone. I had no one to talk to, no way to process so many emotions at one time. It was like all of the hurt and difficulties of all the years came crashing down on me at once. I cried for days and days. I could think of nothing else. Even when I tried to divert my attention with a trip to the store, the pain throbbed on and I felt like a zombie just going through the motions of life.

My husband didn't know what to do to help me. Everything he said just made my pain worse. After several weeks, He invited me to attend the 12 Step support group meetings for spouses, which I quickly assured him I never wanted to attend. He asked me again each week, telling me it would help him with his recovery. I knew it couldn't possibly help him to have me sit in another room during his meeting, but to prove that I was the "good" person in this marriage, I let him drag me to the meeting. I was humiliated and angry, but at the meeting I noticed that the other wives there didn't seem nearly as unable to cope with the situation as I was. I went with him several weeks, and it felt really good to have someone I could tell about the pain and wrongs that I had been given. I began to feel the love and concern of the sister missionaries, and connected with a couple of the other sisters there. I so appreciated their allowing me to be as angry as I needed to be, without shunning me. Slowly I began to hear what they were saying about finding healing and hope. I didn't really believe that I needed to work the 12 Steps, but I listened to their testimonies of turning to the Savior for strength and healing.

I started praying and sharing all my pains and struggles with the Savior. I finally started to feel a tiny glimmer of hope that life could be better someday. Eventually I began working the 12 Steps for myself. It was liberating to feel that the Savior was the one who would fix our mess of a marriage, instead of having to fix it myself. I came to the 12 Step meetings voluntarily, and put on a happy face, and I did feel improvement in our lives, but I think I still held onto a lot of pride in what a good wife I was being to support such a terrible husband, and I kept uncovering hurt and pain that I thought I had overcome. I had worked through Steps 1 - 3, and was wondering what I could write about for Step 4 as an inventory of the things that I needed to address. I didn't want to do Step 4, and I kept putting it off, still feeling my husband was the one who needed this Step, not me.

I came down with what I thought was the flu, and was unable to keep food down for 2 weeks. I was finally hospitalized, diagnosed, and treated for a condition, but the improvement we hoped for never came. Week after week I lay at home or in the hospital, unable to eat, getting weaker and weaker, thinner and thinner. I found myself going through all kinds of emotions and thoughts. There were times when I counseled the Lord and told Him what needed to be done to make me well again. I felt abandoned by God; sometimes I thought maybe I was being punished for my pride and sins. At times I felt satisfaction that my husband finally had to learn how hard it was to care for another person. I experienced many thoughts and feelings that, with time, the Lord was able to replace with more humble, righteous ones. I learned how dependant we are on God for our every breath. I got to the point that it was obvious to me that I had control over absolutely nothing, and so I finally submitted my life and my will to God. After about 5 months of struggling to stay alive, the doctors found a correct diagnosis, and my body began to accept food and the many other physical symptoms began disappearing.

In the healing weeks that followed, I was blessed with profound spiritual healing as well. I learned so much about myself, and the parts of my life that needed to be changed. I understood that my husband's addictions are part of the refining, exalting plan of God, and that I need to love him and let God change and refine him, while I work at changing and refining myself. I learned of the great love the Savior has for me and of His eagerness to help me and teach me better ways to live so that I can find joy.

As I regained my strength, I knew what the Lord wanted me to include in my Step 4 inventories. I have been working my Steps, slowly trying to be thorough and as sincere as I can, and I am now seeing great changes in myself and my relationship with my husband. There are still hard times, hurts, and misunderstandings, but we are more willing to ask for the Lord's help and focus on our own contributions to the problems.

I love the 12 Step program, and the help it is offering me. I don't think I ever really understood the Atonement, and its' power or intimately personal nature, before working the 12 Steps. I didn't know my Savior in the same way I do now. I didn't understand the power of repentance and of the healing power of forgiveness. I gain so much strength from attending meetings and feel the love of the sisters and the Savior so strongly now, that I love going. I love being able to welcome in newcomers and assure them that with the Savior's help they can find hope and peace. I'm so grateful for the love and guidance that God has given me. There can be happiness while dealing with addiction, and there can be healing and recovery through His grace as well.

Story 6:
It's Not My Job to
Rescue My Loved One in Addiction

There were no LDS 12 Step spouse support groups at the time I began seeking help. I looked up S-anon in the phone book and went to my first 12 Step Support Group meeting for wives whose husbands were struggling with sexual addiction. I had an immediate feeling of comfort and relief to talk to other women who understood. At that time I had not told my family, friends, or the Bishop that my husband had a sexual addition. I was in so much shock and isolation that I could not speak of it. I was given a little blue book to take home and read about other women going through this experience. In the book were small steps and tools to regain peace and sanity once more. Furthermore, these women were smiling and actually laughing together!

As I continued to attend meetings I was in shock to find out that they were saying that spouses were often "addicted" to fixing, saving and rescuing others, and they called that behavior "co-dependency". I thought defensively, that's what good wives are supposed to do. Then I read a few more books and the message began to get through. One explained that by constantly trying to "fix, save, and rescue" a loved one in addiction I was being faithless on two counts. I had always felt that I had faith and now I was being told I didn't. First, I was sending the message to my husband that without my "help" he couldn't recover. I lacked the faith that as a child of God, he was capable of finding recovery without my help. Additionally, I was exhibiting a lack of faith in God, that He could save my loved one without my help.

I finally began to see my "addiction" was to rescue and save my loved one. The truth hit me hard. I believed that without my continuous interventions of "kind, sweet, thoughtful, well-meaning, good intentions, advice giving, rescuing, quoting scriptures and Ensign Articles, etc. etc. times infinity...my husband would fail, and I would fail in my responsibilities and stewardship. I resented the words in some books that call it "control or manipulation" because that was never my intention. However that is exactly what my behavior was demonstrating.

As time passed and the 12 Steps began to sink in to my heart, I recognized that my husband felt controlled and manipulated by my efforts to "help", even though my motive was love. Now, I was being advised to put my co-dependant hands in my pockets, detach with love, and walk away from my loved one's life choices. That was harder than I had ever imagined. It felt like walking away from someone who was drowning in a lake, going down for the last count, and I was being told NOT to throw him one more life preserver! How could this be helpful, let alone the right thing to do?

Soon after this, I was imagining the same terrifying scene in my mind of my husband drowning in a frozen lake, going down for the last time, and myself running along the shoreline panicked and desperate beyond belief. Then I envisioned seeing my Father in Heaven standing with the Savior, Jesus Christ on the shore watching. At first I was so relieved they were there to save my loved one. Then, I was despondent as I realized that because of the law of agency and choice, it was my husband that was required to ask for Their help to be saved...not me.

I came to understand that our Savior was the Lord of the vineyard (read Jacob 5), and not only has He never stood idly on the sidelines watching us suffer alone through earth life... He has done everything to rescue us and will never cease striving to reach out to us! He suffered and paid the ultimate price in Gethsemane and died to save and rescue us all. He is the Redeemer, He is enough, and He is everything.

I do not know *how* He does His work, or how He saves all of us drowning children, but He does. Finally, I realized it is not my job to know or understand *how*, it is only my job to *believe it*! I began my journey of practicing Step 3 "letting go and letting God". It wasn't easy, but step by step, little by little, I allowed Him to strengthen and enable me to let go of the burden of my will, and the bondage of co-dependency. I stopped feeling it was my personal "responsibility" to rescue and save my loved one. The "fruits" of letting go of *my* addiction, were delicious to my spirit. A few of these were:

Greater peace and freedom from pain, stress, anxiety, worry, insanity, and suffering in my heart and mind. My burdens have been made lighter or at times they are completely removed. The key word is greater serenity.

Better relationships with my children, friends, extended family and co-workers. They now feel my love and trust in them as valued and capable children of God. They feel safer with me, as I no longer feel it is my stewardship or duty to fix, advise or save them.

Greater love and appreciation for my Father in Heaven and Jesus Christ. I have increased "patience in the process". I do not ask how or why in my prayers. Now my prayers are filled with more gratitude and fewer requests. Trust and faith in His perfect plan of happiness for my life and all those I love has caused a spiritual awakening in me.

These gifts or "fruits" of my own recovery are truly pearls without price! I have thanked my Heavenly Father over and over for the tender mercies in His rescue of me. I now understand that my husband's addiction was not my fault. Now, I am sharing with other sisters the counsel to "detach and go to 12 Step"! *Give your will to God and choose to be changed!* You will feel His arms encircled round about you, and I promise your life will never be the same. I now stand as one more voice and one more witness of these truths: "You will find hope, you will feel peace and you will experience joy again".

STORY 7:
WORKING THE 12 STEPS FOR MYSELF

My husband and I have been married for 18 years. He was up-front with me and told me before we got married that he had a problem with pornography. His sincerity and honesty touched me and I was sure that soon it would be a thing of the past.

At that time, he didn't actively seek out pornography, but whenever he would come across it, he wouldn't resist. I was frustrated because I couldn't see the resolve in him that I thought he should have. I really had no one to talk to because we kept that part of our lives a secret. I told him that I was okay with not talking to anyone if I could talk to him about things, if I needed to. What resulted was an inward struggle. It was hard to sort through my feelings on my own. I didn't want to come across as accusing and mean, because if I weren't supportive, he wouldn't change, right? Through all his many confessions, I never yelled at him, which I prided myself in, but I would always cry.

His addiction took a downward turn when his work required him to be gone for several weeks at a time overseas. Each trip was saturated in pornography. His work had him live away from home for a year during the weekdays and home on weekends. We would go through this weekly cycle of him being away for the week and I would spend my time hoping that he could succeed that week. He would come home on the weekend with a poor report of his activities and our weekends would be me crying and trying to come up with a plan for him to implement in the upcoming week. It was a pattern that we went through week after week for that entire year.

With his increasing use, his testimony started to wane. He came to a point where he told me he was considering leaving the church. My whole world was crashing in on me. My husband's problems still continued. He would find his way onto inappropriate sites at both work and home. I came up with so many plans for him and couldn't understand why he wouldn't just dive into them. I thought that he didn't want to put in the effort needed to change.

Our bishop suggested that we attend the 12 Step program

through LDS Family Services. We couldn't see how that would help with the problem because on our own we were reading books on the subject. If we were to attend the 12 Step program, our secret would be out. Seven months later, our bishop suggested again that we participate in the 12 Step program.

I started to attend with my husband. We went to the weekly meetings. We read together through their materials. We started working through the steps. We'd sit on the bed together with the materials and questions in front of us, answering the questions in our own notebooks. I was seeing to it that my husband was working the program. Even though I was participating in the program, I wasn't doing it with the mindset that I needed to change my life. Nothing was really changing in either of our lives.

Logically, I understood that I wasn't the cause of the problem, but every time that my husband would confess something to me, I would hear my inner voice shout, 'You're not skinny enough!' The truth was that I've always had a thin body. But my inner voice and fear increased my mistaken need to be thinner. I started to skip meals and not eat enough calories in the day. I enjoyed the mistaken feeling that I was in "control." In reality, my life was getting way out of control.

I decided that I was going to work through the steps, again. This time I wanted to change. I wanted to feel close to my Heavenly Father, to feel the divinity within me. I prayed to know who should be my sponsor and I started to seriously try to work through the Steps. My husband, at that time, was attending the weekly meetings, but was not working the Steps. This did not matter to me. I was humble enough to want to make changes in my life without looking over my shoulder to see how he was doing.

I found the Steps to be quite difficult to internalize. How could I say that I was powerless when I am a woman of power? I struggled through that concept until I really believed it. I can now say, "I am powerless" with conviction and joy, knowing that I truly am powerless, and that that is a good thing.

Each Step continued in the same manner. Some concepts were harder than others for me to grasp. I spent some time with each step, but made sure that I worked on a Step daily. Naturally, as I internalized these Steps, my life changed for the better. My husband recently passed through several months where he was succumbing to his addiction. I did not jump on the roller coaster and allow my emotions to ride up and down with how he was doing in his life. My self-worth was not wrapped up in his addiction. I would tell him that he was doing great even though his actions might have said otherwise. I really believe, though, that he is a different person than before. Maybe, though, since I had detached myself from his addictive behavior and allowed myself an identity of my own, I could see him for who he truly was.

I did tell him that I didn't want him to report to me anymore how he was doing. He now has a sponsor to whom he reports along with our bishop. Our current bishop has been a great support to my husband and me. He attended a 12 Step meeting with my husband to better understand the program. My husband is on the recovery path and doing well. I have been attending the 12 Step meetings for three years now. I am going through the Steps for the third time. The steps are a way for me to better understand the Atonement and apply it in my life. I don't think that I have ever been in a happier place in my life than now.

STORY 8:
MY STORY OF HAPPINESS

I want to share my personal story of happiness. As I write this story, I am in my small cozy cottage, overflowing with love and peace in the most beautiful countryside. I am surrounded by my wonderful family and friends who are close in many different ways, but it has not always been this way.

We are told that to appreciate joy, we need to experience sorrow. My life has not been exempt from challenges and heartache. I married my eternal sweetheart in the temple after he served an LDS mission. Soon after our marriage, my sweetheart was called to serve his country in the military. These were the days before emails, cell phones and all the luxuries we have today, so personal contact was sparse at best. We were separated for almost 2 out of the 4 years he served. These were hard times, but with many friends doing the same thing, it didn't seem to be all that difficult.

While we were separated during this period of time, my husband, like most of the other guys overseas, decided that looking at pornography was a better alternative than infidelity. Of course, I didn't realize this same rationale was his reasoning for participating in this practice as a teenage boy. I was aware that my husband received little or no physical affection from parents and family as a child, and that he felt lonely and without much self-worth. I was somewhat aware of his ways but thought at the time that "boys will be boys" and that it was just what guys did occasionally. Little did I know that this was a destructive addiction that would create tremendous pain and sorrow for our marriage and family.

As time passed, I realized there was something missing in our relationship. I bought many books on how to improve our sexual relationship with the hope that this information would benefit our marriage. I was trying to figure out how to create a bond that just didn't seem to be happening naturally in our marriage. I now know that a complete and whole marital relationship is not possible when a partner's sexual addiction is present. We came to understand that reality and fantasy, love and lust, are not harmonious to one another.

Our ability to emotionally connect is something we are still working on almost 50 years later. There were occasions throughout our marriage when our struggle was very evident and alive, and there were times when all seemed to be well. I remember telling my husband how wonderful it made me feel towards him when I saw him studying his scriptures. This created tender, loving feelings towards him. However, I still didn't fully understand the real problem we were dealing with.

His use of pornography became more frequent when we were experiencing hardships such as job loss, money troubles, etc. I became more aware of his problem and we addressed it with one another, several bishops and professional counselors. Sadly, I never really felt any peace or resolution from our efforts. During one of these particularly hard times, his addiction lead to more than fantasy—it lead to an affair. During this time we lost almost everything—our love, our trust, some of our children as they chose poor paths, his job and our home. Ultimately, we became bankrupt in every way.

Starting over was hard, but not everything we experienced was bad. I kept repeating the scripture, "Know thou, my 'daughter,' that all these things shall give thee experience, and shall be for thy good." One of my theme songs was from *Carousel* - "When you walk through a storm, keep your head up high, for you never walk alone." I became aware of my Savior carrying me and walking beside me through these hard times. After losing almost everything, we pushed forward with our deep abiding love and testimony of our Savior sustaining us. We survived our situation with our last four children by living in an old small RV. We lived there for six months in a park where mostly the homeless and downtrodden lived. We pretended we were camping and made the best of our challenging situation. We built a small 3-level bunk bed with a small couch on the other side for our four children to sleep as comfortable as possible. Little by little, we found work, were able to rent a house, and started to rebuild our lives.

During all this, my eternal sweetheart's tender spirit was so discouraged, that he had thoughts of suicide. It was a long, hard road of counseling, medication and many other facets of healing. Death seemed an easier alternative for him, and he actually came very close to death many times when he suffered various illnesses. Thank heaven for the prayers of numerous friends and family members, priesthood blessings, our Savior's love and many miracles that transpired to save his life. His real healing and progress began when we both came to the realization that his pornography habit was an addiction.

Pornography addiction has been so hurtful to not only my husband's soul but also to my tender heart and the hearts of our children. Unlike other serious illnesses, this situation is one that we have had to face, for the most part, on our own. No casseroles were brought into our home for this illness. It seems that pornography addiction is often suffered in silence for fear of losing friends, family, reputation, job and much more. However, as difficult as it has been, we have at times shared with others our addiction recovery path and have found love and support. Because this is a deeply misunderstood challenge with many misconceptions and fears, there is always a risk of having friends and family shun you when they find out the problem you are dealing with.

During the process of confronting the addiction, we once faced an especially complex situation. We had traveled a great distance to rejoice in the birth of a new grandchild and participate in the baby blessing. However, just a few days prior to the blessing, we all became aware that my husband had experienced a relapse. This presented a dilemma of worthiness to participate in a priesthood ordinance, and hence it was decided to postpone the baby blessing. While driving home, we had many hours to honestly discuss this problem at great length, which was a rare occasion in our marriage. With this addiction, it is very difficult to openly talk about the challenge and deep feelings. In reality, his relapse, experiencing the consequences of his relapse, and the open discussion that followed helped to start him on a more successful recovery path. He began to recognize his powerlessness over his addiction, and we prayed that we might find additional help.

One of the Lord's greatest blessings to us was in directing our paths into the LDS PASG (Pornography Addiction Support Group) 12 Step Addiction Recovery Program almost three years ago (visit *providentliving.org* and click on the "Social and Emotional Strength" link for more information). There were support group meetings for the husbands in addiction, and separate support group meetings for their spouses. I wasn't sure why I needed to go to those meetings. After all, I thought I had led a pretty obedient life and followed the gospel principles in the best way I knew how, so why did I need to attend a meeting? But for whatever reason, I was prompted by the Spirit to participate in this program.

I became involved in a PASG 12 Step pilot program that had been written to specifically help the spouses find healing and to know how to deal with these devastating emotions. I began to learn to stop focusing on my husband's addiction. I learned that I needed to focus on my own life and what my Heavenly Father needed *me* to do to become all He wanted me to be.

I answered the questions at the end of each of the 12 Steps. I kept a gratitude journal. I wrote my personal inventory that is part of the fourth step. My scripture study became more meaningful and my life began to change. Through this process, I learned the lessons of trust, hope, and forgiveness that were critical to my personal success and happiness and that this program was necessary in my life to come unto Christ in a very concise and specific way. I did all these things for myself, without regard to my husband's progress and problems. I learned to accept that what my husband needed was to desire to seek recovery for himself, which he did. I had to repeat over and over many times, "Let go, let God." The one thing I had the power to do was to focus on the one person who I could help—myself. I became less critical of my sweetheart while I gradually started recognizing my own weaknesses and challenges. I did so with the help of my Savior, and the interesting, paradoxical result was that as I healed and changed, the light within me influenced my husband's confidence so he could get better. It has been an awakening that has led me to a greater level of peace and happiness.

The first Step taught me I was powerless. It took many times through the 12 Step program for me to internalize my "powerlessness" over his addiction and many other circumstances in my life. As I talk with women with other life challenges, whether it is divorce, death, illness, etc., the 12 Step principles are the gospel in action, and they work for every situation. So when I pray every day to be an instrument in our Heavenly Father's hands, I truly have a powerful application of the gospel principles to follow. When other brokenhearted sisters come to our weekly meetings, I have the opportunity to share my heart and empathy by sharing these principles and my testimony of how these Steps have changed my life and given me peace, hope and a depth I never knew possible. There is hope, there is healing, there is love and joy abounding as we follow these simple and powerful gospel principles. The Lord's education process was not a quick fix, it involved learning and progression, line upon line, here a little and there a little.

Many times divorce seemed eminent, but through much prayer, temple attendance, priesthood blessings and counseling, I was assured this was not the path my Heavenly Father wanted me to personally take. And so where am I today? By obtaining a greater understanding of this addiction, our lives have been directed on a path that has led us to greater happiness, addiction recovery, and physical, emotional and spiritual healing. This journey has provided me wisdom and deeper spiritual understanding to be able to reach out to others. I have friends and family members that, through the light, peace and joy that I presently feel and show, they too want to experience this same happiness. It is another opportunity to share the sweet principles of our very powerlessness, trust, and hope in our Savior that I have learned and experienced in my life.

My husband is now free of the Goliath that plagued his life for so many years, and is a loving, tender companion. I too am free! Free to act for myself, free to understand the sweetness of powerlessness and turning it all over to my Heavenly Father. Together we have reached a happiness that is indescribable. My husband lives. He has not only been healed physically, but he has been healed spiritually and emotionally. It is a miracle to me that I now have a wonderful husband and friend. Our family has a loving father and grandfather. He has become empowered through these challenges and through the blessings of the Lord to become who he truly is and was meant to be. I know the battle against the adversary will continue until Christ comes again. My husband realizes he must remain focused every day on the spiritual principles that have brought him recovery and freedom from his addiction.

To me happiness is a manner of traveling, not a station reached in life. It has not been an easy journey, but the joy I feel with the loving relationship my husband and I now share has been worth every effort. I cherish the sweetness of our little cottage that we built together with the laughter and fun of children, grandchildren and friends. Life still has its challenges for us, and we are still learning the lessons of mortality to assist us in coming closer to our Savior. I would not want to walk this path again, but I certainly appreciate the opportunity and blessings that have been mine as I have lived and learned the 12 Step principles. We are still married and loving it. I never thought I would see this day arrive and yet, through our Savior, all things are possible. I love to share the "good news"—Christ lives and through His atoning power we all can live and experience great joy today and forever.

CLOSING THOUGHTS:
TRIALS CAN BECOME BLESSINGS

If given a choice ahead of time, no one would voluntarily choose to be the spouse of someone in addiction. Who would be willing to agree to the sorrow, pain and suffering that inevitably comes when you have a loved one in addiction? Our instinctive choice would be to avoid this at any cost.

President Spencer W. Kimball explained it this way: "Being human, we would expel from our lives physical pain and mental anguish and assure ourselves of continual ease and comfort, but if we were to close the doors upon sorrow and distress, we might be excluding our greatest friends and benefactors. Suffering can make saints of people as they learn patience, long-suffering, and self-mastery." (Faith Precedes the Miracle, Salt Lake City: Deseret Book Co., 1972, p. 98).

However, when spouses of those in addiction find healing and recovery for themselves, they often report that their lives have changed for the better, they feel blessed because of the experience, and they would not go back and change things. One wife shared the following: "If someone said they would be able to erase the whole pornography problem out of our lives, I would say, oh no don't do that. I have learned so much; I have come so far in the past two years. I never ever dreamed I could be this close to my husband. I never knew I could be this close to my Savior. I wouldn't trade this experience for anything in the world."

Spouses and their loved one in addiction are both in a battle with the enemy of their souls. This is a real war. But there is help and there is hope. The war can and will be won if we turn to the Lord, Jesus Christ, who literally is our Savior. We may all take comfort in the wise counsel of President Thomas S. Monson: "We are waging a war with sin, my brothers and sisters, but we need not despair. It is a war we can and will win. Our Father in Heaven has given us the tools we need in order to do so. He is at the helm. We have nothing to fear. He is the God of light. He is the God of hope. I testify that He loves us—each one." *(*Thomas S. Monson, "Looking Back and Moving Forward," *Ensign*, May 2008, 87–90)

For further information send a request to:
www.healingthroughchrist.com

APPENDIX H

MISCONCEPTIONS ABOUT PORNOGRAPHY AND SEXUAL ADDICTION

The following misconceptions are actual statements that have been made by various family members, friends, and ecclesiastical leaders of those in addiction. These misconceptions, together with brief responses, were prepared by David and Toni Handy while serving as LDS Family Services missionaries in the PASG Addiction Recovery Program.

Pornography is not addictive. Recent medical studies have documented the chemicals that are produced in the brain when viewing pornography and have shown that these powerful chemicals are drugs that impact the brain and create addictions. President Gordon B. Hinckley was correct when he stated in his conference talk of October 2004, "Continued exposure leads to addiction that is almost impossible to break." However, there is hope and there is help. There are principles that can help those struggling with sexual addiction to overcome this challenge if they are willing to seek help.

Shaming or embarrassing those in addiction will motivate them to stop. Quite the opposite is true. Shame, embarrassment and condemnation tend to cause those in addiction to hide their addiction by going into greater secrecy in order to avoid exposure. In an effort to help those in addiction to confess and seek recovery we need to create an atmosphere of love and support, bear witness of the Savior's mercy and love, and direct them to the available programs that can help them find recovery.

Getting married will solve the problem. Having an intimate relationship in marriage does not cause the sexual addiction to go away. Many of those in addiction have reported that their addiction returned very soon after their marriage began. In addition, this addiction will eventually destroy any true intimacy in the marriage relationship.

If a man is addicted to pornography, it is the spouse's fault. This is one of the greatest untruths of all. Many, if not most, of those who struggle with pornography had their first exposure in their youth, long before their marriage. Never blame the wife. Never make her feel it is her fault. Counseling her to lose weight or become sexier for her husband incorrectly puts the blame upon her, and it does not contribute to the recovery of the one with the sexual addiction.

Pornography and erotic materials will help a couple to enhance their marriage. Pornography is a distortion of a true intimate relationship. It increases fantasizing and alienates the husband and wife rather than bringing them closer together. This is one of the adversary's great lies to harm a marital relationship.

If someone in sexual addiction is preparing for a mission or temple marriage and is able to refrain from this addiction for a few months, they are ready to move forward. Not necessarily. The addiction must be addressed first. If someone "white knuckles" (trying to stop by will power alone) or goes without viewing sexual images for several months, that does not mean they are in recovery. Abstinence for a time does not mean recovery. Unless true recovery occurs, a person can return quickly to his addiction during his mission or after marriage. Correct recovery measures should be taken first.

If a husband has a sexual addiction, the wife should always divorce him because he will never change. Divorce is a personal decision and should be considered after prayer and careful spiritual guidance. Many marriage counselors recommend that if the one struggling with sexual addiction is willing to seek help, then divorce should be postponed for a time. Marriages have been healed when those who are in addiction seek recovery, healing, and help, and when the spouse is also willing to seek help and healing from her wounds. However, if one in addiction is involved with sexual addiction on the level that puts any of the family members at risk, then measures should be taken to protect the innocent family members.

If someone quits going online to view sexual images, they are no longer addicted. Not necessarily. The problem is not just in the viewing of images. The problem is a sexual addiction of "lust." Pornography is just one tool that one in addiction may use to satisfy this addiction to lust. You can have lustful thoughts without viewing pornography. We need to realize that we are dealing with a sexual addiction that is very complex and will take time and the Savior's healing power to find complete recovery.

If every home gets the right filter on their computers, there will be no exposure to pornography. Although filters are helpful and serve their purpose for limiting the amount of pornography that enters your home, it will not prevent the viewing of pornography at other locations. In addition, there are ways to get around even the best of the filters available. Getting a filter will not prevent or cure a sexual addiction. Pornography can also be accessed through cell phones and iPods, and in many other ways.

Children can't get addicted. We have seen children as young as seven or eight years of age who are already addicted to pornography. Some studies show that many of those with this addiction began between the ages of five and fifteen. Some children were molested at an early age and introduced to pornography by their molester. Many have reported that as children they did not understand the powerful feelings of euphoria they experienced when viewing pornography. But, later, when they were experiencing fears, sorrows, or anxieties, they would revert to viewing pornography to get those same feelings of euphoria, as a way to escape from the difficulties of life. It is important to understand that the pornography industry is targeting children to entice them into addiction.

Sexual addictions only occur in inactive or dysfunctional families. Sexual addiction can occur in any family. This is a plague that is upon our generation. Our society has become highly sexualized. We see it on

T.V., at the checkout stands in the grocery stores, on the Internet, and virtually everywhere we turn. Very fine sons and daughters of God are caught up in this whirlwind of sexualization. It would be a mistake to assume that our youth have not been exposed, simply because of their young age. Many of those who have been pulled into a sexual addiction have testimonies, love the Lord, and want to be free of this addiction, but they also feel great shame because they know it is wrong. This shame creates within them a fear of being discovered, which leads them to go to great lengths to keep their problem hidden, even while they continue to be active in church. They need to know where to turn for help.

If I am active and faithful in my church calling, the Lord will protect me from this addiction. Being active and faithful in the Gospel will be a shield and protection for you. However, sexual addictions can find their way into any member's life regardless of their testimony and activity. Family, friends, and church leaders must be careful to not delve into the world of pornography in a naïve attitude of trying to better understand the one struggling with addiction and to try to figure out how to save him or her. They too can be caught in the snare of sexual addiction.

My husband went to the Bishop and confessed some time ago, so why is he still struggling with his addiction? Shouldn't his confession be enough? Though confession is an essential part of recovery from addiction. It is only one of the beginning steps of the recovery process that needs to take place. Healing the soul and changing the heart takes time and comes through the power of the Atonement of Christ.

If someone struggling with sexual addiction goes to a therapist and 12 Step Recovery Support Groups, they should be better in a few months. Overcoming sexual addiction takes a serious commitment in applying the principles of recovery, and it also takes a great deal of patience. One would not expect a cancer patient to recover quickly — you would anticipate years of therapy and constant monitoring to stay on top of the problem and immediately take action if it returns. In much the same way, the process of addiction recovery is challenging, difficult, and requires time. But it can be obtained if one is willing to try and is committed to doing it in the Lord's way. Family members can best assist by lovingly encouraging and patiently supporting those seeking recovery. Healing is on the Lord's timetable, not ours.

If one in recovery relapses or slips, then they will never be able to stop. Addictions have great power over the brain and it takes time to fully recover. Slips and relapses may occur but that does not mean all is lost. Relapses should be viewed by those in addiction, and their families as an opportunity to learn principles that will help them to be stronger in the future. It is important to understand that we should never give up on those who are truly seeking recovery from addiction.

As an ecclesiastical leader my counsel to those with sexual addiction is to tell them to pray more earnestly, to attend the temple, and to read scriptures to get better. That's all they really need to do to find recovery. Prayer, temple attendance, and scripture study are essential tools in recovery. But many who have found recovery report that these tools alone were not enough. They found that they needed additional tools to break the power of the addiction. In some cases an experienced counselor was able to help. Many have found additional tools for recovery in the LDS 12 Step PASG program (Pornography Addiction Support Group) or in the SA (Sexaholics Anonymous) Community Support Groups. These programs provide a step-by-step approach for applying gospel based principles of recovery so that a person can draw closer to God and receive His power, which will help them overcome their addiction and find peace and healing for their soul.

If someone is addicted to pornography, he or she is probably a molester. We should not label those who have an addiction to pornography as molesters. Because all addictions are progressive in nature, there are those who will eventually try to act out the vile images they have seen by molesting others. Those who are molesters are undoubtedly a small percentage of all those who have a pornography or sexual addiction.

Those who are addicted to pornography can recover, but they can never really be spiritual again. Full, complete and total recovery from the soul destructive addiction of pornography is possible. In General Conference, President Boyd K. Packer reminded us, *"There is no habit, no addiction, no rebellion, no crime exempted from the promise of complete* *forgiveness."* (Boyd K. Packer, *Ensign,* Nov. 1995,18-21) In addition to this promise, we have personally witnessed the cleansing and healing power of the Savior, made possible by His Atonement. We have witnessed the miracle of total healing and watched as those in recovery have become spiritually powerful. When the Lord spoke to the prophet Jeremiah, He asked, "Behold, I[am] the LORD, the God of all flesh: is there anything too hard for me?" (Jer. 32:27) And the answer remains the same today, as it was more than 2500 years ago, "No, there is nothing that is too hard for the Lord."

It cannot be emphasized enough that the foundation of true recovery from addiction is based upon turning to Jesus Christ and through His Atoning power receive His mercy, love, grace, and healing to overcome the destructive power of addiction. If those in addiction are willing to humbly seek recovery, through the Savior, recovery is possible. Many have found help through 12 Step Sexual Addiction Recovery Programs, such as the LDS PASG program or the community based S.A. program. It can also be helpful to seek the assistance of qualified professional therapists who are experienced in helping those in sexual addiction.

ABOUT THE AUTHOR

Donald L. Hilton, Jr. has practiced medicine for fourteen years in San Antonio, Texas, specializing in neurological surgery. Dr. Hilton graduated from Lamar University with highest honors, and from medical school at the University of Texas Medical School at Galveston with honors, where he was elected to the Alpha Omega Alpha National Medical Honor Society. He completed his neurosurgical training at the University of Tennessee at Memphis in 1994, is board certified by the American Board of Neurological Surgeons, and is a diplomat of the American College of Surgeons. He has been named to *Best Doctors in America*.

A pioneer in the field of minimally invasive spinal surgery, he has published book chapters and journal articles with original contributions in this field, and lectures nationally and internationally. He has taught courses on this topic at the American Association of Neurological Surgeons and at the Congress of Neurological Surgeons, and is currently a Clinical Associate Professor of Neurosurgery at the University of Texas Medical School at San Antonio.

Brother Hilton and his wife, Jana, currently serve as LDS Family Services program coordinators in San Antonio for those who struggle with pornography and sexual addiction and their spouses. They are the parents of five children and have two grandchildren.

Forward Press Publishing
P.O. Box 592681
San Antonio, TX 78259

email:
info@forwardpress.org
website:
www.forwardpress.org